TORY SPY

A NEW YORK FRONTIER FAMILY'S WAR AGAINST THE AMERICAN REVOLUTION

By

Daniel Lovelace

"There was madness on the earth below
And anger in the sky,
And young and old, and rich and poor,
Came forth to see him die."

HERITAGE BOOKS
2009

HERITAGE BOOKS
AN IMPRINT OF HERITAGE BOOKS, INC.

Books, CDs, and more—Worldwide

For our listing of thousands of titles see our website at
www.HeritageBooks.com

Published 2009 by
HERITAGE BOOKS, INC.
Publishing Division
100 Railroad Ave. #104
Westminster, Maryland 21157

Copyright © 2009 Daniel D. Lovelace

All rights reserved. No part of this book may be reproduced or transmitted in any form or by any means, electronic or mechanical, including photocopying, recording or by any information storage and retrieval system without written permission from the author, except for the inclusion of brief quotations in a review.

International Standard Book Numbers
Paperbound: 978-0-7884-5025-9
Clothbound: 978-0-7884-8293-9

For Joan,

my favorite editor and critic.

Figure 1:
An artist's conception of a typical Revolutionary War execution by hanging.

CONTENTS

List of Illustrations ix;
Preface and Acknowledgements xi;

Introduction

The Execution of Loyalist Provincial Corps Officer Thomas Loveless 1;

Chapter 1.

The American Revolution as a Civil War 3; Levels of Loyalist Commitment 6; New York Loyalists: Numbers and Distribution 10; The Personal Background of Thomas Loveless 15; The Jessup Brothers and Albany County 19

Choosing Sides—1775-1777

Chapter 2.

The Strategic Context 22; The Revolution/Rebellion Comes to Albany County 23; Early Patriot Attempts to Deal with the Loyalist Threat 29; Why Did Thomas Loveless Decide to Fight for the Crown? 33

Chapter 3.

Thomas Loveless' Loyalist Military Career During 1776-1777 43

Changing Sides—1778-1780

Chapter 4.

The Strategic Context 53; Fears of a Second British Invasion Lead to More Anti-Tory Measures and Tougher Laws Dealing with Espionage 55; What Happened to

Thomas Loveless and his Family after His Return to Canada? 65

Chapter 5.

The Origins, Leadership, Missions, and Capabilities of the "Tory Secret Service" (TSS) 72; The Impact of the Arnold/André Case upon TSS Operations 108

Settling Scores—1781-1783

Chapter 6.

The Strategic Context 114; Intensified Efforts to Counter Loyalist Intelligence Support Operations in Albany County 117; Rebel Arrests of Loyalists' Dependents Force the British to Kidnap Americans 121

Chapter 7.

Why Thomas Loveless' September, 1781 Intelligence Mission Was Doomed to Fail 123; The TSS Leadership's Failure to Recognize the Dangers Posed by John Stark's Resumption of Command in Albany 136

Chapter 8.

Thomas Loveless' Last Operation: Its Objectives and Betrayal 143; The Trial and Execution of Thomas Loveless 152; The Reactions of Tory, American, and British Leaders to his Hanging 158

Chapter 9.

The Final Years of the Tory Secret Service 161; The Impact of the News of Cornwallis' Surrender at Yorktown 162; TSS Operations During 1782 166

Chapter 10.

A Garbled Story: The Capture, Trial, Execution, and Burial of Thomas Loveless: As Described by Eye-Witnesses, 181; The Strange Travels of the Tory Spy's Skull 185; The Tory Spy's Career as Described by Historians 189

Chapter 11.

What Happened to Thomas Loveless' Wife and Children Following His death? 198; What Happened to Other Players in this Drama? 211

Analysis

Chapter 12.

Why General Stark Decided to Execute Ensign Thomas Loveless: Some Enabling and Precipitating Factors 219; The Influence of Divided Family Allegiances 226

Chapter 13.

Why Was the Tory-Rebel Conflict in Northern New York State So Unusual, and What Can This Teach Us about the American Revolution? 238; Why Has the Topic of Revolutionary War Espionage Executions Been Ignored by American Historians? 253; Why Were Loyalists So Often the Target of Patriot Espionage Executions? 256

APPENDICES:

I. Thomas Loveless: A Personal Chronology 269

II. Photocopies of American Documents Captured by the Tory Secret Service 275

III. A Glossary of Relevant Intelligence Terminology 284

NOTES: 287

BIBLIOGRAPHY: 310

INDEX   327

LIST OF ILLUSTRATIONS

Figures

1. Artist's conception of a typical Revolutionary War execution by hanging — iv

2. Rebel loyalty oath — 32

3. British Provincial Corps recruiting poster — 35

4. Alonzo Chappel's painting of the British/Tory Surrender following the Battle of Bennington — 45

5. Portrait of General Sir Frederick Haldimand — 76

6. Copy of Thomas Loveless' hand-written report dated September 2, 1780 — 95

7. Contemporary print depicting the execution of Major John André — 111

8. Engraving after Trumbull's portrait of Major General Philip Schuyler — 125

9. The Opposing Chains of Command in the "Spy Wars" conducted in Albany County, New York during 1778-1783 — 128

10. Alonzo Chappel's engraving of Brigadier General John Stark — 139

11. Newspaper article of October 4, 1781, containing the Orders captured with Thomas Loveless — 146

12. Copy of Private Daniel Colton's certificate of discharge from Edward Jessup's Loyal Rangers   180

13. Photo of the display case in which Thomas Loveless' skull was exhibited for more than fifty years.   190

14. Portrait of Major General John Stark   221

15. The execution of Nathan Hale, as conceived by Felix Darley   232

Maps

#1. The key towns in Albany County in 1781   21

#2. Albany, Charlotte, and Tryon Counties in the mid-1770s   28

#3. Detail from an 18th Century map showing New York Colony's northern frontier during the French and Indian War   80

#4. The Tory Secret Service's theater of operations   87

#5. A 19th Century map of Old Saratoga/Schuylerville, showing the locations of Burgoyne's surrender and Thomas Loveless' hanging   157

#6. The principal areas of Loyalist resettlement in Canada   205

PREFACE AND ACKNOWLEDGEMENTS

This is a story for our times—it is about people responding to the pressures of revolutionary change. Their world was coming apart, and the outcome was unpredictable. In approaching this book, the reader should ask him/herself: "What would you and your family do if your neighborhood gradually became a war zone torn apart by invading armies, battles, and increasingly lethal 'intelligence warfare' and you were viewed by your neighbors as a potential spy or combatant?"

Most Americans have heard of the "Tories" or "Loyalists" who opposed the Founding Fathers' efforts to leave the British Empire and create a new country called the United States of America. Dozens of scholarly books and articles have been written about the Loyalists, but few of these have dealt with Tory involvement in armed conflict or espionage activities. Even fewer researchers have highlighted the experiences of Tory families of "the middling sort"—yeoman farmers, shopkeepers and artisans—who risked their lives for the British cause.

A few years ago, the movie *The Patriot* brought the subject of Loyalism to the public's attention by depicting Rebel-Tory warfare in the Carolinas during 1779-1780. This book deals with a similar topic, but the action takes place in Albany County, New York. Located astride the principal invasion corridor between Canada and the U.S., and a hotbed of Rebel-Tory conflict, Albany County eventually become a battleground between a cadre of Tory-managed "spies" based in Canada and their Rebel former neighbors.

Most scholarly studies of Loyalism have focused upon the Loyalist elite--the ones who kept diaries, wrote letters and pamphlets, and attended rallies protesting Rebel initiatives and intimidation. With a few notable exceptions, prominent Tories seldom risked life or limb to help defend The Crown from its enemies. As a result, what little we know about the opponents of our War of Independence has come from the top twenty percent of North America's Tory population—i.e. "from the top down." This book, however, attempts to tell the Loyalist story "from the bottom up," and with greater emphasis upon the personal risks involved.

For more than two hundred years Americans have been taught to believe that their revolution was achieved with a minimum of violence and social disruption, especially in comparison to those of France, Russia, or China. Only recently have the civil war aspects of the conflict begun to be uncovered and debated by a new generation of Early American historians. What has been missing, however, is a "human face" on the "Loyalist dilemma"—a case study of what happened to the family of a typical yeoman farmer who gambled on a British victory and ultimately lost friends and family, property, and a future as Americans. When I discovered the story of Thomas Loveless and his family, I knew that I had at last found that "human face."

Americans traditionally have been reluctant to admit that their revolution was in part a bloody civil war, often fought by mobs and partisan bands, with great ferocity on both sides. Never a majority, but in colonies such as New York and the Carolinas amounting to over twenty percent of the population, the Tories were appropriately viewed as a serious threat by Rebel leaders. For this reason, during the war they were subjected to varying degrees of surveillance, intimidation, and punishment by Patriot authorities. At the end of the conflict, the wealthiest and most committed Loyalists turned out to be the biggest losers. By 1783 many of the "brightest and best" in the Thirteen Colonies of 1775 had lost their homes and fortunes and been driven into exile throughout the British Empire.

Unfortunately, it has taken Americans a long time to acquire a more balanced view of those who resisted the tide of America's creation. The historians of the Early Federal Period were not much help—the passions of the revolutionary struggle were too close at hand, and they obtained far too much of their information from confused and biased local sources. As a result, much of the original conventional wisdom about the Loyalists has turned out, in retrospect, to have been wrong or badly skewed. For example, the Tory elements in the Thirteen Colonies were initially viewed as a wealthy, largely urban, self-serving elite; the "running dogs" of an arrogant, bungling, and occasionally despotic British colonial administration. However, in recent years, more rigorous scholarship has revealed that Loyalist sympathies could be found at many different levels of Colonial American society, and that the patterns of multi-class Tory participation varied greatly from colony to colony.

This book surveys the problems faced by a northern New York Loyalist family during the American War of Independence, with special attention to the role they played in the little-known "Intelligence War" fought by British and American spies along the US-Canada border during 1779-1783. It analyzes the career of one Tory provincial corps volunteer who risked everything (his property, his life, his marriage, and the lives of three of his five sons) in the course of six years of service to the British Crown. It focuses upon what I call the "high risk" (i.e. life threatening) aspects of Loyalism, and especially upon those risks associated with espionage. This story will deal with such topics as:

- The choices of allegiance and participation made by Thomas Loveless and his family.

- The kinds of official scrutiny and harassment suffered by Albany County Loyalists in the course of the war.

- The origins, missions, and effectiveness of a British-sponsored, but Loyalist-led "Secret Service" component (which I have designated the "Tory Secret Service," or "TSS") based in Canada that conducted a wide variety of intelligence operations behind Rebel lines during 1781-1783.

- The dangers faced by the families of those Loyalists in the frontier areas of New York who served in British-sponsored military units or supported British espionage operations.

- The gradually increased effectiveness of the security and counterintelligence activities conducted by Patriot civil and military authorities in the Albany County area.

- The unique role that espionage executions played in the conflict between Rebel and Tory factions in revolutionary New York.

An integrated analysis of these subjects will help the reader to better understand the lives of ordinary people who were forced to cope with unprecedented, fast-moving political and military changes in their communities during a seven-year war. "High risk" Loyalist volunteers like Thomas Loveless were among the last to be eliminated in this underground conflict between brothers, cousins, and neighbors. This book's approach allows the reader to witness the Tory-Loyalist struggle at the grass roots, rather than the elite level. As a result, one is constantly reminded of the multi-layered conflicts that coexisted within the greater war—from the formal battles between armies, to the repression and reprisals of the civil war, to the warfare between intelligence services, to the endless competition for manpower, war materiel, foodstuffs, and public opinion.

Acknowledgements

Many people have aided my research on this topic over the years, and the following list must not be considered wholly inclusive: The Superintendents and Curators (during 1996-2006) of the Saratoga National Battlefield Museum, the research staff of the Museum at Fort Ticonderoga, Saratoga County Historian Karen Ufford Campola, Ottawa archivist and genealogist John E. Ruch, Dr. Bill White of the Colonial Williamsburg Foundation, Monica Gray of the New York State Archives, and Dora Winter of Library and Archives Canada. In addition, I have benefited by the support of the Reference and Special Collections staffs at the following libraries: The U. S. Library of Congress, The Library of Virginia, The Colonial Williamsburg Foundation's The John D. Rockefeller Library, the Earl Gregg Swem Library at The College of William and Mary, the New York State Library (Albany), the Crandall Library in Glens Falls (New York), and (via Interlibrary Loan) the Archives of the New York Historical Society, The University of Michigan, The University of Ontario, and The National Library of Canada in Ottawa. Genealogist Steve Ward provided valuable details on the family and personal background of "Thomas the Spy." My wife Joan, a former managing editor of *The John Marshall Papers* at the Marshall-Wythe School of Law at The College of William and Mary, gave me invaluable editorial guidance. Mike Geoghegan and Gerry White provided vital advice concerning publication venues, while Ted Tether, Sean Fitzpatrick, and Rod Lenahan generously reviewed the manuscript at various stages of its development.

Daniel Lovelace
Williamsburg, Virginia

INTRODUCTION:

THE EXECUTION OF LOYALIST PROVINCIAL CORPS OFFICER THOMAS LOVELESS

In early October, 1781—four years after Burgoyne's defeat at Saratoga and less than two weeks before the British expeditionary force under Cornwallis surrendered to George Washington's Franco-American army at Yorktown—a middle-aged farmer and veteran Tory/Loyalist soldier named Thomas Loveless was marched to a bluff overlooking the Hudson River near present-day Schuylerville, New York and hanged by the Continental Army as a British spy. An eyewitness account described the event as follows:

"It was the windiest day I ever saw. A large concourse of people was assembled. He was taken out of the guardhouse; his coffin was placed cross-wise on top of the box of a cart drawn by oxen, a rope around his neck, and a mulatto—a slave of General Schuyler's, I think—holding the end of the rope, who made him walk close up to the cart. The guards surrounded him, forming a hollow square; thus they marched towards, half a mile, to the gallows. The gallows was formed of two long forked stakes drove into the ground and a pole placed across the forks. The cart drove under the gallows and stopped. (Loveless) got up into the cart, and also the minister, Mister Tanner, I think, a Baptist, who was preaching then up Battenkill. He talked and prayed with him, shook hands with him, bade him farewell, and then descended. The Negro then tied the rope to the pole; the cart drove out from under and he hung till he was dead. Then he was cut down and the guards marched away.

"The negro took off the white frock which he had over his clothes. He then twitched his (the corpse's) silver shirt sleeve buttons out, and pocketed them, next stripped off his vest. Then took hold of the bottoms of his pantaloons, and with a violent yank, which drew the corpse a foot or two forward, pulled them off; and then exposed his legs, the skin scarcely to be seen through the coating of glossy black hair which grew upon them. Some of the spectators could endure the negro's brutality no longer and kicked him—and forbade his taking the shirt from the corpse. So the negro desisted." [1]

After stripping the corpse of valuables, according to local legend the crowd buried it head downward—it was believed that this would ensure an early arrival in Hell—in an unmarked and soon-forgotten grave.

Thomas Loveless' execution was the culmination of "a war within a war, within a war" fought by partisan factions in northern New York during 1776-1783. Conducted in the shadows of the greater war, Albany County's Tory-Rebel violence also included 'intelligence warfare' sponsored by the American authorities in Albany and British military leaders in Canada. This 'warfare' involved paramilitary and agent operations, courier missions, ambushes, kidnappings, assassination attempts, and espionage executions. Still unknown to most students of Revolutionary War history, this covert conflict produced hundreds of casualties and thousands of refugees.

During 1779-1781, Thomas Loveless was a major participant in this brief, but bloody campaign against Patriot forces in northern New York conducted by a British-sponsored, and ultimately Tory-led "Secret Service" based in Canada. His Loyalist military career and the circumstances surrounding his death are testimony to the extraordinary social dislocation and the personal sacrifice that accompanied the birth of the United States of America.

CHAPTER ONE

THE AMERICAN REVOLUTION
AS A CIVIL WAR

More than thirty years ago, during the bi-centennial of the American War of Independence, historian Michael Kammen commented as follows:

"Until quite recently, with the partial exception of Civil War historiography, the literature of American history has not been notable for a sense of the tragic. Much more attention has been devoted to progress and success in our national past. Alongside our newly heightened understanding of the suffering involved in chattel slavery . . . we may come to view the American Revolution as a crisis of conscience. In addition to the displacement of persons, the separation of families, and the arbitrary confiscation of property, there is a history of inner turmoil which is suffused with tragic power because it is so very personal and deeply felt. Ultimately, it can be appreciated only case by case, family by family, and community by community. It is an intimate part of the painful birth of our nationality—a story not without voices of anguish." [2]

As was typical of most 18th Century European-style warfare, the American Revolution did not produce large numbers of fatalities on either side (perhaps 7,000 Americans and 5,200 British and their mercenaries were killed in battle). Much larger numbers of men died of wounds and disease, however, so that that the total number of US military casualties during the War of Independence was probably more than 25,000 out of the estimated 100,000 men who served in the Continental Army from 1776 to 1783.

Yet during the same period a bloody civil war was also being fought in British North America, for which even less precise casualty figures are available. In the course of this "war within a war," some fifteen to twenty percent of the colonies' population tried to defeat the estimated thirty percent of their fellow colonists who actively supported the Revolutionary cause. During any given year of the struggle, the majority of the people living in the thirteen colonies remained neutral, trading with both sides and awaiting the outcome of events. A large number of these "fence sitters" were able to change sides several times as the war progressed. But for those Loyalists or "Tories" who were the most fully committed, the risks and sacrifices of the protracted conflict were very real indeed.

Because they were always a conspicuous minority, the Loyalists were vulnerable to both vigilantism and official Rebel harassment, and during the war they were forced to make great sacrifices, losing both kinfolk and personal property. Hundreds were executed or imprisoned for real or imagined treason or espionage, and thousands provided the British military or civil authorities with information about their Patriot neighbors. Tens of thousands of Tories joined British Regular, Militia, or Provincial Corps units and fought alongside British troops. At the war's end, hundreds of thousands of Loyalists lost their property in North America to official confiscation and some 80,000 chose (or were forced) to emigrate to England, Canada, the West Indies, or other parts of the British Empire.

In the last century the world's most violent Revolutions, and especially those in Russia and China, involved protracted civil wars. Even the fairly brief civil wars in countries such as Spain (1936-1939), and Greece (1946-1950) produced unusually high civilian casualties relative to their national populations. Often pitting fanatical political or religious groups against each other, these kinds of conflicts divide families, both by generations and among siblings, and their warfare usually involves larger percentages of undisciplined, or "irregular" partisan forces who tend to commit more atrocities.

Several factors make it possible for a civil war to be carried on within a larger, more conventional conflict. If the larger war is protracted or stalemated, both sides end up competing for recruits, weapons, food, transport and other necessities. As partisan conflict behind the lines intensifies the timely collection of intelligence information becomes increasingly vital for both sides, and espionage becomes a more dangerous enterprise. As a result of such pressures, the cost in human lives tends to escalate.

In some civil wars, the presence of sizeable numbers of dissidents behind the lines of one or both parties to the conflict can add an additional dimension of threat. During the American Civil War (1861-1865), for example, the Confederate States of America had to deal with numerous enclaves of pro-Union, or "Unionist" elements, some of which—like the famous "Empire of Jones" in rural Mississippi--remained intact throughout the war. The CSA also was the target of many volunteer spies for the Union-- such as Elizabeth Van Lew--in major cities such as Richmond and Charleston. On the Union side, Rebel spies infested Washington, D.C., Baltimore, and other northern cities, resulting in the imprisonment of thousands of "Copperhead" southern sympathizers and a few notorious female spies.

The escalating importance of Intelligence to both sides during protracted civil wars leads to increased conflict between their Intelligence Services. While much of this competition will remain non-violent, some of the missions involved—including paramilitary operations, sabotage and kidnapping—inevitably will involve the use of force. Even if direct exchanges of fire can be avoided, the normal levels of competition for "secret" information—plus the counterintelligence and security measures organized to protect such secrets—will often produce activities that look very much like "a war within a war."

During the Revolutionary War neither side's military leaders had access to the kinds of elaborate intelligence support which modern armies take for granted. Roger Kaplan describes these limitations as follows: "The typical eighteenth-century army possessed a very rudimentary intelligence-gathering organization. No staff section existed to advise the commander; instead, the commander was his own intelligence officer, usually seconded by an aide or adjutant. Moreover, he could rely on very few groups trained in reconnaissance. Armies possessed only a handful of topographical engineers, and only few military units devoted themselves primarily to scouting." [3]

Levels of Loyalist Commitment

For over 230 years the American public has had an ambivalent attitude toward the Tories who sided with the British during what London called "The American Rebellion." Although most Anglo-American families with deep roots in North America have ancestors who fought on both sides of the "Revolutionary War," many are reluctant to admit it, or they treat their Loyalist kin as "Black Sheep." At the same time, like the Confederate losers of the Civil War, the losers of the Revolution have always generated a certain amount of public curiosity in the United States. After all, who could possibly have thought that a political movement committed to the pursuit of "Life, Liberty, and the Pursuit of Happiness" was not truly noble and good?

Of course, the opposite was once the case in Canada, where being able to trace your lineage to one of the "United Empire Loyalists" as the Tory refugees who came to Canada after 1783 were called, traditionally conveyed a certain amount of social prestige because of the role their descendents played in the founding of independent Canada.

Because the Tories preferred to remain loyal to the British Crown, they were also called "Loyalists," or (in British Colonial terminology) "Friends of Government." These Tories/Loyalists represented all classes of society, from British Colonial officials, great landowners, and wealthy merchants, to the owners of small farms and businesses. Most of them benefited economically from the prevailing colonial system in some direct or indirect way, although a minority opposed "the Rebellion" for reasons of political philosophy as well as self-interest.

The burst of interest in Tory/Loyalist historical issues generated by America's 1976 bicentennial produced a wave of new scholarly attention and findings about the groups that openly opposed the American Revolution. This second look at the subject discovered a narrower base of Tory support (probably no more than fifteen to twenty percent participation in most colonies), but a much more complex set of Loyalist roots. Instead of the generally accepted "Rich vs. Poor" or "Urban vs. Rural" or "Free Trade vs. Mercantilism" dichotomies, this research revealed a split more often driven by personal allegiances grounded in economic, religious, ethnic, political, and cultural values and interests which divided families as well as neighbors. In short, the Tories were a true mixed bag, the contents of which varied from colony to colony.

In the early phases of the war against the British, many Tories publicly resisted the efforts of their Rebel neighbors with political ploys and arguments, but as the hostility against them mounted, more Loyalists began to take concrete actions to support the British civil and military authorities. Soon the Tories were providing logistical support and intelligence information to British forces, and eventually they began to join Provincial Corps and Militia units designed to fight alongside regular formations of the British Army. These "militarized" Tories were viewed as a serious threat by Rebel leaders, especially in the Hudson and Mohawk River Valleys, The Carolinas, and along the Canadian border.

The American War of Independence was a protracted conflict that lasted nearly seven years, during which the fortunes of both sides rose and fell and the outcome of which, even following the French-American Victory at Yorktown, remained in doubt. Although US citizens today are reluctant to admit the fact, there was nothing inevitable about the success of the American colonists' rebellion against British rule. Indeed, if it were not for George Washington's tenacious leadership, France's cynical generosity, the growing support of the Whigs in Parliament, and some crucial good luck, the whole enterprise could easily have failed.

The Loyalists gambled on a British victory, but they did not do so blindly or foolishly. The conventional military and economic wisdom of the day made it look like a low-risk option. After all, the British possessed large, highly experienced land and naval forces, and to that date no large colonial possession of a European power had yet fought its way to independence. But in the long run, the war turned out to be an ugly surprise for the Tories, many of whom had expected it to be over within less than a year. For both Loyalists and Patriots, the uncertain outcome of a long war led to morale problems, doubts, and often faltering allegiances. After an initial period of enthusiastic volunteering and self-sacrifice, supporters on both sides began to waver, and, depending upon the risks and the economic benefits, cooperated with "the enemy" or even changed sides. This trend in turn intensified the civil war dimensions of the conflict, and violent partisan warfare escalated, especially in New York, New Jersey, and the Carolinas.

Throughout all the colonies, levels of personal commitment varied widely within the Loyalist community. The vast majority, either out of fear or because of lack of opportunity, resisted passively. Others engaged, to the extent they were able, in meetings, publications, protests, and other political actions designed to counter their "Patriot" enemies. Many refused to sign Patriot loyalty oaths and resisted being drafted into Rebel militia units. Beyond this, Loyalist resistance took various forms of what I choose to call (in descending order) "The Pyramid of Risk," as follows:

- Directing or Conducting Intelligence Operations

- Enlisting in British Regular Army Units

- Enlisting in Loyalist Militia or Provincial Corps Units

- Supporting British or Tory Intelligence Operations

- Joining Tory Vigilante Groups

- Informally Gathering and Passing Intelligence Data to the British

- Providing Logistical Support to British Forces

All of these activities entailed a certain amount of personal risk, but only the top four entailed a high probability of losing one's life. Espionage was especially dangerous, and both the British and American Intelligence systems, while highly informal and ad hoc by today's standards, took steps to protect their agents from detection. Unlike the specialized bureaucracies of today, Revolutionary War Intelligence activities were largely directed by Commanders in Chief, with the help of staff officers, or "aides-de-camp." George Washington was his own spymaster throughout much of the war, with the help of officers such as Lt. Col. Thomas Knowlton and Colonel Benjamin Tallmadge. British Generals Howe and Clinton depended upon subordinates such as Major John André and Colonel Oliver DeLancey to manage such affairs.

Because the British were often fighting in unfamiliar territory, they were especially eager for "actionable" tactical intelligence about Rebel troop movements, as well as strategic intelligence dealing with enemy logistics, political vulnerabilities, and morale. Not surprisingly, British colonial leaders hoped that the Friends of Government would be able to provide much of this valuable information. Consequently, engaging in intelligence activities was to become the ultimate proof of Tory allegiance. Several prominent Loyalist military commanders such as Cortland Skinner and Beverly Robinson ran their own intelligence networks, and individual Loyalists provided sanctuary for British spies and military couriers as they transited Rebel territory.

New York Loyalists: Numbers and Distribution

In sheer numbers, New York was the most loyal of the thirteen colonies. Alexander Flick estimated that up to 90,000 of New York's inhabitants remained loyal to the Crown, and that 35,000 of them emigrated at the war's end.

In an article entitled "The New York Loyalists: A Cross-section of Colonial Society," Esmond Wright pointed out of the 5,072 Loyalist claims for financial compensation put before the British Commissioner between 1784 and 1789, 1,107, or almost twenty-five percent, were submitted by New Yorkers, two out of three of which claimed to have served in the armed forces.

Other scholars have noted that New York's Tories had a very high level of military participation during the war, providing more military volunteers for service with the British Army (an estimated 15,000) than any other colony. If volunteers for the Loyalist Militia and Provincial corps units are included, the estimated total comes to 23,500 men. In combination with Loyalist units raised in Nova Scotia and Canada, New York's Tory Provincial Corps regiments, in Wright's opinion, ". . . probably constituted a half or more of all Loyalists in arms during the war." [4]

Loyalists were not evenly distributed throughout the colony. Wallace Brown noted that ". . . the great concentrations of Tories were (in numerical order) in Tryon County, Albany County, Charlotte County, New York City, Dutchess County, and Westchester County; this area included the heart of New York running north from Manhattan up the east bank of the Hudson as far as the southern boundary of Albany County, and then on both sides of the river up to Lake Champlain (with notable concentrations around Albany and Saratoga)," as well as sizeable numbers in the Mohawk Valley and on Long island.[5] Moreover, Brown noted that two New York counties alone (Tryon and Albany) accounted for about fifty percent of the total claimants for post-war compensation from the British Government in 1786.

The Loyalists of northern New York were quite different from those living in New York City and along the lower Hudson. As Wright puts it, "New York City's Loyalism was simply a consequence of its location.. . .As the major British military stronghold throughout the seven years of war, it became in fact a Fortress Britannica, part refuge, part port, and part supply base for the British Army. . ."[6] As a result, from late 1776 onward the city remained a bastion for both local and refugee Tories, and, with a few exceptions, its wealthy Scots and Anglo-Dutch American business community supported Governor Guy Carleton and his governing officials.

On the Lower Hudson River, Many of the great landlord families, and especially those of Dutchess and Westchester counties, aggressively supported the Crown, creating and leading elite Tory military units such as DeLancey's Brigade, The King's Orange Rangers, and The Prince of Wales Regiment. In the "Neutral Ground" of Westchester County, political competition between two major factions—Tory Episcopalians led by the Delancey family and Whig Presbyterians led by the Livingstons— eventually degenerated into skirmishes between lawless bands known as the "Cowboys and the "Skinners

However, Loyalism's base was much less aristocratic along the Upper Hudson and north of Albany. Here, a number of politically-prominent families, such as the Schuylers, sided with the Rebels early in the war, and the Tory leadership came mostly from regional British Colonial officials such as Sir John Johnson of the Mohawk Valley, and from frontier entrepreneurs and land speculators such as Philip Skene and the Jessup Brothers.

New York Loyalists participated in three of the four types of British-sponsored military units that fought alongside each other during the American Revolution:

- Sixty-three British-manned Army regiments (Administratively part of the British military's "Regular" military establishment, and hence, closed to "Provincials").

- Five British and Loyalist-manned regiments that were formed during the war and were eventually granted "Regular" establishment status.

- Thirty-one Loyalist-manned Provincial Corps units which were equipped and trained for combat, but remained part of the "Provincial" Establishment. The strength of British-sponsored Provincial Corps troops varied greatly during the Revolution.

The following table appears in the Appendix of Piers Macksey's The War for America, 1775-1783: [7]

Provincial Rank and File in America

December 1777	3,738
June, 1778	4,628
December 1778	6,326
June 1779	6,504
December 1779	6,757
December 1780	8,201
May 1781	8,151

- Dozens of British-equipped Loyalist Militia units that usually performed garrison duties in forts and cities.

Philip Katcher claims that during the war New York provided 23,500 men to British Regular Army, Provincial Corps, and Militia units. This figure is only slightly lower than the 27,781 New Yorkers who served in Continental Army or American Militia units during the conflict. The majority of New York's pro-British volunteers served in ten Provincial Corps units, of which Thomas Loveless's unit, The King's Loyal Americans, (or Jessup's Corps), was one. The other units included Robert Rogers' King's Rangers (later renamed the "Queen's Rangers"), Beverly Robinson's Loyal American Regiment, Butler's Rangers, the King's Loyal Regiment of New York, John Coffin's King's Orange Rangers, the King's American Regiment, Delancy's Brigade, the British Legion, and the Westchester Refugees. [8]

Each of these Provincial Corps units was initially subordinate to one of the four regional Command Areas in North America established by the British War Office: either the British Army's Northern Department headquartered in Quebec or its Central Department based in New York City. Like the British General in charge of New York City, the Northern Department's Commander was also responsible for civil administration as "Governor-General," in this case of the Province of Canada.

With a few exceptions, the Loyalist Provincial Corps, or, as they were called, "Colonial," units were considered inferior to, and were used as auxiliaries in support of, British Regular units. Because their performance on the battlefield proved to be uneven, they were considered unreliable, and (as George Washington had personally discovered during his French and Indian War service) their officers were seldom treated as professional or social equals by the British officer corps. Moreover, since only a handful of Provincial Corps units were granted "Establishment" status, the pay, disability, and retirement benefits of most New York Provincial Corps soldiers remained lower than those of British regular troops, especially in the early years of the war.

In addition, Loyalist military units often were the last to receive adequate weapons, uniforms, and military equipment. The following extract is from a 26 July 1779 letter to Canada's Governor-General from 60-year old Captain Daniel McAlpin, who had recently been placed in command of the poorly-equipped Loyalist Corps then stationed at Sorel, near Montreal:

"When I got the Command of the Corps of Loyalists the most of them were then and still are employed in the works, Sundays not excepted, and I had no opportunity to see them under arms. Except Capt. Leake's Detachment, whose arms I found in very bad order...Upon examining the arms of the remainder of the Corps left here [at Sorel] I found them much in the same condition [mostly old French muskets without bayonets]. I need not explain to His Excellency the figure an old greyheaded fellow will make at the head of a parcel of raw undisciplined people with bad arms in their hands. My old withered face blushes at the thought of it. I hope the General will be good enough to prevent me from appearing in this mortifying situation by ordering good arms to be delivered to us." [9]

The Personal Background of Thomas Loveless

The limited information available suggests that "Thomas the Spy's" father was James Loveless of Rhode Island, who was born in Connecticut in 1716. This James Lovelace subsequently bought land during the 1730s in North Kingstown, Rhode Island and married a woman named Lydia sometime prior to June, 1738. James was a leatherworker or shoemaker, as he was listed as a "Cordwinder" when he sold ninety acres to an apparent cousin, Joseph Loveless, "husbandman" in December, 1737. He then relocated to South Kingstown, R.I., where during the years 1738 and 1743, James and Lydia produced at least two sons: Thomas (1739/40), James Jr., (1742). Young Thomas may have been named after his uncle Thomas Loveless, who also owned land in the Kingstown area and had married a woman named Isabel in November, 1734.

Tax lists indicate that James Loveless senior moved to Lower Dutchess (Putnam) County, New York in 1745/46, where he owned a farm. In the course of the next fifteen years, James senior volunteered to join three different British colonial or Provincial Militia units in campaigns against the French during 1746-47 and 1756-58. Military records show that he served with units organized in New London, Connecticut, as well as Albany and Dutchess County, New York. In each of these cases, James Loveless appears to have served as a Private soldier, rather than as a commissioned or non-commissioned officer.

All of this suggests that Thomas Loveless' father was a strong supporter of the interests of the British Crown in North America—a loyalty which may have rubbed off on at least one of his sons. James Loveless senior is probably the man listed among soldiers from New York who had died in 1760, leaving their heirs to collect their pay. Between 1760 and 1773 a Thomas Lovelace (most probably his son), was listed in the Dutchess County tax lists, suggesting that James Loveless was indeed dead by 1760, and that Thomas was afterward in charge of the family farm. We know nothing about the Tory Spy's formal education, but the personally signed, hand-written intelligence reports found in the Haldimand Papers prove that, unlike many of his colleagues in the "Tory Secret Service," Thomas Loveless could read and write.

The French and Indian War lasted eight years, but most of the action in North America was over by 1760.

British military records show that Thomas Loveless was 42 years old at the time of his execution in October 1781, so he could have been born in either 1739 or 1740. During 1755-1760, he would have been 15-20 years of age—old enough to have volunteered for duty with a British Provincial Corps or Colonial Militia unit fighting the French and their Indian allies. Thus it is possible that he served in one of several "irregular," or Ranger units formed in New York and New England during the war. Because of their smaller numbers and the high turnover of their personnel, the surviving rosters of Ranger units are much less complete than those of militia formations.

Trained to fight "Indian style," the Rangers were primarily used for frontier defense, intelligence-gathering, or to support the operations of British Regular forces. Six colonies (Virginia, Massachusetts, New Jersey, New Hampshire, Connecticut, and Rhode Island) created Ranger units during the war, and several were organized and funded by the Commands of British Armed Forces in North America. The most famous of these irregular units sponsored by the British was commanded by Major/Colonel Robert Rogers, and was known as "Rogers' Rangers."

Only a few of the rosters listing the names of the Private soldiers serving in Roger's Rangers have survived, but other military documents prove that Rogers and his lieutenants regularly recruited men from Rhode Island, Connecticut, and New York. The Tory Spy was born in Connecticut and raised in Rhode Island and northern New York. If Thomas Loveless joined a company of the Rangers during 1755-1760, he would have taken part in British-directed military reconnaissance and combat operations in the area between Albany and the border with French-controlled Canada.

By 1775 "Thomas the Spy" and his family (he had married a woman named Lois prior to 1762) had moved further up the Hudson River Valley, where he purchased two 100-acre parcels of "wild" (unimproved) land, both located west of the Hudson River near today's Saratoga Springs. One of these parcels was purchased from a private party in Palmertown. The other, located in "Jessup's Patent," was purchased from the Jessup brothers. On the property near Palmertown Loveless cleared thirty acres and built a typical frontier farmstead, consisting of a log house and a barn. With such meager, privately-purchased holdings he did not fit the conventional mold of a wealthy Tory landowner whose prosperity was the result of the Crown's largesse.

The Loveless family was typical of the thousands of settlers who had moved into the northern and western frontier areas of New York after 1763 in search of cheap and fertile land. The vast majority of these immigrants were farmers living on small land holdings. Janice Potter-Mackinnon has described the supporters of the Crown who came from this group as follows: "Only about 1 percent of the Loyalists held more than 500 acres of land, about 50 percent held less than 200 acres, and approximately 35 percent less than 100 acres. Further, even these figures exaggerate the affluence of the farmers since many holding 100 or even 200 acre farms would have cleared less than twenty acres. Over 40 percent of Loyalist claimants [for British compensation] for example, stated that they had cleared less than ten acres of land. The majority of Loyalists, then, lived on the frontier and engaged in non-commercial, family-based farming." [10]

Although no deed or map remains to pinpoint its exact location, we have indirect evidence indicating the general area where Thomas the Spy's `101-acre farm was situated in 1775. His son James' 1786 petition for compensation for his father's lost property in New York is supported by the sworn statement of witness Captain Jonathan Jones, an officer in the Queen's Loyal Rangers. In the course of his testimony, Captain Jones claimed that "The late Thos. Loveless lived within a few miles of the witness in Albany County." The summary of the statement goes on to describe the Loveless property as follows: "One hundred acres of land near Palmer Town, (or "Palmertown" located 9 or 10 miles northwest of the town of Saratoga) with a house and improvements, about 20 or 30 acres were cleared. Captain Jones knew it well."[11]

In documenting his own claim for compensation from the British Government, Captain Jones describes three items of real estate "lost to the Rebels." One of these is described as "A lot containing about two acres at Fish Creek 36 miles from Albany," which he purchased in 1770. In addition, he purchased "84 acres adjoining" in 1773. If "Thomas the Spy" lived within a few miles of Jones's property, then his farm must have been situated fairly close to "Fish Creek" or "Fish Kill" which runs into the Hudson River from the west. The largest other landowners in that area were the Jessup brothers.

The Jessup Brothers and Albany County

Born in Connecticut and raised in Dutchess County, New York, Edward and Ebenezer Jessup were Albany-based land speculators who had benefited from their close relationship with Colonial Governor William Tryon during his 1771-1775 tenure. In 1772 the Jessups and their consortium obtained 40,000 acres in the mountains of the upper Hudson, establishing the township of Hyde. They owned large parcels of land both north and south of the Sacandaga River, as well as at Jessup's Landing (where the Schroon and Sacandaga Rivers join the Hudson near modern

Corinth) and a large parcel of land known as Palmertown (near modern Wilton). The Jessups' holdings were part of a much larger piece of land known as "The Kayadrossera Patent" which had been purchased from the Mohawk Indians in 1768.

Many colonial militia veterans of the French and Indian War bought or leased land from the Jessup brothers and established farms in the Luzerne/Wilton/Palmertown area after 1771. Some of these early settlers came from Dutchess County NY and Rhode Island. The Jessups facilitated immigration into the area by building a road from Fort Miller on the Hudson River, through Palmertown and north to Luzerne. In addition to large tracts of raw land, the Jessup brothers' industrial holdings in the Saratoga area were extensive, and included timber transfer facilities, lumber mills, grist mills, forges, and other economic operations requiring water power.

Enriched by the profits obtained from these investments, the Jessup brothers reportedly built palatial, log-timbered homes some ten miles north of today's Glens' Falls, New York. In contrast to the frugal frontier farmers surrounding them, the Jessups lived in luxury, filling their homes with elegant furniture and costly paintings, and decorating their tables with fine linens and silver plate. Thanks to their real estate and business operations, the Jessups were in a strong position to influence the loyalty decisions of their customers, tenants, and business associates when the war broke out. Unlike Thomas Loveless, the Jessups were Tories whose personal and economic future depended entirely upon defeating the American Colonies' attempt to throw off British rule. In short, they had nothing to lose if they took action to resist their Patriot neighbors.

Map # 1:
The key towns in Albany County in 1781

CHOOSING SIDES--1775-1777

CHAPTER TWO

The Strategic Context

At the outset of the American Revolution, neither side fully understood what it was up against. Even after they were forced to evacuate Boston, the British believed that they would easily be able to re-assert control over the small percentage of the thirteen colonies' two and one-half million inhabitants (some 500,000 of whom were free or enslaved Blacks) who had been misled by a few radicals and malcontents. Until the retreat of Washington's army from New York City, a majority of the Continental Congress felt that England could be leveraged into an early political compromise of some sort. During the war's first two years, British complacency was matched by the inexperience of Patriot leaders, and patriotic zeal remained high in both camps.

By the fall of 1776, however, the war seemed to be going London's way. As a result, the pulse of Loyalism began to accelerate, and thousands of Loyalist volunteers flocked to New York City to fight for the Crown. They were welcomed by the British civil and military authorities, who had always believed that the Friends of Government would help turn the tide of war in their favor. New York City became a Tory bastion, and the British set about recruiting Loyalists for service in the Regular Army, additional Provincial Corps units, and newly-formed militia companies for the defense of the city itself. Attracted by the prospect of becoming commissioned officers, wealthy Tories in counties along the Hudson began to form infantry and cavalry units. These units were funded, armed, and equipped by British military headquarters, but remained organizationally "Provincial," rather than part of the "Regular" British Army.

However, early Loyalist military recruitment in the area north of Albany did not fulfill official expectations, even when stimulated by General Burgoyne's invasion of northern New York in the summer and fall of 1777. Stephan Stratch has noted that ". . . throughout the campaigns of 1776 and 1777 it is estimated that no more than 1,000 able-bodied Loyalists ever came forward in active support of the British forces operating in the Lake Champlain and Upper Hudson Valley Region." He attributes this shortfall to fears of property losses and a reluctance to leave one's family to the mercy of roving bands of Indians or Militia. Stratch concludes that "Those Loyalists who did choose to gamble and actively support the King's Army for the most part lost all of their worldly possessions either before or after the failure of the Northern Campaign of 1777." [1]

The failure of Burgoyne's expedition to obtain sufficient Loyalists support in the Upper Hudson region proved costly. Roger Kaplan noted that "The Loyalists of northern New York were too dispersed and too disorganized to provide much information, and Burgoyne's Indian allies proved too unreliable to be used on detached operations. Since his light infantry was incapable of conducting extended patrols, Burgoyne became aware of the rebel build-up only when two Hessian regiments were annihilated at Bennington." [2]

The Revolution/Rebellion Comes to Albany County

In comparison with the rest of New York State, the war came late to the frontier region between Albany and the border with Canada. A vast area stretching from Dutchess County to Lake George, in 1775 Albany County was New

York Province's largest and fastest growing county, with a non-native population of 42,706, including 3,877 slaves. Over one-third of the county's residents lived in or near the City of Albany, with others concentrated in the well-established agricultural settlements located on the east side of the Hudson River, including the townships of Kinderhook, Schaghticoke, Hoosick, Half moon, and others. The most recently settled and more sparsely populated areas of the county were located north of Albany City, in and around the remote hamlets of "Old" Saratoga (modern Schuylerville), Ballstown, Cambridge, and Fort Edward.

Further north, focused upon Lake George and the Champlain Valley and including the garrisons at Fort George, Fort Ticonderoga and Crown Point was Charlotte County, which had been carved out of Albany County in 1772. At the war's outbreak it remained sparsely settled, with a population of just 4,456 people, most of who were living on isolated family farmsteads or in small frontier settlements. To the west, and also created from Albany County in 1772, Tryon County included settlements along the Mohawk River such as Johnstown, Stone Arabia, and Fort Stanwix, as well as in Cherry Valley.

In 1775 the vast majority of the people living in the frontier settlements of northern Albany and Charlotte counties were chiefly concerned with the immediate problems of building log cabins and outbuildings, cutting trees and removing stumps to clear fields for crops, and protecting themselves from Indian attacks. In addition, they were worried about their land titles. Conflicting British land grants issued during the French & Indian War had later led to title disputes between settlers allied with New Hampshire (known as "Yankees") and those allied with New York ("Yorkers"). The granting of several large land patents to speculators such as Thomas Palmer and the Jessup brothers in the early 1770s was followed by an influx of new settlers, many of whom were born in Scotland, Ireland, and New England. This increased the friction over competing land claims. Consequently, as the region slowly became "a seat of war," its residents often harbored local grievances that had little to do with the larger issue of supporting or resisting British imperial policies. [3]

News of the escalating conflict elsewhere in New York and in other North American colonies usually reached the homesteaders of New York's frontiers by word of mouth, rather than via newspapers or broadsides discussing current events. Historian Wallace Brown has commented that "The New York countryside was never alerted in the way the Massachusetts hinterland was. Rural New York had an almost feudal air; there was no vigorous local government, no town meeting, no Samuel Adams in New York City to bestir and organize the country dwellers." [4]

Given their relative isolation, it is likely that Thomas Loveless and his neighbors learned of the early battles of the Revolution, even those that took place in and around New York City in the fall of 1776, a week or two after they had taken place. Church services were often important venues for the dissemination of current political and military information. For example, on April 30, 1775 the parishioners of the Dutch Reformed Church of Schuylerville heard the news about the skirmishes at Lexington and Concord (April 18-19th) in a speech delivered there by General Philip Schuyler.

As the war progressed, key military events in the region fueled tensions between Patriots and Friends of Government. Early Rebel victories such as the 1775 capture of Ticonderoga and Crown Point led a hundred Charlotte county residents (including Dr. George Smyth and his brother Patrick, who later became Loyalists) to sign an "Association" (a pledge) in support of the Continental Congress. By the summer of 1775, eighteen colonial militia regiments (one for each district) had been organized in Albany County. General Philip Schuyler soon became the commander of the Continental Army's Northern Department, and Albany's militia companies had begun to contribute soldiers to the New York Line's four Continental regiments.

Albany also served as headquarters for the Patriot Army's first attempt to invade Canada. In hopes of recruiting a "fourteenth colony" to help them wage war against the British, in late June, 1775 the Continental Congress approved the creation of a 1200-man force under the joint command of Generals Philip Schuyler and Richard Montgomery. This ambitious campaign hoped to create a Provincial Congress in Canada that would send deputies to the Continental Congress and become part of the "United States of America." Documents subsequently captured from the Rebels by the British revealed that "If he [found] the Canadians disposed, Schuyler was ordered to raise a regiment at the expense of the Continental [Congress] and to select such officers as shall be agreeable to them and fit for service." By 1775 Thomas Loveless' neighborhood in northern Albany County had thus become part of the regional US-British conflict over control of the Province of Quebec that would last throughout the war.

The American expedition departed Albany in August, on its way to attack Montreal, which was taken without resistance on November 13th. Luckily, Schuyler's precarious health saved him from participating in the subsequent siege of Quebec, in the course of which Montgomery was killed. Led by Benedict Arnold, the American army and its small contingent of Anglo-Canadian allies (known as the "1st Canadian Regiment" organized by James Livingston) was forced—by disease and the arrival of British reinforcements when the St. Lawrence River's ice melted in May—to abandon its siege and retreat to northern New York.

Albany County's first Loyalist Provincial Corps units were raised in early 1776, as wealthy Tories began to assert themselves politically and prepare for the defense of their holdings in the area. That summer Loyalists clashed near Crown Point with elements of the 5000-man American force as it retreated from Canada. Albany County Loyalists must have been disappointed by the withdrawal to St. Johns of General Carleton's 13,000-man army following Benedict Arnold's spirited defense at Valcour Island in mid-October.

By mid-August, 1777 many of the Loyalist troops from Albany and Charlotte counties had received a bloody lesson in the realities of combat as a result of their defeat at the Battle of Bennington. However, the long-expected arrival of General Burgoyne's 7,500-man expeditionary force on the west side of the Hudson in mid-September raised the morale of the region's Loyalists, some of whom began to provide intelligence and logistics support to the British.

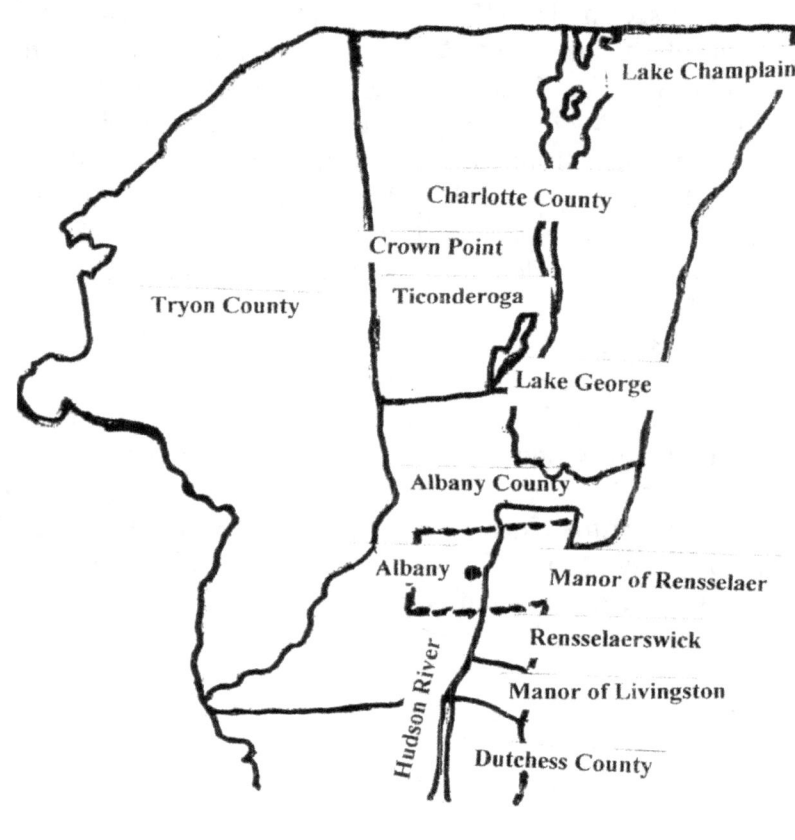

Map #2:
Albany, Charlotte, and Tryon Counties in the mid-1770s.

Early Patriot Attempts to Deal with the Loyalist Threat

Why didn't the supporters of the Revolution simply ignore their widely dispersed and vastly outnumbered Tory opponents? Henry Steele Commager has offered the following explanation: "The very strength of loyalism in America condemned it to persecution. Had the Loyalists been few in number, weak and disorganized, the Patriots might have ignored them, or have contented themselves with making sure that they could do no harm. But they were numerous and powerful, strong enough at times to take the offensive against the Patriots and endanger the success of the Revolution. It was not, therefore, surprising that even before Independence the Patriots moved to frustrate, intimidate, punish and, if possible, wipe out loyalism." [5]

From the point of view of some Patriots, the traitorous loyalists were more dangerous than enemy troops. In a February, 1777 letter about Tories sent to his friend James Warren, the firebrand Samuel Adams declared that: "In my opinion, much more is to be apprehended from the secret machinations of these rascally people than from the open violence of British and Hessian soldiers, whose success has been in great measure owing to the aid they have received from them…Indeed, my friend, if measures are not soon taken, and the most vigorous ones, to root out these pernicious weeds, it will be in vain for America to persevere in this generous struggle for the publick [sic] liberty." [6]

In Albany, Continental Army Northern Department commander General Philip Schuyler was also becoming increasingly aware of potential "fifth column" threats posed by Loyalists. As Don R. Gerlach describes Schuyler's dilemma in late 1776, "Meantime, The watch on Lake Champlain, like that on the Mohawk Valley, continued until early November. The enemy was not, however, confined to these two frontiers. Loyalists at Schuyler's rear threatened disruptions of the civil scene, defections to the enemy, and infection of the militia." [7]

Such fears led to paranoia about the dangers posed by Tory activities, and a number of tests that could be applied to determine a person's Loyalist sympathies. Chief among these was any unwillingness to serve in the Patriot militia. Other offenses that would draw the attention of one's Rebel neighbors included speaking ill of the Continental Congress, refusing to sign the "Association" barring trade with Britain, selling proscribed goods, refusing to take continental currency, praising the King, and trading with the enemy

Military participation was an important test of loyalty to the Patriot cause. New York adopted a new militia law on August 10, 1776 which ordered the drafting of every fifth man in the New York militia into the Continental Army. According to James Biser Whisker, "Those drafted and not wishing to march could pay a fine of 30pds. to be used to acquire a substitute. The law provided for the inclusion of all able-bodied men into the militia and for arming and equipping them." [8] The state's militia forces had grown to some 3000 men by late summer of 1776. Those who tried to escape militia duties or fines (especially Quakers) were the focus of increasing official pressure as the war continued.

One of the other tests imposed upon suspected Tories was a loyalty oath, several versions of which were applied during the war. It is possible that Thomas Loveless refused to swear to the following "Oath of Allegiance to The State of New York" a hand-written copy of which is preserved in the Haldimand Papers:

"I do solemly [sic] and without any mantal reservation or equivocation whatsoever swear and call God to witness that I believe and acknowledge the State of New York to be of right a free and independent State and that no Authority or power can of right be exercised in or over the said State but that is or shall be granted or derived from the People thereof. And further that as a good subject of the said free and independent State of New York, I will to the best of my knowledge and ability faithfully do my duty and as I shall keep or disregard this Oath so help and deal with me Almighty God." [9]

By early 1776 Loyalists in New York were the targets of official policy as well as popular wrath. As in other colonies, Albany County's Tories were first watched by local "Committees of Safety" and other quasi-legal "anti-conspiracy" bodies whose purpose was to intimidate and harass Loyalists. Until the New York Legislature took action to legalize such operations, these vigilante groups were responsible for much of the early violence directed at Tories. The fact that Thomas Loveless' family was forced to evacuate to Canada following his enlistment in the Jessup brothers' Provincial Corps unit suggests that high levels of violence and intimidation were being applied by Rebel sympathizers against their Loyalist neighbors in the Saratoga area by late 1776.

In 1776 armed bands in northern New York began to conduct raids against "Enemies of Liberty" that often involved summary arrests, beatings, and other forms of mob justice. Barns began to be burned, and livestock and other

OATHS[1]

I................ do solemnly swear and declare in the presence of Almighty God that I ought not and do not acknowledge any Allegiance to the King of Great Brittain, his Heirs or Successors or any power or Authority of the Parliament of the said Kingdom of Great Brittain, and that I will bear true faith and Allegiance to the State of New York as a free and Independant State, and that I will in all things to the best of my knowledge and Ability do my Duty as a good Subject of the said State ought to do, So help me God,

          Ebenezar Allen   Joseph Greenman
          Adam Vrooman   Benjamin Greenman ju[r]
          Daniel Chase   Mindert Van Hoesan
                his   Jeremije mullr
          Jonathan X Chase   his
             Mark   William X Bartel
          James X Lake   Mark
          Daniel Mosher   his
[Signatures]Ishmel Reynolds   Mathewis X Pool
            his   Mark
          John X Van Hining   his
            Mark   Tobias X Salsbury
          Charles Near   Mark
            his   John Cobham[2]
          Nicholas X Boss
             Mark
             his
          Jacob X Finehout
             Mark
             his
          Peter X Finehout
             Mark

Figure 2:
A Rebel Loyalty Oath
(Published by the State of New York in 1909)

Tory property stolen. Hazel Mathews's book provides a dramatic example of this sort of violence. The home of Loyalist John Gibson senior was attacked by a party of "Liberty Men" who fired a volley of musket fire through the door of his cabin. According to Mathews, Gibson ". . . instantly dropped himself into the cellar, and his wife Janet, uttering a shriek, crept under the bed, to escape being hit by the balls. When a barrel of beer was pierced John thought that the warm beer dripping on him through the cracks in the floor 'was puir [sic] Janet's bluid . . . and that she was surely kilt." John Gibson and his wife later fled to Canada. [11] As Albany County's "Committee of Correspondence" began its own aggressive campaign against them, some local Tories began to look to Canada as a refuge.

Why Thomas Loveless Decided to Fight for the Crown

According to Paul Huey, at the outbreak of the Revolution the situation in Charlotte County ". . . was so confused …that people's allegiances are difficult to explain. Many picked a side and remained firm in their loyalty throughout the war. Some residents (and patentees) switched from the American to the British side; others did the opposite. Too often, the reasons are unknown and can only be conjectured." He notes, however, that ". . . many people lived in patent-based, closely-knit communities with distinctive cultural origins," and that such communities often agreed to support one side of the Revolution," As examples, Huey cites the Patriot preferences of congregations of Baptists and Presbyterians and the tendency of Anglican communities to support the Crown. [12]

Recent scholarship has concluded that political ideologies probably did not play a very large role in helping people in greater New York to make up their minds about whom to support. In the words of history professor Sung Bok Kim, "The political choices the New York tenants made during the Revolution were at once more simple, more mundane, and more subtle than many scholars have suggested. The least important was the role of republican or Tory ideas and radical class interest." [13]

The factors that drove Thomas Loveless to volunteer for Tory military service were likely numerous and conflicting. As a yeoman farmer possessed of two hundred acres of land which he had purchased with his own money, he was not a direct beneficiary of The Crown. On the other hand, he had benefited indirectly from British post-1763 Indian policies—and especially the Fort Stanwix Treaty of 1768—which reduced the threat of Indian attacks on settled areas east of the Treaty Line. He probably also expected to benefit economically from British efforts to encourage English-speaking settlements along the frontier between Canada and the colonies of New York and New Hampshire, as well as the disputed "New Hampshire Grants."

In addition, Thomas' father had served in British-sponsored Militia or Provincial Corps units during previous conflicts, and Thomas himself was very likely a veteran of the later campaigns of the French & Indian War. Based upon his previous contact with British regular forces, he probably believed that Britain's military professionals would have little trouble putting down a rebellion fomented by "Whig" political radicals and led by military amateurs. He may have also been attracted by the prospect of receiving "bounty land" that the British had announced would be confiscated from the Rebels and given to Loyalists troops following suppression of the Patriot uprising.

TEUCRO DUCE NIL DESPERANDUM.

First Battalion of PENNSYLVANIA LOYALISTS, commanded by His Excellency Sir WILLIAM HOWE, K. B.

ALL INTREPID ABLE-BODIED

HEROES.

WHO are willing to serve His MAJESTY KING GEORGE the Third, in Defence of their Country, Laws and Conſtitution, againſt the arbitrary Uſurpations of a tyrannical Congreſs, have now not only an Opportunity of manifeſting their Spirit, by aſſiſting in reducing to Obedience their too-long deluded Countrymen, but alſo of acquiring the polite Accompliſhments of a Soldier, by ſerving only two Years, or during the preſent Rebellion in America.

Such ſpirited Fellows, who are willing to engage, will be rewarded at the End of the War, beſides their Laurels, with 50 Acres of Land, where every gallant Hero may retire, and enjoy his Bottle and Laſs.

Each Volunteer will receive as a Bounty, FIVE DOLLARS, beſides Arms, Cloathing and Accoutrements, and every other Requiſite proper to accommodate a Gentleman Soldier, by applying to Lieutenant Colonel ALLEN, or at Captain KEARNY's Rendezvous, at PATRICK TONRY's, three Doors above Market-ſtreet, in Second-ſtreet.

Figure 3:
A British Provincial Corps Recruiting Poster,
The Pennsylvania Ledger, November 12, 1777

Although he would not have known of Burgoyne's plans to invade New York in the coming year, Thomas Loveless would certainly have heard about the recent British victories over American forces in New York City and New Jersey and the Patriot militia units being formed throughout Albany County. He may also have heard about a regiment recruited in Albany made up of refugees from Canada who had supported the US invasion of that province in 1775. Created by the Continental Congress in January, 1776 and commanded by former Canadian resident Colonel Moses Hazen the 200-man unit known as "The 2nd Canadian Regiment," enjoyed the support of Philip Schuyler, who had strong business ties in Canada and had been General Montgomery's co-commander during the invasion of 1775-1776.

In addition, Ranger companies had recently been stationed at Ballstown and several other "pro-British" townships in an effort to seek out and counter Tory resistance. Finally, like many other Loyalists, Thomas may have volunteered to fight for the British simply because his neighbors were doing so, or because he was tired of being harassed and intimidated by Rebel informers, committees, and vigilante groups.

It must be remembered that yeoman farmer Thomas Loveless was living in a rural area that was uniquely pro-British. In his article on the loyalty choices of American farmers during the Revolution, Canadian historian Wallace Brown noted that, in general, "The Loyalist position appealed most to some rich, urban and urbane conservatives and was not compatible with the "spirit of equality" which characterized the rural areas," and that "Throughout America most leading farmers were . . .Whig." However, Brown discovered that the farmer-Loyalists of northern New York were a conspicuous exception to this rule. His study of the

American Loyalists' post-war claims submitted to the British Government found that nearly 75 percent of New York's claimants were farmers. New Jersey's percentage was 50, and in the Carolinas the percentages were in the mid-40s.

While Brown cites factors such as negative personal experiences, economic self-interest, faith in British military superiority, and the proximity of major British forces in New York City after 1776 as motivations for New York Loyalists, he concludes with the following general assessment: "Most humble farmers throughout America were not against the Revolution, but a good many were loyal. The reasons for the loyalty of most of them will never be known; many may not even have known themselves." [14]

The Jessup brothers' headquarters near Corinth on the Hudson was a rallying point for local Tories, and the brothers had been promised commands in the Royal provincial service by their patron, Governor Tryon. Both Ebenezer and Edward Jessup sponsored the formation of Loyalist provincial corps units in Albany and at Fort Edward, but the paucity of volunteers resulted in a single battalion, designated "The King's Loyal Americans" KLA) or "Jessup's Corps" led by Ebenezer, granted the rank of Lieutenant Colonel, with Captain Edward Jessup second in command, and the youngest Jessup brother, Joseph, a Lieutenant in charge of one of its six companies.

A document entitled "Muster Roll of Captain Edward Jessup's Company of Loyal Americans from New York" (i.e. the KLA) shows Thomas Loveless as having enlisted on 4 November, 1776. The Muster covers an eighty-two day period (4 November, 1776 to 24 January, 1777), and describes the unit as follows: "Mustered present in Captain Edward Jessup's Company of Loyal Americans: One Lieutenant, Two Ensigns, one Sergeant, One Corporal, and twenty-three Private Men." [15] Ebenezer Jessup had used the prospect of land bounties to attract recruits, reportedly pledging "…24,000 acres of his land to those who 'would serve faithfully during the war…and 20,000 more to such of my officers as should merit the same by their good conduct."[16] As the father of five sons and the owner of only two hundred acres, Thomas Loveless could easily have been convinced to join the KLA by such generous offers of post-war "bounty land."

As originally conceived, the King's Loyal Americans was to consist of ten companies, each containing sixty men. When fully officered and recruited, the unit would have had a total strength of 650, but this number was never achieved. Each company commander was responsible for recruiting his own men, and officers' commissions could only become official after the battalion had reached two-thirds of its target strength. The KLA was commanded by Lt. Colonel Ebenezer Jessup from 1776 to the autumn of 1781, when it was combined with elements of the Queen's Loyal Rangers, or "Peter's Corps" commanded by Colonel John Peters to form a new regiment called the Loyal Rangers, whose commander was Major Edward Jessup.

When the Jessup brothers delivered the KLA's 80 men to a surprised Sir Guy Carleton at Crown Point in November, 1776, the General had been given no appropriate orders to deal with Loyalist-sponsored volunteer units. The Jessups insisted that they had raised their own regiment in order to "conquer our enemies and re-establish civil government for the honour of the Crown and the true interest of the Colonies." Although Carleton would have preferred that they return home and await further orders, he had no choice but to provide the Loyalist volunteers from New York with provisions, shelter, and clothing. When Carleton moved his forces into winter quarters, the still officially unrecognized KLA was moved to Chateauguay (near the Falls of St. Louis, south of Montreal) to spend the winter, where its ranks were reduced by smallpox and other illnesses.

Although the Privates of the King's Loyal Americans were not yet formally soldiers in General Carleton's army, they were paid 6d. per day in "Halifax Currency," minus deductions for their rations, clothing, and hospital costs. They continued to refer to themselves as "Jessup's Corps," and demanded (unsuccessfully) the right to choose their officers. Their numbers were still quite small—eleven officers, six non-commissioned officers, a surgeon's mate, and sixty-two privates. [17]

The KLA's officers could not formally receive their commissions until their unit had reached two-thirds strength, and so the unit was temporarily attached to a Canada-based Provincial Corps unit, the King's Royal Regiment of New York, commanded by Sir John Johnson. As a consequence, recruitment of additional personnel became the principal peacetime priority of prospective KLA officers. In a July, 1777 report to Lord Germain in London, General Burgoyne commented that: "Mr. Peters and Mr. Jessup, who came over to Canada last autumn, one from the neighborhood of Albany, the other from Charlotte County, are confident of success as the army advances. Their battalions are not in embryo but very promising; they have fought with spirit."[18] Meanwhile, Ebenezer Jessup had to meet many of the unit's expenses from his own pockets. A year later he was still lobbying General Burgoyne for reimbursement for past expenditures, and reminding the General of the KLA's services to himself, General Carleton, and Carleton's successor, General Frederick Haldimand. [19]

The uniforms worn by Thomas Loveless' Provincial Corps unit were similar in design to Regular British Army uniforms, but had their own special color combinations. The initial colors of the King's Loyal Americans' uniforms were reportedly as follows: "First (coats or jackets) uniforms red, trimmed with green, red, then green." These colors were not always available, however. Information regarding other items of the unit's uniforms and equipment (such as headgear, waistcoats, breeches, canteens, cartridge boxes, belts, shoes, and other leather items) is scarce, and no original image of a typical KLA officer, non-commissioned officer, or private soldier has survived.[20]

The style and quality of uniforms issued to the Tory Provincial Corps units varied, especially following their arrival in Canada. In December of 1778, Captain Jessup was forced to write General Haldimand about "the danger to the loyalists of wearing the clothing in the store (blue faced with white) as it is the same as the uniform of some of the enemy's troops," and asked that his men be again supplied with red uniforms.[21] René Chartrand notes that a year after the King's Loyal Americans was combined with the Queen's Loyal Rangers to form "The Loyal Rangers," its men were issued "green coats faced with red, shirts, hats, and moccasins." However, as the majority of the unit's men were employed at the time as "artificers" building roads, houses and fortifications, most of them probably did not wear their uniforms every day.

The Consequences of his Enlistment for his Family

Once Thomas Loveless joined the King's Loyal Americans, his family would have found themselves under much greater suspicion and scrutiny by the Patriot authorities. Wallace Brown's summary of the persecution endured by Tories elsewhere in New York gives us an idea of what the Loveless family might have faced: "No province passed harsher laws against Loyalists than New York. Numerous examples of unofficial and illegal persecution are found in the claims commission testimony—burnings, mobbings, and, in New York City, 'Grand Toory [sic] Rides,' as a contemporary called the grisly riding on a rail. Only one tarring and feathering is mentioned but there certainly were others." Brown references examples of the harassment of Loyalist dependents and the confiscation and sale of Loyalist lands during the war, and notes that the 1783 Peace Treaty did not immediately put an end to such persecution.[22]

By the end of 1776, New York State authorities faced a new kind of Loyalist threat, and had begun to devise more effective ways to deal with it. With the British occupation of New York City, the center of Loyalist activity shifted to the Hudson Highlands, which became a source of Tory volunteers for British military units in Long Island or Manhattan. In addition to concerns about Loyalist threats to the state's northern and western frontiers, Albany leaders feared a Tory uprising might take place at some future critical moment.

It was to head off such prospects that on September 21, 1776 New York's Provincial Convention created its first major Loyalist suppression organization, a standing committee "…for the express purpose of enquiring into, detecting, and defeating all conspiracies which may be formed in this State, against the liberties of America." Led by a staff of six and supported by both "secret service" and military components, this "First Commission" would remain active from December 11, 1776 to September 23, 1778. As a result of its investigations, hundreds of Loyalists were arrested, tried, imprisoned, released on bail, or deported to other states.

We have no details with which to document the Loveless family's experiences in their father's absence, but the following view of the plight of other Loyalist dependents probably applies: "Loyalist women's experiences during the Revolution were more disorienting that those of the Patriots. Like their Patriot counterparts, they had to care for their families when their husbands or fathers were gone but many had to do so after their property had been plundered or confiscated. They had to cope as well with the uncertainty and haphazard nature of Patriot decisions about their future. Also, they were forced to leave their homes, extended families, and communities and make their way to British lines…" [23]

We do not know the date on which Lois Loveless and her seven children finally abandoned the family's farm in Palmerstown for the safety of Canada. However, it was most likely during the first six months of 1777—a period when fears of a British invasion from the North were at their height. We can only guess at the route, the means, and the weather conditions of the Loveless family's journey, but the surviving accounts of such escapes by other Loyalist families reveal that these transits were often traumatic, especially for infants and younger children.

CHAPTER THREE

THOMAS LOVELESS' LOYALIST MILITARY CAREER DURING 1776-1777

Because the King's Loyal Americans was at only one third strength during the Burgoyne expedition of 1777, a few of it's men saw action on the flanks of the army during the two battles at Saratoga, while most worked with the batteaux (supply boats) bringing up supplies for the British forces. Evidence from General Burgoyne's orderly book indicates that once the British invasion force arrived at Crown Point in late June both Jessup's Corps and Peter's Corps had initially been placed under the command of Baron Friedrich von Riedesel, perhaps because the Loyalists corps included a number of German-speakers. During the next two months both of the Tory units were probably used as foragers, responsible for obtaining food, fodder, horses and wagons from local sources.

The Tory Spy's unit was lucky in that it did not participate in the disastrous British/Tory defeat at the Battle of Bennington on August 17th, 1777. Unaware of the growing strength of Rebel militia units in the area, General Burgoyne had ordered Lt. Colonel Fredrick Baum to lead a large-scale raid that would (in addition to obtaining horses and badly-needed food and forage) "try the affections of the country" and "complete Peter's corps"—two objectives designed to increase Loyalist recruitment. Burgoyne was apparently hoping that prominent local Tories would be especially helpful to this expedition. In his instructions to Colonel Baum, Burgoyne noted that "Col. [Philip] Skene will be with you as much as possible, in order to assist you with his advice; to procure the best intelligence of the enemy; and to choose those people who are to bring the accounts of your progress and success (i.e. reliable military couriers)." [1]

The Bennington clash involved large numbers of men from locally-recruited Patriot militia and Loyalist units. As a result, the battle's aftermath provided a bizarre kind of "family reunion." Writing in 1848, 92-year-old Thomas Mellen, a veteran of the Bennington fight, described the post-combat situation in the following words: "When the smoke cleared away, those who had vanquished the tories beheld, among the captives, among the wounded, among the killed, their neighbors, and in some cases their kinsmen. My own mother's father was in the battle under Stark. My stepmother's father, but for an accident, might have fought in the same engagement under Baum; and these, my two 'grandfathers' were cousins." [2]

Another example of the civil war aspects of the Bennington battle can be found in the post-war "Narrative" written by Lieutenant Colonel John Peters, who was in command of the Queen's Loyal Rangers. In Peters' words: "A little before the Royalists gave way, the Rebels pushed with a strong party on the Front of the Loyalists where I commanded. As they were coming up I observed a Man fire at me, which I returned. He loaded again as he came up and discharged again at me, and, crying out: 'Peters, you Damned Tory, I have got you,' he rushed on me with his bayonet, which entered just below my left Breast, but was turned by the Bone. By this time I was loaded and I saw that it was a Rebel Captain, and old school-fellow and playmate, and a Cousin of my Wife's. Tho' his Bayonet was in my body, I felt regret at being obliged to destroy him." [3]

Figure 4:
Alonzo Chappel's painting of the British/Tory surrender following the Battle of Bennington

The treatment of the Loyalist prisoners captured at Bennington provides a classic example of the levels of the Rebel militia's hatred for Tories. According to one summary account, following the battle: "The men of Peter's Corps [the Queen's Loyal Rangers] here discovered for themselves how Provincial soldiers could expect to be treated by the rebels. One of them, half dead with his left eye smashed open by a musket-ball, was slung on a captured horse with a similar wound and led around for the amusement of the rebel militiamen. Other prisoners were ordered tied in pairs and attached by traces to horses, driven by Negroes. The state government ordered them to tramp their way through deep snows to make roads for the rebels to use—while clad only in thin shoes, or actually barefoot." [4]

Those Loyalists who survived the Bennington defeat did not gain any benefit from their comrades' sacrifice in the eyes of General Burgoyne, who blamed the debacle on the Loyalists, rather than upon Lieutenant Colonel Baum and his own regular forces. In a letter of August 20th to Lord George Germain "Gentleman Johnny" acknowledged the defeat, but claimed that the Rebel losses at Bennington were "more than double ours." He went on to blame the "misfortune" upon the military weaknesses of "professed Loyalists" and the mistakes of "a Provincial gentleman of confidence" [most likely Philip Skene] who betrayed Colonel Baum's design and misjudged the strength of Rebel militia.[5]

Regardless of the Bennington defeat, the morale of the British and Tory survivors in Canada remained high. John Peters recounts the reaction of his wife to an early (and erroneous) report that both Peters and his eldest son had been wounded and had died following the battle. In response to this bad news from a senior British officer, Mrs. Peters reportedly said: ". . . my calamities are very great, but, thank God, they died doing their duty to their King and Country. I have Six Sons left who, as soon as they shall be able to bear Arms, I will send against the Rebels, while I and my daughter will mourn for the Dead and pray for the living." [6]

In the month prior to the Bennington disaster, one of Thomas Loveless' fellow soldiers in the King's Loyal Americans, Lieutenant David Jones, had an even more unpleasant experience when on July 27th his fiancee', twenty-three-year old Loyalist Jane McRae was killed and scalped by a party of General Burgoyne's Indian allies who were escorting her from Fort Edward to Fort Ann. Legend claims that Lt. Jones later recognized his fiancee's " blonde tresses" hanging from the trophy belt of an Indian at Fort Ann. This notorious incident was disputed at length by both sides, with much outrage, but little detailed information about how the crime was committed.

General Horatio Gates, the newly appointed commander of the Northern Department, sent a letter to Burgoyne (who had previously complained to Gates about the inhumane treatment of Tory prisoners at Bennington) charging that "The miserable fate of Miss McCrea [sic] was particularly aggravated by her being dressed to receive her promised husband, but met her murderer employed by you." Burgoyne replied with sympathy, but claiming his "insight into the Indian mentality" refused to execute the culprits. [6] Contrary to legend, Lieutenant David Jones did not go insane with grief or desert to Canada, but remained on duty with the KLA and ultimately joined the "Tory Secret Service." Lorenzo Sabine claims that David was the brother of Jonathan Jones, who served in the Queen's Loyal Rangers and was probably the Jonathan Jones who witnessed young James Loveless' claims petition submitted to the British Government in 1786.

The arrival of General John Burgoyne's 7500-man army in northern New York in September frightened many Patriots in the area, but was viewed by Loyalists throughout the state as the prelude to inevitable victory over the Rebels. An article in a Loyalist newspaper in New York City on September 29th described these prospects in the following terms:

" From Albany we learn the beginning of this month Gen. Burgoyne's army was advanced as far as Saratoga, about thirty-two miles northward of that place . . . it was expected that General Burgoyne would reach Albany in this month, . . . that the Loyalists in that quarter had acted with much spirit, upwards of two thousand having joined the Royal army; many others in the rear of the Rebel army, that could not join, were collected in small parties in different parts of the county of Albany, . . . frequent skirmishes happened between Rebels and Loyalists, in one of which about one hundred and fifty loyalists were attacked by twice their number of Rebels. . . may those brave loyal sons soon be supported, and enabled to retaliate their injuries on those rebel tyrants." (This article also appeared in the Pennsylvania Evening Post on October 30, 1777)

Although the Jessups found it harder to recruit in the Albany area after Burgoyne's expeditionary force began to move south in the summer of 1777, according to Mary Beacock Fryer the strength of The King's Loyal Americans had increased to 272 men by late July. By October 7th, casualties, prisoners, and desertions had reduced this number to 175. While few details concerning the KLA's participation in the crucial battles fought at Saratoga on September 19th and October 7^{tth} has survived, Thomas Loveless was apparently a member of a company (fourteen men under Captain Hugh Munro) of Tory teamsters and bateaux men providing vital logistics support to Burgoyne's army.

This was no small task, as these land and water supply lines were being closely guarded by a force led by newly-promoted Brigadier General John Stark, "The Hero of Bennington." The KLA logistics company's bateaux support was especially vital when Burgoyne's retreating army encamped at Old Saratoga, seven miles north of Freeman's Farm on October 7th. Short of supplies and without winter clothing, Burgoyne's troops were in no condition to make the planned march to Fort Ticonderoga in cold, stormy weather. Until the surrender ceremony on October 17th, the exhausted British troops depended upon whatever supplies could be brought in at night by bateaux on the Hudson.

As a result, the KLA boatmen became some of the very few Loyalist soldiers who served alongside the "Provincial Marine," a small force (some 300 men) of Loyalists and Canadians led by officers seconded from the Royal Navy. The Ontario Archives' French Papers contain a later certificate from Captain John Schanck stating that Major Edward Jessup ". . . was attached to the Naval Department on the Hudson's River by order of His Excellency General Burgoyne for the purpose of guarding and navigating the Batteaux [sic] and during that service he shew'd great Zeal and attention to the orders given him for the provision of the Provision etc." [8]

Luckily, Loveless was not one of the Jessup's Corps soldiers involved in the futile defense of the Breymann Redoubt at Saratoga on the night of October 7th. Thus he was one of 796 Provincial Corps soldiers (more than half of them prisoners of war) who survived the two Saratoga engagements. Like his fellow Loyalists, he turned in his weapon (to the jeers of a hostile crowd who reportedly recognized the Jessup brothers) at the formal surrender ceremony on October 17th. In order to obtain his parole, he was required to sign an oath (known as "the Convention") promising no further participation in the war. While the Regulars in Burgoyne's Army (except for the officers) were marched off to prisoner of war camps near Charlottesville, Virginia, the Loyalist volunteers were allowed to return to Canada.

On their way to Boston, General Burgoyne and his staff officers visited Albany, where they were lavishly entertained at the mansion of General Philip Schuyler, who until recently had been Commander of the Northern Department. Burgoyne was reportedly overwhelmed by Schuyler's hospitality in light of the fact that, as it passed through Fishkill (near Old Saratoga) in mid-September, the British Army had destroyed Schuyler's mills and summer home, which were valued at some £10,000 Burgoyne's visit lasted three days. According to the diary of the Baroness Von Riedesel, whose husband was a senior British staff officer, Burgoyne told his host "You are too kind to me, who have done you so much injury," to which Schuyler replied "Such is the fate of war; let us not dwell on the subject." [9]

While the King's Loyal Americans had emerged relatively unscathed from the defeats at Bennington and Saratoga, this was not the case for Captain John Peters' Queen's Loyal Rangers. The Monthly Returns for this unit for the periods 7 August and 2 October, 1777 show a decline in total unit strength from 262 men (of whom 180 were designated "present and fit for duty" on August 7th) to 154 men of all ranks (of whom 46 were designated "present and fit for duty" on October 2nd). By that date, only twelve of the company's original twenty-one Sergeants remained on duty, and one Captain and thirty men were Rebel prisoners. After the second battle of Saratoga five days later, the unit was reduced to sixty-two men of all ranks, some thirty-five of whom, led by Peters, escaped through Rebel lines to Lake George and returned to Canada.

Following the British surrender and parole ceremonies, which were held less than a mile from the site where he would be hanged four years later (See map on page 172), Thomas Loveless and his Tory colleagues returned to Canada via Fort Edward and Fort Ticonderoga, and went into winter quarters near Lachine. By this time the King's Loyal Americans had shrunk to 130 officers and men (83 of whom were temporarily on parole, or "under convention"), with 16 men listed as "prisoners of the rebels." The situation of Captain Peters' Queens Loyal Rangers was much worse, with only 89 officers and men fit for duty, (with 11 "under convention"), and 79 "prisoners of the Rebels." New recruits were becoming hard to find, and KLA men were frequently assigned temporarily to other Loyalist under-strength units. For the next three years these Loyalist soldiers would spend most of their time on garrison duty at Pointe-Claire, Lachine, or Sorel near Montreal building fortifications, roads, and homes for refugees, and foraging for hay.

With the possible exception of small-scale incursions such as the one against Fort Edward in the autumn of 1780, the survivors of the KLA and The Queen's Loyal Americans took no part in offensive military operations after 1777. For many Loyalist soldiers, and especially those whose families had not yet relocated to Canada, life "in garrison" must have proved a bit monotonous. However, for those with the right skills and experience, the war was not over. Within a year of his return to Canada, Thomas Loveless was employed helping British Army scouts transit and infiltrate what was to them unfamiliar territory in northern New York.

Perhaps because of his age and previous military experience, Thomas Loveless appears to have been treated from the outset as a senior enlisted man with leadership potential. An undated document submitted to Haldimand's Headquarters by Edward Jessup entitled: "Account of Provisions Furnished by Edward Jessup in the Year 1776 to bring Loyalists from the Province of New York to Canady, and of cash paid to different men for transporting them thirty-six miles into the woods," is verified and signed by Thomas Loveless and five other men, including a Lieutenant, an Ensign, and a Sergeant. [9] A Return of the Officers and Men of the King's Loyal Americans commanded by Lieutenant Colonel Ebenezer Jessup from the 25th of June to the 24th of October, 1777 lists Thomas Loveless as a member of the Company in that unit commanded by Major Edward Jessup, Esquire. Loveless is listed just three lines below the Company's three officers and only sergeant, Martin Kelley, suggesting that he is a senior or trusted enlisted man. [11]

CHANGING SIDES—1778-1780

CHAPTER FOUR

The Strategic Context

In early 1778 the Board of War had proposed another invasion of Canada, although the idea was opposed by George Washington. Command of the operation was given to Lafayette, and troops and Albany again became the focus of recruitment of men and supplies for the expedition. However, when fewer than 1200 men volunteered and the necessary logistics support failed to appear, Congress accepted Lafayette's recommendation that the project be abandoned.

Meanwhile, along the frontiers of Pennsylvania and New York, another "war within a war" was about to escalate as the British fully unleashed their Indian allies in the summer of 1778. Now Seneca, Mohawk, and other Iroquois forces, often supported by Loyalist units such as Butler's Rangers raised by the Butler brothers or "Johnson's Greens" (also known as The King's Royal Regiment of New York) raised by Sir John Johnson began to terrorize frontier homesteads and settlements, applying the ambush and scalping tactics of what historian John Grenier has called "The First Way of War." He notes that, unlike the Tory vs. Rebel struggles in other colonies, ". . . as Patriots and Loyalists skirmished and killed one another along the New York frontier, frontiersmen were in the midst of a larger war of conquest, and the Indians were in a ferocious war of anti-colonialism, on the same frontier."[1]

According to Grenier, this British decision was inevitable: "The British disaster at Saratoga and the French Alliance that ensued changed the character of the war, especially on the New York frontier. Just as in the Seven Year's War, necessity forced the British to turn to American rangers and the Iroquois. British commanders in Canada, with the loss of 7,000 regular troops and no prospect of acquiring a replacement for Burgoyne's army, found that they had too few men on hand to use in other than defensive roles. They therefore had no choice but to use the rangers for offensive operations." [2]

Although George Washington purposely overlooked the use of similar harsh tactics by his own Indian allies, the British command's ultimate approval of such extreme measures against civilians caused severe "blowback" for the Tories of New York. After the massacres in the Wyoming and Cherry Valleys, and following the retaliatory Sullivan-Clinton campaign against the Senecas in the summer of 1779, Butler's Rangers and other Tory ranger units had become infamous and the targets of Patriot outrage. This same hostility would now be faced by all those identified as Loyalists, especially in New York and Pennsylvania.

By 1779 the larger war had become a stalemate in which neither side seemed capable of achieving a decisive victory. Defeated in their early efforts to divide and conquer the northern colonies, the British had re-deployed their major land and naval forces to the south, hoping to capitalize upon what they perceived as stronger Tory support in the Carolinas. With the capture of Charleston and Savannah, this strategy seemed about to pay off, although the region's Loyalists had turned out to be more of a burden than an asset. For their part, the American forces had enjoyed few battlefield triumphs since Saratoga, and the long-term impact of the French alliance remained uncertain. Meanwhile, within the Continental Army a general war weariness and growing frustration with the shortcomings of the Continental Congress were beginning to generate serious mutinies, increased desertions, and in the case of Benedict Arnold, treason.

Fears of a Second British Invasion Lead to More Rigorous Anti-Tory Measures and Tougher Laws Dealing with Espionage

Rumors of impending attacks by Canada-based British forces persisted in both Albany and Charlotte counties during 1778-1779. Some of these were generated by Loyalist agents in the area, who in February, 1778 circulated anonymous messages in Albany warning that the British were planning ". . . to burn your City, all your Stores and all your Mills, as soon as the River opens; a great many negroes are enlisted, Regular Soldiers, Tories." From the British perspective, such disinformation served the dual purpose of keeping local Militia and Continental Army units off balance and heading off any offensive operations by US forces against Canada. However, because of these threats, the economic, social, and legal status of northern New York's Loyalists was becoming increasingly precarious.

As A.C. Flick described it, the system for repressing Loyalists throughout the colonies was both multi-tiered and complex: "From the sovereign Continental Congress to the pettiest district committee there was a comparatively uniform procedure, based on continental and provincial regulations and supplemented by precedents. Authorization came from the supreme representative bodies, but the enforcement of the scheme was left to minor boards. The Continental Congress laid down the program on general lines, but let each colony devise its own ways and means."[3] Ironically, the increasingly aggressive "Tory Control" measures adopted by Patriot authorities often created many newly-mobilized Loyalists while in the process of suppressing Tories already resisting Rebel rule.

By April, 1778 the State Legislature had created the "Board of Commissioners for Detecting and Defeating Conspiracies in the State of New York "Although all seven of the County Boards which functioned in New York during the war were required to keep records of their proceedings, only the Albany County Board's <u>Minutes</u> have survived. In the course of its deliberations, the Albany Board arrested and tried some 1000 Loyalists for treasonous activities. The transcripts of the Board's sessions provide a revealing glimpse into the American side of the Loyalist-Rebel "civil war" in Albany County, as well as the "intelligence war" fought between the Canada-based Tory Secret Service and its Continental Army opponents during 1781-1782.

Stefan Bielinski has summarized the Albany Board's activities as follows: "Informants were cultivated in each district, as the commissioners gathered information on potential internal enemies. Evidence on dozens of suspected Tories was evaluated. Militia detachments were sent into the countryside to bring in suspected Tories for examination. Many with ties to upstanding revolutionaries typically were required to post bail guaranteeing their good behavior. Strangers were ordered to leave the country." [4]

Staffed by current or former court officials, the Albany Board was essentially an investigative body tasked with determining the seriousness of threats to the Patriot cause posed by "disaffected" individuals or groups. Separate from military courts-martial jurisdiction and proceedings, the Board none-the-less had the power to arrest, try and incarcerate suspected Tories. <u>Minutes</u> editor V.H. Paltsits describes the system's operations as follows: "A warrant for arrest was issued in most cases after charges preferred by some Whig. It was of course the duty of every true citizen of the state to reveal the identity of disloyalty in any form.

When persons refused to reveal information which was requested of them, they were themselves sent to prison. Under these circumstances it was not unusual that suspicious persons construed Dame Rumor to the damnation of their neighbors, and that revengeful spirits were afforded an outlet." [5]

Although some suspects surrendered themselves, the Board's four Commissioners usually ordered their arrest by militia parties or small teams of specially-hired Rangers. Once the Board had interrogated the subjects brought before it, it discharged them in a variety of ways. According to Paltsits: "Accused persons were fully exonerated, or allowed to go at large on their honor, or were kept within certain bounds, or were put under recognizance and bail for their future good behavior, or required to appear before the Board or a Commissioner daily or monthly or when called upon, or to present themselves at the meetings of designated courts. Some were enlarged [freed] on condition of their joining the Continental Army Bail varied all the way from 40pds to 5,000pds." [6]

The accused could improve their bargaining position if they agreed to sign a loyalty oath or offered to spy for the Board if they were released. Those prisoners deemed sufficiently disaffected and dangerous—both male and female—were sent to prison for various periods, but were often released in less than a year. Because prisoners were sent to Albany from other counties, the Albany jail was frequently overcrowded and usually unhealthy. Security was sometimes lax, and escapes by the more experienced of its prisoners were not uncommon.

The following description of one of these escapes is based upon the memoir of Simon Bloodgood, who, as a lad of thirteen in 1778 witnessed the execution of seven 'disaffected men, who, to bad political principles, had added crimes against society which even a state of war would not justify.' According to Catherine Crary, "These men had escaped once; as prisoners once again, they had taken bricks from the fireplace, had barricaded the door of the Albany prison against the sheriff, and had laid a line of stolen gun powder so as to blow up their adversaries along with themselves, should the door be battered in. Guards cut a hole through the ceiling and introduced a fire hose which quickly inundated the powder. A brave Irishman jumped in with a cudgel and, followed by other intrepid citizens, subdued the captives." [7]

The property of Loyalists also became the target of official sanctions. In October, 1779 the New York legislature passed an Act of Attainder which permitted the confiscation and sale of the estates of fifty-nine "Persons who have adhered to the enemies of this State," specifically listing the property of wealthy Albany County Tories such as the Jessup brothers and Philip Skene. For the time being, the New York authorities did not target minor land-owners and yeoman farmers such as Thomas Loveless, but the Act of Attainder was a sign that, even in the event of a British victory, the post-war return of Loyalists to their properties in New York would be difficult. By the war's end, nearly forty percent of New York State's 851 Confiscation Judgments would involve properties in Albany and Charlotte counties. [8]

Eight months later the Albany Board took new steps to counter future British intelligence-gathering efforts in the Northern Department. On June 30, 1780—three months prior to the arrest of Major John André and the discovery of his role in Benedict Arnold's treason—the Board passed an act stipulating that all persons who came from the British lines and were found lurking secretly in any part of the state, were to be tried as spies. [9]

The cumulative effectiveness of these anti-Tory measures would prove to be crucial to the success of the Revolutionary movement in New York State. Draconian as these measures may seem today, they eventually achieved their purpose. In the summer of 1782, Alexander Hamilton wrote Gouverneur Morris, claiming (a bit inaccurately): ". . . that while half of the state had been loyal to the king in the early years of the war, the energy of its government had suppressed much of the opposition and reduced the faction to one-third." [10]

The strengthening of the laws dealing with treason and espionage put the "stay-behind" Tories under greater scrutiny and pressure. Those Loyalists who chose not to evacuate to Canada became an increasing source of concern for Patriot authorities following the Battle of Saratoga. While there is no way to accurately determine their numbers, many of the Tories who remained behind to protect their properties actively supported British courier and Intelligence operations. Some of these people were the relatives (including wives and children) of local men who had joined Provincial Corps units and retreated to Canada. Others had been recruited in the Northern Department as "agents in place" by British Intelligence, and a few had been brought to Canada for training and sent back to their old neighborhoods. Their support functions included management of the "letterboxes" and "safe houses" used by Haldimand's Quebec-New York City courier network, support for Tory-led scouting and kidnapping operations, collection of local intelligence, dissemination of propaganda and other misleading information, and helping Loyalists secretly escape to Canada.

Although Rebel paranoia often exaggerated the seriousness of Tory fifth column threats, the Albany Board's

Minutes reveal a broad spectrum of potentially dangerous local Loyalist activities, many of which appear to have involved the Tory Spy's neighbors in Jessup's Patent, Palmertown, and other parts of the Saratoga District:

--On April 27, 1778 Jonathon Pettit was required to post 100 pds. Bail for Christopher Bennet of Parmerstown, who was "confined to gaol and extreamly [sic] ill." Pettit promised to return Bennet to jail once he had recovered.[11]

--Early the next month, John Stiles of Parmertown was "permitted to return to his place of abode" upon his entering into a "recognizance for good behavior and monthly appearance [before the Board]." [12]

--On May 27th, Stiles and two other men from Parmertown—Samuel and John Perry— "heretofore eliberated" [sic] [i.e. set free] made their appearance before the Commissioners.[13]

--On June 18, 1778, John Boyd Jr. and Alexander McAuley who ". . .were apprehended by a party of Continental troops at Jessup's Patent on their way to Canada" were ordered to be "closely confined." (They were later "liberated on recognizance" after paying 200pds. in bail each). [14]

-- In September of the same year, the Board ordered Albany Militia officers to maintain lists "…of the names of the persons within their respective Beats [Districts]" who had "lately gone over and joined the enemy." [15]

--The Board noted the receipt on August 19, 1779 of a letter from General Philip Schuyler, who claimed that "several of the inhabitants of Palmertown" have been guilty of harboring and concealing "a party of men from the Enemy," and asked the Board to investigate. [16]

--On September 22nd of the same year a man named Blackman Browning was described by the Board as "A spy sent by Major [Philip] Skene into General Stark's army, for which piece of service he received twenty dollars." [17]

--In early October of 1780 the Board ordered militia Colonel Cornelius Van Veghten [sic] to arrest Hans Peter Snyder of Fishkill at Saratoga, who "has and still keeps up a correspondence with the enemy and harbors persons passing through the country who are coming from the enemy." [18]

--The Board's Minutes of October 22, 1780 noted that Major General Schuyler was sending to Albany, "under guard," two inhabitants of the Saratoga District "for harboring and concealing spies sent from the enemy," and one James Van Driesen, "who has come from the enemy in the character of a spy." [19]

--Two months later, the Board ordered Colonel Gansevoort to apprehend "John Cobham, John Stiles, and the man living at a place called the Halfway House in Jessup's Patent [who] are concerned in forwarding in forwarding intelligence to Canada." [20]

The Roles of Blacks and Indians in Rebel-Tory Conflict in Albany County

The varied roles played by Blacks and Indians in Albany County's Rebel-Tory Conflict demonstrate that race was a dividing factor. Ultimately, the names of over five hundred "Negroes" were included in the Canadian Honor Roll of the Tory refugees known as United Empire Loyalists. The majority of these arrived as part of the more than 7,000

Loyalists evacuated by the British from New York City to Nova Scotia during 1783, but a few had come to Canada from northern New York. At the start of the war, Blacks constituted about ten percent of Albany County's population, or about 4,300 persons, few of whom were Freedmen. Most of these African-Americans lived in the more densely-populated, rather than the rural, parts of the County. While slavery was widespread, the majority of Albany County's slaves were owned by a few wealthy families.

During the war, people in both contending factions in Albany County owned slaves, and the allegiances of Blacks often paralleled those of their Masters. A number of the Tory families who moved to Canada after 1776 brought their slaves with them, and the names of Black men (such as "Scipio," "Nero," or "Prince") can also be found in the muster rolls of New York Provincial Corps units. A man who listed his country of origin as "Africa," Private John Jacobs, served as a soldier in a company commanded by Loyalist Justus Sherwood. Volunteering to fight for the British could be a dangerous option for Black Tories. A newspaper article dated Newport, Rhode Island, May 29, 1775 reported that "Two tory Negroes have been lately hanged in the province of New-York, and several others were to be tried for their lives, they have been detected in joining the tories, and engaging to murder their masters who were supporters of Liberty."[21] On the Patriot side, there were Black volunteers serving with local Continental Army and Albany County militia companies in various capacities, and some African-Americans regularly informed Patriot authorities of the activities of their "pro-British" fellow slaves.

Living as a conspicuous minority in the midst of a politically divided and racially segregated population such as that of Albany County was not an easy task. Attacking the

Loyalist minority in the Albany area was a good way for Blacks to curry favor with the Rebel majority and exact revenge, as did Thomas Loveless' hangman. Yet, for some younger Black men the war offered an opportunity to escape from bondage in the United States to the relative safety of Canada, where (at least as promised by British authorities) they might hope to eventually obtain their freedom. However, the <u>Haldimand Papers</u> contain evidence that some Indian allies of the British sometimes sold captured "Patriot" negroes to people in Canada. Moreover, on February 16, 1781 Private William Parker of the King's Royal Regiment of New York wrote to inform the Governor General that ". . . black people, loyalists from the Colonies, have been made slaves in Montreal."[22]

For the majority of Blacks who continued to live in the "no-man's land" of the Northern Department, however, survival became increasingly risky. The <u>Minutes</u> of the Albany Board of Commissioners contain many examples of their predicament:

--On June11, 1778 a warrant was made out for the arrest of a blacksmith named Thomas Anderson, who was accused of "encouraging Negroes to desert from their Masters to go over to the enemy." [23]

--In January of 1779, "Tom, the Negro of Henry Hogan" was ordered taken into custody for "endeavoring to stir up the minds of the Negroes against their Masters." [24]

--The Board's Minutes for July 10, 1780 mention that although "a number of Negroes" who had been apprehended on suspicion of intending to burn the settlement of Half Moon denied the charge, they admitted that they planned to go to Canada, "to which they were induced by William Loucks and a Hessian named Coonradt, and that they had been told "that when they got to Canada they would be free." The Board requested that an official at Half Moon "send down his Negro wench who has given information concerning the above mentioned Negroes in order that she may be examined." [25]

On May 4, 1781 the Commissioners had received a report that several Negroes "intend shortly to go off to Canada with Joseph Bettis [a well-known Tory Secret Service scout]." The Board wrote a letter requesting to have six slaves (all men) apprehended, and ordering the arresting officer "keep them separately and bring them before us at the City Hall of this City."[26] Joe Bettis was not the only Tory officer who was actively helping groups of Blacks to plan their escape to Canada. According to Janice Potter-MacKinnon, "The Loyalist sheriff of Tryon County promised to 'protect and defend all slaves and negroes that would resort to him and put themselves under his protection." [27]

By 1776 Albany County's small Native American population was continuing to decline, but the State Capital's leaders were eager to strengthen their relations with the Oneidas and the Tuscaroras, with whom they had an alliance. As a result, Philip Schuyler and his fellow Indian Commissioners frequently petitioned the Continental Congress and the New York legislature for food and clothing for the two tribes. Thanks to the pre-war successes of Indian Agents such as Sir John Johnson, and the wartime leadership of Walter Butler and Joseph Brandt, the British enjoyed the support of the Mohawks and other tribes of the Iroquois Confederacy throughout most of the war. With the intensification of Indian and Indian/Loyalist attacks against forts and settlements to the west of Albany in 1778, the Albany Board's Commissioners also began to pay attention to potential Native American security threats.

The Minutes of the Board contain many references to fears of Indian attacks in the Albany vicinity, the possibility of local fallout from aggressive Tory-Indian operations in the Mohawk and Cherry River Valleys, and the potential use of Indians by Tory Secret Service officers to support their intelligence activities in northern New York. This latter concern was the focus of the Board's inquiry into a bizarre incident that took place in Albany in mid--August of 1781:

"An Indian woman living with Mrs. Gibbons in this city having reported that she saw in the woods a dead man who appeared to be murdered, and his Worship the Mayor of this city (Abraham Ten Broeck) having gone out to view the dead body and not being able to find the same, and we being of [the] opinion that Mrs. Gibbons her Mistress whose husband is gone off to the Enemy has caused the said Indian Woman to raise the said report with a view to draw the Mayor out of the city in order to his being carried off by persons prepared for that purpose, therefore resolved that the said Indian Woman be apprehended." The woman later acknowledged under examination that there was a party of men in the woods who told her to go to the Mayor and inform him that there was a man murdered in the woods, and she was "committed" [i.e. incarcerated]. [28]

What Happened to Thomas Loveless and His Family after his Return to Canada?

Once back in Canada, the provincial corps units from northern New York begun to increase their manpower, making use of both Canadian and American volunteers. By December, 1778 a list of the men "In Barracks and Doing Duty at [Sorel]" commanded by Ebenezer Jessup contained the names of eight officers, two sergeants, and 35 men. Two years later a logistics document dealing with the clothing required by Loyalist provincial corps units showed that Ebenezer Jessup's unit still had eight officers, but it now contained seven sergeants and 92 "rank & file." When these troops were added to the total number of non-commissioned officers and privates in the three Tory other provincial corps units from Charlotte and Albany counties, the grand total of Loyalist military manpower in Canada in late 1780 (excluding officers) amounted to only 22 sergeants and 231 men. [29]

The Kings Loyal Americans and the other New York Provincial Corps units remained in administrative limbo for more than two years following their escape to Canada, largely because British Military leaders could not decide what to do with them. Mary Beacock Fryer describes their situation as follows: "Until a shortage of reinforcements for Haldimand's regular regiments caused him to attempt enlarging his provincial units, the officers and men of the below-strength bits and pieces suffered a lengthy period of uncertainty, leading a precarious existence, paid for whatever work they did, provisioned and sheltered when they were not employed, shunted about to build a blockhouse here, a sawmill there, or to forage for hay." [30]

Like the remnants of the other Provincial Corps units raised in northern New York, the KLA was placed under the temporary command of Sir John Johnson (of Indian Alliance operations fame) and posted to St. Johns for the winter. In September of 1778 the base for the King's Loyal Rangers and other Provincial Corps troops was shifted to Sorel, where the Richelieu River joins the St. Lawrence, northeast of Montreal. Because they were not mobilized for active duty, men like Thomas Loveless were being carried on the British Command's "Subsistence List," the cost of which for three months (June-July-August, 1779) was a total of £1,634 pounds. 8s. 10d. for all of the small Provincial Corps units in Canada. [31]

In late 1780 Haldimand decided to restore the Tory Provincial Corps units to active status, on the assumption that their officers would be able to find more recruits to fill their ranks. The several original Loyalist units were first organized into a single regiment, under the temporary command of Major John Nairne of the Royal Highland Emigrants. However, Tory-based recruitment numbers remained low, and within a year the Governor-General again modified his command's Table of Organization by combining Ebenezer Jessup's King's Loyal Americans and John Peters' Queens Loyal Rangers to form a new regiment called the Loyal Rangers.

By the fall of 1780 Thomas Loveless had begun to make his bid to become a junior officer (an Ensign) by attempting to recruit additional men for his company. A document submitted by Ebenezer Jessup on September 7, 1780 entitled "Return of the names of the officers of the Corps called the King's Loyal Americans, showing the units that they respectively served in, in the year 1777, and also the names of two other gentlemen who have an opportunity to raise men, to entitle them to the Offices to which they are here nominated" described Private Loveless as follows:

"Mr. Thomas Loveless came with me to Canada in 1776 & has been employed frequently in going out as a guide. He was employed as overseer of teams of horses with General Burgoyne. In all his service he has merited some credit and is now out recruiting in hopes to bring in men that he may be an Ensign with me." [32]

Mary Beacock Fryer describes how this recruiting system, known as "raising for rank," worked for officers within the Provincial Corps: "A captain had to raise a full company, and numerical strength varied from 50 to 60 men...A lieutenant was required to raise half a company, an ensign a quarter [i.e. fifteen men]. Sometimes, bounties were paid to recruits, or a man might be promised 50 acres in lieu of cash. Enlistments were for two years or until the end of the war."[33]

Other than officers' pay, the rewards for becoming a provincial corps officer were minimal. When serving with Regular units of the British Army, provincial corps officers were ranked junior to Regular officers in the grade below theirs, and officers of the provincial corps could not hold permanent rank in the British Army or retire on half pay if their regiments were "reduced" in times of peace. While these restrictions were removed in early 1779, and minimal medical and disability benefits added to the package, the number of recruits enlisted as Privates was never great enough to satisfy the ambitions of those seeking commissions.

How did the Loveless Family Fare as Tory Refugees?

No official or family documents survive to illuminate the daily lives of "Thomas the Spy" and his family once they arrived in Canada, but we can assume several things about their lifestyle. Until they received the news of the British defeat at Yorktown they probably continued to believe that they were on the winning side and that they would eventually be allowed to return to their farmstead in New York. Meanwhile, their housing, food, and other necessities were being provided by the British Army authorities in Canada—an arrangement which was seldom generous or equitable. When Ebenezer Jessup came to Quebec in 1777 he claimed to have been accompanied by ". . .a brood of unfortunate women and children...many of which were possessed of very good livings at their homes." While this was probably an exaggeration aimed at increasing the rations of the families of the officers of the King's Loyal Americans, it also highlights a harsh reality: the quality of life enjoyed by Loyalist refugee families in Canada was generally lower than that of their former circumstances in the United States.

Canada's first Loyalist refugees arrived in Nova Scotia following the evacuation of British troops from Boston in 1776. There was an influx of New York Tory refugee families to the Province of Quebec following the British defeat at Saratoga a year later, and most of these were initially housed near Montreal. When General Haldimand decided to concentrate the remnants of his Loyalist Provincial Corps units at Sorel in 1778, he ordered the construction of houses for the refugees' families in the parish of Machiche on the opposite shore of the St. Lawrence River. Eventually schools for Provincial Corps officers' children were created there, as well as at St. Johns and Montreal.

Janice Potter-MacKinnon's studies of the lifestyles of Loyalist refugees after their arrival in Canada paint a grim picture of dependence and subordination. She summarizes their plight as follows: "When Loyalists arrived at British bases, penniless and physically exhausted by the rigors of their journey, they were at the mercy of paternalistic and patriarchal British military regimes…The British government took care of its charges, but expected deference and service in return. The British regimes were military ones that dealt quickly and harshly with dissenters. In return for their keep, men had to fight in the Loyalist regiments, and women had to do washing and other domestic chores for the army. Questioning of the regime was neither common nor tolerated. When a petition was drawn up in Quebec asking for more aid for the Loyalists, for example, the petitioners were advised that if the governor's plans for them were not acceptable, then the petitioners could go to Nova Scotia." [34]

In addition to their quarterly military pay, both officers and enlisted men in the Provincial Corps received benefits for themselves and their families depending upon their position on the British Army's "Provision List," which determined the allocation of foodstuffs and other basic supplies. The supply system within which Loyalists' families were forced to live was well prepared to maintain large numbers of soldiers in garrison or in the field, but not to meet the long term needs of thousands of military and civilian dependents. As a result, shortfalls and inadequacies were inevitable. The threat of cutting people's provisions was sometimes used as a means of punishment or coercion. The quality and quantity of provisions declined as the war continued, and by 1780-1781 Haldimand had begun to reduce the number of people on the Provision Lists as a means of forcing more able-bodied Loyalists to work.

Each member of a family had to petition for a "ration" of flour and meat, with women and children over six receiving one-half of a man's ration and young children one-quarter. Unfortunately, the Loyalists' rations were often haphazardly allocated and inadequately distributed. Moreover, the salt provisions at British bases, the lack of dairy products, fresh meats, and vegetables led to unhealthy diets and outbreaks of diseases, including scurvy, malaria, measles, and smallpox. As a result, according to Potter-MacKinnon, "Loyalists complained that the men were too poorly fed to work effectively, that women and children did not get enough to eat, and that disease and even death were caused by poor and insufficient food. Such claims took on compelling credence when made by officials in charge of Loyalists." [35]

These problems were especially acute during the winter months when it was difficult for the American refugees to grow any of their own food and they were solely dependent upon their British hosts. Loyalist memoirs of this period are full of bitter examples of the hardships faced by their displaced families in Canada during the war. Why wasn't the British Government in Canada able to be more generous to these newcomers? Mary Beacock Fryer notes that "Haldimand had serious difficulties over provisions. The population of Canada was about 100,000 when the war began, the local agriculture inefficient. Thus he was forced to import vast quantities of food, and military actions were frequently curtailed until supply fleets arrived from the mother country."[36] The steady growth of Canada's population during and after the war meant that the Governor-General's administration was always playing "catch up" with escalating civilian demands for material support. According to Canadian census data, Canada's population had increased to over 125,000 people by 1784, and grew to 161,311 persons by 1790.[37]

CHAPTER FIVE

THE ORIGINS, LEADERSHIP, MISSIONS, AND CAPABILITIES OF THE "TORY SECRET SERVICE"

The defeat at Saratoga put an end to British plans to invade the United States from Canada, and the Battle of Monmouth (June 28, 1778) marked the last major engagement in the north between Washington's and Clinton's armies. From that time forward, and especially in the Continental Army's Northern Department, the stalemated war consisted largely of raids, skirmishes, and "intelligence warfare." Nonetheless, military leaders and citizens on both sides of the New York-Canada border remained fearful of a possible future attack.

To forestall such an event, the Northern Departments of the opposing British and American armies kept substantial forces within striking distance of the border. In addition to small garrisons at Crown Point, Fort Edward, and Old Saratoga, the frequently rotated Patriot Commander at Albany controlled a force of some 1500 Regulars from the Continental Line, and three regiments of Militia--a total of about 2000 men--most of which were based in the Albany area. These units were backed up by several thousand more Militia from the upper Hudson River Valley.

On the British side, General Watson Powell commanded a mixed force of regular troops (4,000 Redcoats and 2,000 German mercenaries) supplemented by three under-strength Provincial Corps regiments. However, with the exception of the Loyalist units, these forces were scattered throughout a jurisdiction reaching from Ft. Michilimackinac in the far west to Halifax, Nova Scotia. This effectively left Haldimand with less than 3000 troops with which to defend the cities of Montreal and Quebec against another concerted American assault. Military historian Piers Mackesy has estimated that during the period October 1778 to September 1781, British forces in Canada gradually increased from 6,647 to 8,976 men, [1] but only about half of these troops were available for the defense of Quebec or Montreal at any given time.

As a consequence, British Army Headquarters in Montreal sought to strengthen its intelligence-gathering capabilities as rapidly as possible. Initially, Regular British Army personnel--usually junior officers dressed in civilian clothes--were used for long range reconnaissance missions, but this proved both dangerous and unproductive. Over time it became clear that it would be better to use soldiers from the Loyalist units that had escaped to Canada, and especially those who had once lived in the "no man's land" within fifty miles of the Canadian border.

When General Sir Guy Carleton was replaced as Governor General and Commander in Chief of Canada by 60-year-old Lieutenant General Frederick Haldimand in June, 1778, British policy along the border with New York became more pro-active. A Swiss professional soldier who had succeeded in the British Army despite his difficulties with the English language, Haldimand had previously held several high-level commands in North America, including that of Governor-General of East (British) Florida. Although he never married, during his tour of duty at St. Augustine, Haldimand had evidently been the focus of at least one lady's attentions. On August 1, 1767 he received the following romantic "receipt" (i.e. recipe) in a letter sent by a "Mrs. Tayler":

A RECEIPT FOR A HASTY WEDDING

Take of the flower of youth a good quantity,

73

Of resolution the same,
Of the quintessence of opportunity three drams,
Of canonical time one sprig,
Of reasons for love, twenty drams,
Of merry conceit, three quarts,
Let these be well mixed in the pipkin of harmony,
And boil over the fire of love,
Keeping it constantly stirred with the ladle of affection---

Make use of it as soon as possible;
If kept too long it will spoil…

The letter closed with the following message: "Mrs. Tayler presents her complements to General Haldimand and has enclosed (a receipt for) a wedding which she hopes will be of (interest to) him by and by….or tomorrow." [2] Alas, the General chose to remain a bachelor.

    Haldimand approached his new assignment in British Canada with a combination of gusto and caution. With fewer than 2500 British Regulars immediately available, Haldimand feared the prospect of another American invasion of Canada. He thus set about strengthening the defenses of existing southern posts such as Isle-aux-Noix and St. Johns, and (in the summer of 1781) ordered construction of a new facility designed to support more ambitious intelligence operations. Located on North Hero Island, just below the US border and on the shore of Lake Champlain, the "Loyal Blockhouse" benefited from *de facto* British naval supremacy on the 100-mile-long lake, which also provided Haldimand's raiding parties and spies with year-round speedy and covert access to targets in northern New York.

    As more risky Intelligence activities were attempted, the limitations of using British military personnel for such missions became increasingly apparent. They "didn't know the territory," and their foreign accents tended to give them away when they were behind Patriot lines. In 1779 British military leaders began to identify a few "chosen men" from the Tory refugee ranks to be used as clandestine couriers and guides (one of whom was Thomas Loveless) for scouting parties. This effort intensified during 1780, as the tempo of British Army-directed intelligence operations below the Canada-US border speeded up.

By the end of 1780 General Haldimand had decided to strengthen the capabilities of his command's Secret Service component by turning its management over to experienced New York and Vermont Loyalists. Although Tory-directed, this reorganized Secret Service would make use of personnel detached from both Provincial Corps and British Regular Army units. Tasked by and reporting directly to Haldimand, the Loyalists in charge of this new Intelligence effort would be able to make good use of the Governor-General's name in obtaining the men, money, and materiel required for their operations. They also had been given tacit approval to increase the number of Loyalists that would be taking part in missions conducted on their "home turf." in New York

An important caveat is required here. British documents of the period contain no references to the "Tory Secret Service" because the TSS was in fact part of Haldimand's existing Intelligence resources, collectively known as the "British Secret Service, Northern Department." As a result, neither the British authorities nor the Loyalists in charge of the new service used the title "Tory Secret Service" in their correspondence. Nonetheless, I have chosen to use the TSS designation in order to emphasize the important role played by Loyalists in Haldimand's new intelligence scheme, and to emphasize its significance in determining the fate of Thomas Loveless.

Figure 5:
A Portrait of General Sir Frederick Haldimand,
Library and Archives Canada, 1996-156 C-003221

In a letter of 10 December, Haldimand's secretary, Captain Robert Mathews informed Edward Jessup that "...Captain Sherwood will furnish Major Jessup with a list of men for Secret Service which His Excellency has directed should form a part of the garrison at the Loyal Block House—they are chiefly at St. Johns, and Colonel St. Leger will have directions to forward them." [3] By 1 January, 1781 Mathews was informing Jessup of this new mission:

"Sir: I am commanded by His Excellency General Haldimand to acquaint you that he has sent Captain Sherwood to reside at St. Johns to carry on the business of the Loyalists at that fort, with which he has hitherto been entrusted, and with particular instructions to provide the several Corps of Loyalists intelligent and fit men for Scouts as often as the Commanding Officer shall require them. Mr. Sherwood being well acquainted with the abilities and sentiments of those people in general His Excellency desires you will afford him every assistance in your power by ordering such men as he shall from time to time require, immediately to join them, notwithstanding their being employed in any other service whatsoever." [4]

A January 22nd letter from Captain Robert Mathews to Justus Sherwood made it clear that Haldimand wanted the Tory Secret Service to accomplish multiple objectives: "...Major Jessup has permission to send men into the colonies upon the Recruiting Service, and at the same time to procure Intelligence—and has proposed that they should call upon you for such hints or instructions as you may think most likely to promote success in the latter." [5]

The General with the heavy accent had another objective in mind as well. By early 1781 the British were looking for new ways to covertly respond to diplomatic initiatives made by Ira and Ethan Allen, leaders of the

"Republic of Vermont." Claimed by both New York and New Hampshire, and known until 1777 as "The New Hampshire Grants," Vermont was now attempting to play both ends against the middle. In addition to approaching Haldimand regarding Crown Colony status for their "Republic," the devious Allen brothers were simultaneously negotiating with the Continental Congress, hoping to achieve Vermont's acceptance as the fourteenth state. For their part, the British were eager to prevent Vermont from joining the American war effort against the Crown. Because of the extreme sensitivity of the Vermont negotiations, it was decided that the Tory-led Secret Service would also serve as a "cut-out" between the Allens and British officials in Canada. The "cover" for this effort would be Sherwood's official duties as the British coordinator for prisoner exchanges.

Thanks to his experience during the French and Indian War, the geographic area within which General Haldimand planned to deploy his newly-augmented Intelligence assets was familiar to him. The immediate theater of TSS operations would focus upon the region between Albany and the Canadian border, which was the northernmost segment of a traditional invasion corridor stretching from Montreal to the city of New York. This corridor begins with the Saint Lawrence and Richelieu Rivers, connects south via Lake Champlain and Lake George, and ends in the waters of the Hudson River. Hazel Mathews once described it as "...the military highway between Canada and the American colonies," pointing out its use by such varied campaigners as the St. Francis Indians, the Marquis de Montcalm, Lord Jeffrey Amherst, James Wolf, and Continental Generals John Sullivan and Benedict Arnold.[6] Haldimand was also aware of the importance to the British of the Champlain Valley as a vital channel of communications linking their two most important military headquarters—the cities of Quebec and New York.

The area's geography also favored access for Intelligence operations. Sir Guy Carleton's and Sir Henry's relatively secure bastion in New York City allowed the British to mount espionage operations against Rebel targets on its periphery (Long Island, Connecticut, and New Jersey). Likewise, Haldimand's somewhat less secure Canadian bastion provided the British with the opportunity to mount a wide variety of intelligence operations against Patriot targets along a two hundred-mile-long border with New York, Vermont, and New Hampshire.

By 1778 Lieutenant General Frederick Haldimand had served with the British Army for more than three decades, becoming a naturalized British subject. Fluent in French and German, he had proven to be both a successful field commander and a competent military administrator. As a Colonel he had taken part in operations during the French and Indian War and had commanded the British garrison at Fort Edward. He was stationed briefly at Albany, where he and young Philip Schuyler served in the same British Army unit. In subsequent "flag rank" assignments he served as the British Commandant in both Canada (at Trois Rivieres) and East Florida (at St. Augustine), and had commanded British forces in New York during General Thomas Gage's temporary absence in 1773-1775. Haldimand's accent and former nationality apparently prevented him from becoming Gage's successor. As Governor-General his headquarters in Quebec City was located in the imposing former French governor's palace known as the "Chateau St. Louis."

Map #3
Detail from an 18th Century map showing New York Colony's northern frontier during the French & Indian War

Like George Washington, Haldimand seems to have taken a personal interest in the creative tasking of Intelligence operations, and he paid unusually close attention to the activities of the Tory Secret Service. A payroll document of the Civil Government of the Province of Quebec shows that General Haldimand's salary for six months (from 1 November, 1781 to 1 May, 1782) was £1000 pounds, or £2000 pounds per year.[7]

General Haldimand's military secretary, Captain Robert Mathews, was a newly-commissioned British Army officer who had just arrived in Canada. Among his other duties during the next six years he would provide the essential communications link between the leaders of the Tory Secret Service and their Commander in Chief. In this capacity he screened incoming correspondence from Sherwood and Smyth and drafted Haldimand's responses, orders, and other documents relating to the Loyalists' intelligence operations. Evidence in the Haldimand Papers reveals that Mathews was an energetic and resourceful secretary and executive officer, and that Sherwood and Smyth were the frequent beneficiaries of his direct and indirect support. The same documentary source reveals that by June, 1782, Captain Mathews was receiving (in addition to his base pay as an officer in the British Army), £188 pounds per year in salary as a member of Quebec's "Civil Government."[8]

A native of Connecticut, Justus Sherwood was one of the early pioneers of the New Hampshire Grants and a friend of Ethan Allen, with whom he helped capture Fort Ticonderoga in early 1775. Disillusioned with the Patriot cause, he later offered his services to British Governor William Tryon. After being arrested and escaping from Connecticut's notorious Simbury Mines Prison, he sought refuge in Quebec. In May, 1777 he joined Lt. Colonel John

Peters' Queen's Loyal Rangers, with the rank of Captain. Barely escaping with his life from the Battle of Bennington, he was active with Peter's unit during the Burgoyne Expedition, and was wounded during the second battle of Saratoga.

After his return to Canada, Sherwood was temporarily in limbo because his oath under the "Saratoga Convention" kept him from engaging in combat or recruiting additional men for the company he commanded in the Queen's Loyal Rangers. When the Convention was declared invalid by Governor Carleton in June 1778, Captain Sherwood volunteered for courier missions to Albany and New York City. Over time, he became increasingly involved with prisoner interrogations, and the exchange of prisoners with military authorities in both New York and Vermont. This experience, plus his aggressive and resourceful personality recommended him for more ambitious intelligence work. Of equal importance were his equities with and knowledge of the unpredictable leaders of the "Republic of Vermont," which was now of growing interest to British officials in Quebec.

An Irish surgeon who had immigrated with his family to New York in 1770 and moved to Fort Edward five years later, Dr, George Smyth had planned to practice his profession in nearby Albany, but politics and the war intervened. Initially a Patriot, he was elected a representative to New York's Provincial Congress in June, 1775 and signed documents in support of the Continental Congress. By late 1779 he had lost faith in the American cause, and had begun to pass intelligence information about Rebel activities in Albany area to Haldimand, using the pseudonym "Hudibras"—the hero of a 17th Century satirical poem by Samuel Butler. For nearly two years while he was employed in an Albany hospital Smyth acted as an "agent in place" for the British, providing vital support for Loyalist couriers and reporting on Rebel political and military developments in New York and Vermont.

During his time in Albany, Smyth reported on the latest military and political developments in northern New York and Vermont. Proof of this can be found in the variety and detail of his reports preserved in the Haldimand Papers, as well as in a few of Smyth's messages which were captured from British couriers by the American forces. The papers of General James Clinton contain a lengthy intelligence report from Dr. Smyth (intended for Haldimand) which was intercepted by American forces on May 27, 1781. The circumstances of this Rebel intelligence coup are not explained by historian William L. Stone, who included excerpts from the captured report in his 1851 book about famed Indian leader Joseph Brant. Although he apparently had no idea of the identity of the intelligence report's author, Stone none-the-less concluded that "...the character of these communications showed but too plainly that treason was deeply and extensively at work, and, that the enemy was, beyond doubt, correctly advised of the true situation of the country." [9]

This report covered such topics (underlined by Smyth himself) as: General Intelligence (i.e. "No hostile intentions on foot against the Province of Canada"), Saratoga ("A fort [being] erected here by General Schuyler. Two hundred and fifty men at this place"), Albany ("No troops at this post, except the Commandant, General Clinton and his Brigade Major. Work of all kinds stopped for want of provisions and money"), Washington's Camp ("The strength [here] does not exceed twenty-five thousand. Provisions of all kinds are very scarce...The flower of the army gone to the southward with the Marquis De La Fayette."), and Eastern News ("By a person ten days ago from Rhode Island, we have an account that the number of land forces belonging to the French does not amount to more than three hundred"). This report also included paragraphs summarizing recent military events in Schenectady, Fort Stanwix, the Mohawk River Valley, and the "State of Vermont."

After being placed under house arrest and later twice imprisoned by Patriot authorities, he and his wife (but not his son Terrence, known as "Young Hudibras," who remained a prisoner) were extracted by British agents and resettled in St. Johns, Canada in June of 1781. Smyth's arrival caused General Haldimand to send the following letter to Sir Henry Clinton on June 21st:

"Doctor SMITH [sic] of Albany, my best Intelligencer, is just come in having escaped from the Hands of the Rebels on his Way to Jail. He attributes his being seized to his having given You late [recent] Intelligence, and suspects some of your Domestics of betraying him to Washington, who wrote to the Commissioners of Conspiracies that a Plot was on Foot, and SMITH was immediately seized and loaded with irons. Should his suspicion be well founded, I hope he will arrive in Time enough to prevent greater Evils." [10]

One month later, Smyth was approached by General Haldimand to help Justus Sherwood manage the Tory Secret Service. The division of labor between Sherwood and his Deputy initially proved to be a sound one. Differing widely in temperament, talent, and experience, the two men none-the-less formed a highly successful team. Operationally oriented, Sherwood was most comfortable on "the front lines" of the campaign, managing prisoner exchanges, interrogating prisoner and defectors, and planning complex missions. Because of his experience as an active agent behind enemy lines, Dr. Smyth was best suited for managing strategic planning, internal security, counterintelligence, and the processing of incoming information prior to its dispatch to Montreal and Quebec. In geographic terms, Sherwood was to be the principal point of contact for operations in "the East" (especially negotiations with the Allens and other plotters in Vermont) and Smyth would be responsible issues in "the South and West," i.e., New York.

The Headquarters of the TSS was located at Fort St. Johns, a major garrison on the west bank of the Richelieu River about twenty-five miles north of the New York-Canada border. Dr, Smyth and the administrative elements of the Secret Service resided here, while maintaining close communication (via Captain Mathews) with General Haldimand in Quebec. It was here that men such as Thomas Loveless, Abraham Wing, John Walden Meyers and Joseph Bettis/Bettys came to get paid, collect their food and equipment, and relax between intelligence assignments. In order to protect the Secret Service's internal security after 1781, all personnel and visitors who arrived at the Loyal Block House were required to be screened and granted prior approval before their arrival at St. Johns.

However, St. Johns was much too large and "open" a community to serve as a secure jumping off point for offensive intelligence operations. In order to obtain such a facility, Justus Sherwood had decided that an isolated and easily-defended strong-point needed to be built close to the border with New York. In July of 1781 he chose a site on Grand Isle in Lake Champlain for the location of what he called the Loyal Blockhouse . By July 29th Sherwood's men had built a structure of which he was able to boast that ". . . there is not so proper a place on the Frontier as this for the residence and departure of secret scouts." For the next two years this remote facility would play a vital role in both prisoner exchanges and the launch of Loyalist intelligence personnel on courier and scouting missions against Vermont and New York.

The Loyalist rank and file of the TSS probably joined for better pay, adventure, and a chance to visit their old homesteads in Rebel territory. They may also have volunteered in order to escape the boredom of routine garrison and support duties within their much-reduced Provincial Corps units. Some, such as Thomas Loveless, Abraham Wing, Caleb Clossen, Roger Stevens, and Azariah Pritchard, had previously served as guides for British regular troops engaged in courier and scouting missions behind enemy lines. With the exception of basic espionage tradecraft skills, most of these men were veterans of frontier warfare who required very little training.

The number of Loyalists assigned to Secret Service work during 1781-1782 was small—probably no more than a hundred men, half of whom were assigned to guard and logistics support duties at the Loyal Blockhouse. A late 1781 "Recapitulation" (roster) of Jessup's Corps shows that of a total of 137 officers and men, only four were detailed to Secret Service duties, and only five men from Daniel McAlpin's corps were so assigned. Some of the Secret Service's "operations" personnel, like Dr. Smyth, were civilians, and a few were volunteers from Regular British Army units in Canada. In any case, the attrition associated with high-risk espionage and paramilitary operations—due to combat deaths and injuries, incarcerations, and executions—meant that over a two-year period the TSS witnessed a considerable turnover of personnel.

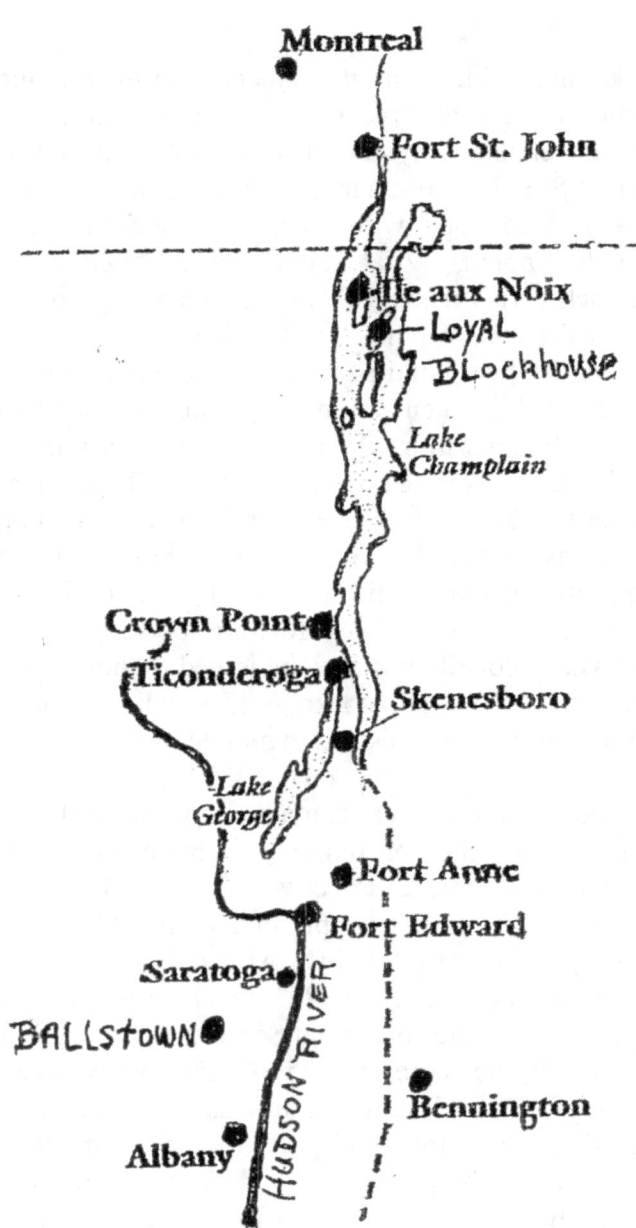

Map #4:
The Tory Secret Service's theater of operations

Like the soldiers in the other Loyalist Provincial Corps units in Canada, Secret Service personnel were equipped and supplied by the British Army. As a result, Sherwood & Smyth's contingent of Intelligence volunteers sometimes had to cope with logistics shortfalls. As Ian Pemberton has noted, "Vital supplies were often lacking, including such varied items as blankets, coats, caps, mittens, leggings, moccasins, candles, butter, treacle (used in the making of spruce beer), andirons, fire shovels and tongs, and medical supplies."[11] When commissary food provided by the Crown—usually consisting of barrels of rum, salt pork, and "hardtack" biscuits, was scarce, the troops had to survive on a diet of locally-brewed "spruce beer (a mixture of boiled spruce needles, molasses and water necessary for the prevention of scurvy), venison, and "moose deer" meat Because of its sensitivity as a forward operational base, Sherwood would not allow rum to be issued to those visiting or assigned to the Loyal Blockhouse, a policy which he noted did little to improve his men's morale.

However, documents contained in the Haldimand Papers suggest that the consumption of large quantities of rum was vital to the overall effectiveness of the Tory Secret Service's operations. For example, a monthly "Return" of the rum consumption of the British Armed forces in Canada covering the period September 25th to October 24th, 1781 shows that "Scout Parties on Secret Service" operating out of St. Johns (usually no more than 25-30 men) drank seventy-five gallons of rum in less than thirty days. This unusually high level of rum consumption by the TSS is illustrated by a document covering the period January 25th to February 23rd 1782 which shows that the entire British Army in Canada (then estimated at some 2100 men) consumed only 497 gallons of rum (plus 707 gallons of Spruce Beer) during a one-month period! [12]

Issues concerning the different kinds and levels of financial compensation received by its officers and men regularly haunted the Tory Secret Service. In addition to his base pay as a member of a Provincial Corps unit, each man assigned to secret service duty received additional amounts of money while engaged in such activity, whether these duties were carried out in Canada or behind enemy lines. Further pay increments were associated with the kinds of operations being conducted (i.e. "guide" work for raiding parties, routine courier runs, or covert scouting that could involve combinations of missions such as kidnapping courier ambushes, and recruiting).

Couriers were usually paid set fees, depending upon the distance and the season. Men sent on "scouts" were paid for the number of days that they spent on the mission, plus financial rewards for success in intelligence collection, recruiting, and other special tasks. This piecework reward system meant that some personnel received more money that others, and this frequently produced friction and morale problems. An example of this problem is provided by the following excerpt from a May 18, 1782 letter from Major Mathews to Dr, Smyth:

"In regard to the complaints of the scouts on Secret Service respecting the former allowance being diminished, there is no remedy—it cannot materially affect those who requite themselves with fidelity and dispatch, and the oftener they are employed and the more expeditious they are, the better they are rewarded—and the services of those who go out and linger their time to procure half a dollar a day, are not worth having..." [13]

The types of activities associated with this new Tory-directed Intelligence effort included all the basic offensive and defensive elements of modern-day military intelligence operations; including reconnaissance, espionage, deception and disinformation campaigns; counterintelligence, the use of "safe houses;" the encryption, concealment, and delivery of secret messages; and betrayals by "double agents." For the most part, the TSS's operations focused upon reconnaissance (scouting) missions, recruiting volunteers for Canada-based Tory units, intercepting Rebel couriers, managing official prisoner of war exchanges and kidnapping Rebel citizens for same, supporting Loyalist spy networks in New York and Vermont, and staffing the courier network linking Haldimand's headquarters in Montreal, Tory elements in Albany, and General Henry Clinton's Headquarters in New York City.

Although his tasking requests were always filtered through Captain, Haldimand took a very "hands on" approach to tasking his command's Intelligence resources. The tasking letters drafted by Mathews were often models of brevity and precision, and contained very specific descriptions of Haldimand's evolving tasking priorities. The kinds of tasks requested varied widely, from identifying and countering "the chief promoters" of the Rebellion in a certain area to obtaining specific information concerning political developments in Albany and Vermont, or the status of French forces in Rhode Island (after the French Monarchy allied itself with the United States in February, 1778 the British feared French troops might be used by the Americans to invade Canada, an event that might have been supported by British Canada's French-speaking majority.) Once instructions such as these had been delivered to Sherwood and Smyth, it was up to them to deliver the goods. Within the limits of Haldimand's tasking, however, the TSS leadership was free to plan and propose a wide variety of operational activities, only some of which required the approval of their Commander-in-Chief.

Both sides along the Canada/New York frontier were eager for information about the strategy, tactics, capabilities and intentions of their enemy, and both mounted a wide variety of Intelligence collection programs. Although the Americans had a few agents and Indians reporting to them from Canada during the war, the British were much more in need of actionable Intelligence, and were therefore more aggressive in seeking to obtain it, especially after 1778. As a result, they took risks and incurred operational losses that their counterparts in the Continental Army were unwilling to accept.

While human source intelligence data obtained from agents in place, scouts of enemy territory, or gleaned from prisoners was highly prized, it was hard to come by, often out of date, and sometimes poisoned by the disinformation efforts of their opponents. As a result, some of the most timely and valuable Intelligence was gathered from the documents and dispatches carried by intercepted enemy couriers and from hard-copy materials such as newspapers, handbills, broadsides, and official proclamations. The tasking memos sent by General Haldimand to Sherwood and Smyth frequently stressed the importance of procuring the most up-to-date Rebel newspapers, even though the information contained in them was sometimes wildly inaccurate, exaggerated, or purposely designed to mislead.

Some Intelligence was gathered from in-coming Loyalists, refugees, deserters from the Continental Army, and prisoners of war in Canada. Debriefing these kinds of sources was one of Justus Sherwood's most important duties. Inevitably, it was difficult to tell real defectors or deserters from double agents, and to confirm from other sources the accuracy of their offered information. The following report was submitted, in manuscript, by two Loyalists, "lately arrived from the colonies" in early September, 1780:

"(After listing the places they had visited in Vermont and New York) . . .in which tour we have visited many loyal subjects by whome [sic] we have been informed that the French Fleet was at Rhode Island to the amount of 36 sail and that they were blocked up by the English Fleet, and that there were eight thousand British troops had set sail from New York to go to Rhode Island and that the main body of Washington's army is at Smith (___), which army contains(___) men." [14]

Most of the Intelligence reports which Justus Sherwood passed on to General Haldimand via his Secretary were in fact written by Sherwood or Smyth, following their debriefings of returning Tory scouts. However, a few of the men, including Thomas Loveless, were able to submit reports written in their own hand, and copies of several of Loveless' original reports from the field have survived. For example:

From St. John's
of 2 September, 1780:

"The information of Mr. Thomas Loveless, who has this day arrived from the District of Saratoga in the Province of New York is as follows...

The rebels have lately erected a block house in the Township of Palmerstown which is about 9: or 10: miles to the westward of Saratoga. Said blockhouse is about 60: by 50: feet, at present no cannon. There is an order of Congress to speedely [sic] erect a picket about said blockhouse: it now contains about 150 men. It is a common report that Washington is driven back by the King's Army and that one forth part of all the militia to the southward of Albany ware called to reinforce Washington and the other three regiments to the North and of Albany are to protect the afforsaid blockhouse. It is also reported that six sail of the French men of war is arrived at Rhods Island with troops on bord, the number to me unknown.

(Signed)

Thomas Loveless [15]

TSS Support for Haldimand's Political Bargaining with the Vermonters, and British Recruiting Efforts in the US

By the spring of 1781, the Tory Secret Service was deeply involved in supporting Haldimand's diplomatic approaches to Vermont. Because of his familiarity with the region's settlement history and its major factions, Thomas Loveless was a logical choice for espionage missions to eastern New York and western Vermont. In a 25 May, 1781 letter to Mathews entitled "Intelligence," Justus Sherwood writes as follows:

"Mr. Thos. Loveless reports, that when he first arrived at Saratoga, the inhabitants E. of Hudson's River had a general meeting to consider of Genl. Allen's handbills, in which he proposed a union with Vermont, at this meeting the majority of the people signed the handbills—that, on the 16th Instant there was a convention at Cambridge, consisting of two delegates from each district, to finally determine on the union with Vermont, and this convention unanimously agreed to establish the union—He says great numbers are moving in, from the other states, many of them men of considerable property, in expectation of a union with Great Britain, or at least (unclear),and some of the most desperate Rebels are moving out, for the same reasons that these move in—He says Genl. Schuyler and Mr. Duer are secretly in favor of Vermont, that the Friends of Government are very active in this plan. He says this infatuation of a peace between Great Britain and Vermont, is so general, and the people's expectations so high, that it prevented him from getting a number of recruits, which he might otherwise have done, and he fears it will be a great damage to the recruiting plan in general." [16]

In a letter of 2 June 1781 to Mathews, Sherwood ends with a reference to the same intelligence report from Thomas Loveless: "I beg you will send me the copies of Loveless [sic], [Thomas] Sherwood's, and [Elijiah] Bothums's reports—I had not time to copy them and I think they may be of service to assist my memory in examining other parties that come in." [17]

By 1781, the Tory Provincial Corps units in Canada were desperately short of personnel. To help fill this gap, TSS officers sent into New York and Vermont were rewarded for enlisting Loyalist recruits in the course of these missions and leading them back to St. Johns. Not the least of such rewards was the possibility of (as Thomas Loveless probably hoped) becoming an Ensign or a Lieutenant if he could recruit enough new Privates into his unit.

Although such recruitments had become much more difficult by this stage of the war, they were still being attempted. A good example of such an effort was a courier trip to New York led by veteran Secret Service officer John Walter Meyers in late May, 1781. On his return up the Hudson, Meyers recruited a dozen Loyalist volunteers and then led them on a June 4th raid against Ballstown, New York, which netted him two more recruits and four Rebel militia officers as prisoners. Few other Secret Service scouts did as well at recruiting, however. Although he was clearly

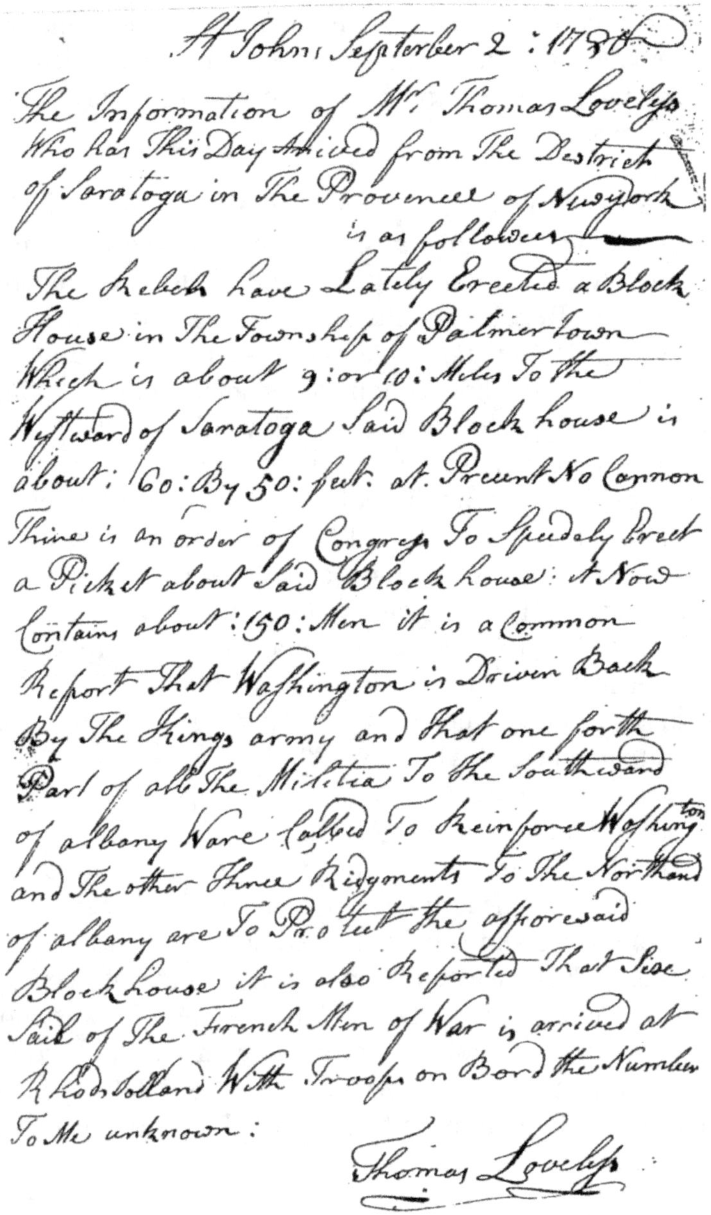

> St Johns September 2 : 1780
>
> The Information of Mr. Thomas Loveless
> Who has This Day Arrived from The Destrict
> of Saratoga in The Province of New York
> is as follows
>
> The Rebels have Lately Erected a Block
> House in The Township of Palmertown
> Which is about 9: or 10: Miles To the
> Westward of Saratoga Said Block house is
> about: 60: By 50: feet. at. Present No Cannon
> There is an order of Congress To Speedely Erect
> a Picket about Said Block house: It Now
> Contains about: 150: Men it is a Common
> Report That Washington is Driven Back
> By The Kings army and that one forth
> Part of all The Militia To the Southward
> of albany Ware Called To Reinforce Washington
> and The other Three Ridgments To The Northend
> of albany are To Protect the afforesaid
> Block house it is also Reported That Sixe
> Sail of The French Men of War is arrived at
> Rhodes Island With Troops on Bord the Number
> To Me unknown:
>   Thomas Loveless

Figure 6:
A copy of Thomas Loveless' hand-written report dated September 2, 1780 (Haldimand Papers)

seeking to become a commissioned officer and command his own company of men, Thomas Loveless does not appear to have had much success recruiting during his brief Secret Service career.

TSS involvement in small-scale British attacks against Continental Army positions in New York usually took the form of providing guides to accompany detachments of Regular and Provincial Corps troops. In mid-February, 1781 General Haldimand sent Major Edward Jessup a letter regarding Haldimand's interest in attacking the Continental garrison at Fort Edward, which recent intelligence reports claimed was defended by only thirty men "ripe for revolt" and ready to defect to Canada. In his letter, the General wants Jessup to tell him "…what numbers you think necessary for this attempt (and) how soon they could be got ready." He suggests that "…in order to avoid suspicion, the party would be marked as a relief & reinforcement for [the British garrison at] Point au Fer," and orders that "…in the mean time…you will not breathe the Intention to any person whosoever."[18]

Long-range penetrations of Rebel territory were extremely dangerous, even when these missions involved sizeable groups of heavily-armed men led by experienced guides. Ambushes and fire-fights were common during such operations, and often wounded men who could not keep up had to be left behind. For these reasons, it was not uncommon for men going out on a scout to leave some "worst case" instructions. Writing from St. Johns on 7 January, 1782, Benjamin Patterson sent the following letter to his superiors:

"It is my earnest request, as I am ordered on a scouting party, and in case any accident should befall me, that you will be pleased to pay Chisholm & Ross of St.

Johns, shopkeepers, the sum of fourteen Pounds, Halifax Currency and deduct the same from my pay, and you will much oblige, Sir.

       Your most Obed't Serv't

          Benj. Patterson

N.B. If any unlikely accident should befall me, pray do not fail to do justice to Chisholm & Ross, as well as to her who is my nearest concern." [19]

 Prior to August, 1775 the supreme command of British forces in North America had been exercised from the British Army's headquarters in Boston. Following the return of General Thomas Gage to England, however, the Board of Trade and Plantations in London decided to create two British Army headquarters, one in Quebec commanded by Canadian Governor-General Sir Guy Carleton, and the other (responsible for the thirteen colonies) in Boston (later removed to New York City) commanded by General William Howe.

 In April, 1776 both Carleton and Howe were named Commanders in Chief in their respective areas of responsibility. This division of responsibilities meant that reliable year-round communications had to be maintained between the Commands, a task which proved to be both difficult and vulnerable to disruption. Even though an overland courier's roundtrip could take more than six weeks, it was often faster than exchanging dispatches via the St. Lawrence River (parts of which were ice-bound in winter) and unreliable coastal shipping. Initially these dangerous courier duties were carried out by specially-trained British military personnel based in Canada. Courier missions were by their very nature extremely dangerous, as General Burgoyne discovered once his expeditionary force entered enemy territory in northern New York on its way to attack Albany. In an August 20, 1777 letter to Lord George Germaine, Burgoyne noted "...the want of communication with Sir William Howe: Of the messengers I have sent, I know of two being hanged, and am ignorant whether any of the rest arrived. The same fate has probably attended those dispatched by Sir William Howe, for only one letter has come to hand..."[20]

After General Haldimand replaced General Carleton, one of the most vital missions performed by the Tory Secret Service was that of carrying official documents and messages (known as "packets" or "dispatches") between Haldimand's headquarters in Quebec and Carleton's Headquarters in New York City. Loyalists from Thomas Loveless's part of New York were uniquely qualified for such operations. Success largely depended upon two factors: a courier's detailed knowledge of the terrain and lines of communication, and his ability to obtain refuge and support at "safe houses" run by fellow Loyalists who continued to live in farms and towns along his route. Usually traveling alone and moving only by night, couriers wore civilian clothes and were armed. They carried their documents in water-proof bladders covered with bark or in concealment devices such as lead balls, knife handles, canes, or quill pens. Successful messengers could earn up to forty guineas [a coin then worth twenty-one shillings] per trip, or about 2s.6d. per day. [21]

When he found himself being pursued or captured, a courier had to find a way to dispose of his incriminating message—a task which sometimes proved impossible, and hence, fatal. Several British and Tory intelligence agents were executed because they failed to destroy their concealment devices before of after being captured. The following after-action report concerning the courier mission of Corporal David Crowfoot, an Oneida Indian, describes a more successful effort of this sort: "Corpl' Crowfoot says, he was taken before he arrived at Arlington [in Vermont], but destroyed his dispatch in a bag of bread & water. He was carried as far as White Creek on his way to Saratoga but on the second night after he was taken he made his escape & went to a friend [of Government] who secreted him till he found an opportunity of coming away."[22]

Several British and Tory couriers plying between New York and Quebec met their deaths because they were unable to destroy or conceal the messages they were carrying at the time of their capture. One of the earliest such casualties was Lieutenant Daniel Taylor, a native of Kinderhook, New York who was serving with the British Army's 9th Regiment. Chosen by Sir Henry Clinton at Fort Montgomery to carry the a message of support to General Burgoyne, Taylor was captured at New Windsor on October 8, 1777 and charged with "lurking about the camp as a spy of the enemy." Written on thin silk, his message was concealed within a bullet-sized silver ball, which he swallowed, but was forced by his captors to regurgitate. In addition to General Clinton's message, Taylor had made the additional mistake of carrying several incriminating personal letters from British officers to their families in Kinderhook. Condemned "Out of his own mouth" as Rebel soldiers jokingly characterized it, Taylor was tried and hanged as a spy.

Some of the Loyalists who continued to live in northern New York after the defeat of the Burgoyne expedition also served as couriers, at considerable risk to themselves and their families. Many years later, Mary Gillespie Bain, the young daughter of one such Tory, told Dr. Asa Fitch the following story which highlights the dangers faced by Tory couriers:

"Father used to carry the packet or letters of intelligence from the Canadian officers to the British officers in New York. A packet would be brought to him from the north, and he would forthwith start on with it to Albany. These packets were done up in a small compass [size] and enveloped in lead—being not more than an inch or two in length...I remember on one occasion it was thought twould [sic] be difficult to get the packet through. Mother...put it into the middle of a biscuit, baking it carefully so as not to burn the paper in the middle. With this and a quantity of similar biscuits for provisions on his journey, he started off. On his route he fell in with a scouting party of American soldiers who were without provisions and hungry. They forthwith appropriated Father's biscuits to their own use. Father, now as they were eating the biscuit, regarded himself as a dead man. But to his joy, they returned it to him unbroken with a part of one or two other of the biscuits, having eaten all the rest...Mother, in baking it, had been very careful not to heat it enough to burn the paper, and probably they observed it was poorly baked and heavy and therefore preferred all the others to this."[23]

The problem with using Canada-based Loyalists for courier work was that while they were fine woodsmen, they often lacked discipline and ignored basic intelligence tradecraft. Many resented the fact that couriers were not permitted to carry private letters, and some were tempted to visit relatives and friends in the course of their missions. In reality, courier work was both difficult and dangerous, for captured British and Tory messengers were occasionally executed as spies by Rebel Army leaders. Often a courier from Canada would arrive at a rendezvous or a "safe house" only to find that his contact or its owners had been arrested or forced to flee. Emergency hiding places used by couriers included hollow trees, the insides of haystacks, and secret cellars built beneath barns and churches. The identification of "Friends" along the route was facilitated by the exchange of tokens or "seals," but these were occasionally compromised by the enemy.

The TSS also had an aggressive courier intercept program, as evidenced by the instructions in this letter of 30 April, 1781, from Mathews to Smyth:

"His Excellency the Commander in Chief having received intelligence that Rebel scouts will leave Cahos? for this Province about the middle of May and that their routes will be to St. Francois, St. Ours, and St. Therese, he is pleased to direct that you will have prepared as many small scouts, consisting of 4 or 6 men, as you shall think sufficient effectively to watch the above routes—they must be conducted by such officers or persons on whose vigilance, knowledge of the country, and good conduct you have a perfect dependence, and they should be on their different grounds by the 10th of May, and remain there until the first week of June..." "[lying near the] paths or parts of the country thro [sic] which the Rebels are expected to pass---and as they will certainly be [...] in their profession, they must be fired upon, if there should be any risk of their escaping—and in pursuing them great attention must be had to observing if they throw away or let anything drop, for if they have dispatches they will naturally attempt to destroy or conceal them---" [24]

The Haldimand Papers reveal that in the course of its operations the TSS captured a wide variety of American civil and military documents, including items signed by Thomas Jefferson, Silas Dean, George Washington, Benjamin Franklin, General Rochambeau, Philip Schuyler, Patrick Henry, John Hancock, and Captain George Rogers Clark (For examples See: Appendix II, pp. 304).

Most Secret Service sabotage operations were aimed at small, regional targets. The few raids conducted against Rebel forts along the Hudson during 1779-1780 usually included the spiking of cannon, demolition of powder magazines, and the destruction of military stores. However, Dr. Smyth's most ambitious sabotage attempt was a long-range strike against a distant target—a 74-gun ship-of-the-line that was being built for the Continental Navy (originally to be commanded by Captain John Paul Jones) in late 1781 at Portsmouth, New Hampshire. Two soldiers serving in the King's Loyal Rangers offered to join the crew constructing the vessel, with the objective of setting fire to it when it neared completion. Smyth approved the scheme and the men joined both the work crew and the small security force guarding the ship.

Samuel Eliot Morrison noted that because the New Hampshire authorities refused to cover such costs, Captain Jones ". . . had to pay the carpenters to do sentry-go at night, to supply them with muskets, powder and ball; and he himself acted as officer of the guard every third night." Thus, America's greatest Revolutionary War naval hero was unwittingly supporting the very men who planned to destroy his new flagship.[25] However, the war was winding down and the pace of the ship's construction was extremely slow. As a result, Smyth's two saboteurs reported that "her inside work was not done she would not burn well" and the arson plan was abandoned. Christened the "America," the uncompleted ship was presented as a token of friendship to the French Navy by the Continental Congress, and was finally launched in late 1782.

The major weaknesses of the TSS involved personnel and operations security. The quality of the individuals engaged in Secret Service work varied widely. Some Tory operatives, such as Loveless, Abraham Wing, Azariah Pritchard, Roger Stevens, Joseph Bettys, Caleb Green, Eli Hawley, John Savage, David Crowfoot, Joseph Wright, and John Walden Meyers proved remarkably tough and resourceful, but the security blunders and bad judgment of others often led to disaster. Dr. Smyth once described three of his less productive operatives as follows: "The first is a simpleton, the second proves himself a knave, and the last, I believe unfit for anything except weaving Lindsey Woolsey." [26]

Maintaining routine operations security was always a problem. Sherwood and Smyth found that their cadre of spies had to be constantly reminded of the Service's many security vulnerabilities. Sherwood noted in a letter to Smyth that in Quebec: "[Our] Messengers arrive—the inquisitive and impertinent flock around them for news, they sit down together to pass the evening, and over their glass make the business they have been upon, the Topic of Conversation—from hence they retire to their homes and renew the subject with their wives and families, and by the first post or express, it is conveyed all over the country, no matter whether by friends or enemies, the effect is the same."[27]

Many of the classic security techniques designed to protect collection from human sources were utilized by the Tory Spies. "Paroles and countersigns" were sometimes used to prevent penetrations of Secret Service base facilities by agents sent by or working for the Continental Army. In addition to the use of "tokens" to prove the bona fides of contacts while in enemy territory and "seals" to protect the exchange of mail with agents, some Loyalist agents in place used pseudonyms such as "Plain Truth" or "True Heart" to protect their identities. Efforts to ensure more secure written communications included the use of book-based cipher codes "sympathetic," or disappearing ink, and code-words such as "black birds" (used to describe suspicious persons or an increasingly hostile CI environment) in "open" messages. Such measures did not work all of the time, but they did succeed in raising the Service's overall level of security awareness.

Another major vulnerability of the TSS was its inadequate counterintelligence, or "CI" defenses. CI is an integral element of covert human source, or "HUMINT" collection operations, which by their very nature involve greater risks than other types of Intelligence activities. When effectively implemented by an intelligence service, CI is both its "sword and shield," protecting its own agents and operations, and undermining those of the service's enemies. It is designed to protect the security of one's own spies as they operate in enemy territory, and to prevent the headquarters of one's own service from being misled or penetrated by enemy agents or their surrogates. CI officers are constantly on guard to detect the efforts of "moles" and false defectors, or "double agents" to infiltrate and betray their organization's personnel, information, and operations.

Although not yet recognized as a separate field of Intelligence specialization, counterintelligence was a well-established component of the Secret Service operations mounted by both sides during the Revolution. Both defensive and offensive in its capabilities, CI seeks to prevent hostile penetrations of its own service's human-source operations while seeking to penetrate, mislead, and disrupt the enemy's collection programs. In addition to catching spies and protecting its own agents, effective counterintelligence can help ensure quality control of HUMINT data collection by preventing the covert transfer of bogus or misleading information by double agents.

In his classic 1965 summary of revolutionary war espionage, John Bakeless concluded that "Both sides in the American Revolution were about equally well served by their intelligence services—and quite as badly served by their counterintelligence." [28] This was certainly true in the case of the Tory Secret Service, which suffered from a variety of serious problems which collectively undermined both its internal and operational security. Many of these weaknesses were self-inflicted--especially the eagerness to believe that they could easily "turn" enemy prisoners or deserters into honest and effective recruits for their cause-- while others were the result of the Continental Army's efforts to penetrate its ranks and disrupt its activities.

This record of failure does not mean that the TSS was unaware of the threat or did not take steps to prevent, detect, and counter hostile activities. For good reason, they were especially concerned about the dangers posed by hostile penetrations and the potential recruitment of double agents. Unfortunately, such problems were never solved, and grew worse over time. From the outset, the Tory Secret Service was vulnerable to American CI operations on two fronts—both at home in Canada, and on enemy territory in northern New York and Vermont. This "dual jeopardy" was made worse by the Service's attempt to combine Intelligence collection with military recruitment, support for Friends of Government still living in New York state, and covert political negotiations with opportunistic Vermonters.

Haldimand knew from the beginning that both his Government in Quebec and its Military Headquarters in Montreal were being targeted by American spies, and that creating the Tory Secret Service would lead to an intensification of such efforts. Both Smyth and Sherwood assumed that their service would immediately come under attack, and took steps to protect the security of its bases and personnel. In addition to turning St. Johns into a headquarters and building the right on the frontier with New York, the two Tory spymasters did their best to screen their services from the rest of the British establishment in Canada, which they had to assume was already penetrated.

Their "Achilles Heel," in the long run, was their inability to accurately screen the <u>bona fides</u> of defectors and prevent the recruitment of double agents who were eventually able to compromise vital operations. The problem was that, in addition to military prisoners taken in combat and civilians taken hostage during periodic raids, Sherwood's prisoner debriefing system was constantly being fed imposters controlled by Rebel Intelligence officers. Several of these individuals would turn up on Sherwood's doorstep each year, seeking asylum as Loyalist refugees or disaffected Patriots and offering valuable tidbits of Intelligence.

For example, an October 22, 1780 letter to General Haldimand mentions a man named John Quin, " . . .who told me himself that he had been working for the Congress till they were indebted to him upwards of six thousand dollars equil [sic] to hard money, which he had lately been to Congress to receive, but could not get so much as would bear his expenses, which induced him to fall in with Government. Doctor Smith, Mr. Shepherd, & Mr. Hudibras desired I would conduct him safe to Canada, as he had been lately to Congress, and might have intelligence that might be of service to Government." [29]

After considerable debate concerning his authenticity, and a brief period of incarceration, this type of plausible individual would be offered the chance to sign a Parole in which he promised:

"...not to say or do any thing which may be contrary to his Majesty's Government, and, being allowed to return to (his) respective province does engage immediately to go there and to look upon the same as (his) prison, and further does faithfully promise that (he) will at any time when required surrender himself to his Excellency General Carleton, or any other of the King's Commanders in Chief in America." [30]

If he also agreed to serve as an agent after returning to the colonies, he would (with Haldimand's approval) be allowed to "escape" and return to his former home, where (hopefully) he would be of some future operational use.

The danger of accepting "turned" Patriot soldiers and civilians was understood by Smyth and Sherwood, but they never seemed to be able to defend their service against this kind of attack. A classic example of this predicament was provided by the case of a kidnapped American officer, Colonel Thomas Johnson, who was seized in Vermont in March, 1781. Seven months after his arrival in Canada, Johnson was able to convince Sherwood he was a true "Friend of Government" and he volunteered to serve as an "agent in place" after regaining his freedom. According to at least one source, after his release Johnson operated for the rest of the war as a double agent, passing information about the British to his fellow-Americans.[31]

Time after time, Tory Secret Service operations were damaged or deflected as a result of the deceit and treachery of Rebel double agents. The problem was to haunt the service until its dissolution. Ironically, Ephraim Crocker, the "turned" Patriot who betrayed Thomas Loveless and his party in September of 1781, had successfully avoided detection and was still being accepted by the Tory Spies' leadership as a loyal supporter a year later.

During its relatively brief existence the Tory Secret Service failed to alter the stalemate between the British and American forces deployed in their respective garrisons on the approaches to the New York-Canada border. Nor did it succeed in persuading Vermont's leaders to ally themselves with England. Haldimand's Loyalist spies none-the-less enjoyed some short-term successes. Smyth and Sherwood's aggressive tactics kept General Stark, General Schuyler, and New York Governor George Clinton in a constant state of uncertainty regarding British military threats from Canada. Likewise, the "Tory Spies" operations boosted the morale of those Loyalists remaining in the northern frontier of the Continental Army's Northern Department by demonstrating that the interests of The Friends of Government in frontier New York had not been forgotten. Moreover, given the geographic and topical breadth of its responsibilities, the service led by Smyth and Sherwood did a reasonably good job of keeping General Haldimand informed of his American opponents' military activities.

The Impact of the Arnold/André Case upon TSS Operations

Knowledge of the circumstances surrounding Major John André's capture and execution for espionage is central to understanding the fate of Thomas Loveless and the TSS. Like General Haldimand, André was a Swiss citizen who joined the British Army and rose rapidly in its ranks. Arriving in Canada in 1774, he was captured by Rebel forces at St. Johns a year later and held under parole at Lancaster, Pennsylvania until his exchange in 1776. Perhaps because he was a talented amateur poet and painter, some historians have tended to ignore André's more ruthless side. As Aide-de-Camp to General Charles "No Flint" Grey, André planned and participated in what came to be known as "The Paoli

Massacre" of September 21, 1777 a night attack during which more than a hundred of General Anthony Wayne's troops were killed or wounded by British soldiers armed with unloaded muskets and fixed bayonets.

At that time the British held Philadelphia, and in the course of his duties there the charming André cultivated prominent Loyalists, including 18-year-old Peggy Shippen, who was later to marry the Commander of American forces in Philadelphia, the recently-widowed, partially disabled (he had been seriously wounded twice in the same leg), and increasingly embittered Benedict Arnold. After joining the staff of General Henry Clinton in 1778, André became Clinton's head of Intelligence in April 1779. Within a month (probably with Shippen's help) he had recruited Benedict Arnold and was managing Arnold's encrypted correspondence with General Clinton.

Promoted to Adjutant General, André's role was that of a "case officer" who managed spies, rather than an "agent" or spy himself. Under normal circumstances, he would have had no reason to meet an agent like Arnold "in the field." Unfortunately, that became necessary after Arnold (no longer physically able to accept a field command) was placed in charge of West Point in August of 1780. In mid-September Arnold insisted upon a personal meeting with André during which Arnold would hand over the plans of West Point's defenses in exchange for a promised reward of £20,000 pounds. A British ship brought André behind American lines, and the meeting took place. But the plan to pick up André failed, and he had no choice but to return on horseback under very thin civilian cover. All went well until, apparently by coincidence, he was stopped, searched, and arrested by three local militiamen in neutral territory a few miles from the British lines.

Unlike Nathan Hale, Major André did not believe he was a spy, and he did not confess to having conducted any espionage. Technically speaking, he was correct. He was, in fact, acting as an intermediary between the British Army and its most skillful, well-placed, and valuable spy. On the other hand, on the morning of September 23rd he had been apprehended emerging from American territory, in civilian attire, using the pseudonym "John Anderson," with a pass signed by his agent in his pocket and the Defense Plan for West Point in his boot. Most important of all, the agent himself had managed to escape. Under these circumstances, André's disavowal of his role in Arnold's espionage plot carried little weight.

None-the-less, perhaps because of André's popularity among many American officers, George Washington summoned a Court of Inquiry made up of six Major Generals and eight Brigadier Generals to determine if André had acted as a spy and to recommend proper punishment if necessary. Presided over by General Nathaniel Greene, this panel included such experienced officers as William Alexander (Lord Sterling), the Marquis de Lafayette, Baron Von Steuben, and Arthur St. Clair. The list of Brigadiers included Henry Knox, John Glover, James Clinton, and John Stark.

Without intending to do so, André made the mistake of "confessing everything." Although General Henry Clinton and Benedict Arnold privately intervened on his behalf, claiming that André had been acting "under a flag of truce." The clueless André insisted this was not the case, and that in fact he was simply a prisoner of War. For this and other reasons, no witnesses were called by the Court of Inquiry. André may have hoped that his position as Adjutant General would prevent his execution, but the final decision lay with Washington, who after the British rejected his offer to

Figure 7:
A contemporary print depicting the execution of Major John André

exchange André for Arnold, decided that "the most rigorous" judgment (i.e. death by hanging, rather than a firing squad) was required. In a formal military-style ceremony, André was publicly executed on October 2, 1780.

The fact of Arnold's escape made it almost impossible for George Washington to let André live. Only strong action would do at this moment of crisis. As Washington himself had exclaimed, the country faced the question: "Who can we trust now?" The shock waves reverberated throughout the Continental Army. As Washington' Aide-de-Camp Colonel Alexander Scammell, a former subordinate of Arnold's, put it, "Heavens on Earth! We are all astonishment, each peeping at his next neighbor to see if any treason was hanging about him; nay, we even descended to a critical examination of ourselves. The surprise soon settled down to a fixed detestation and abhorrence of Arnold...as the veriest [sic] villain of centuries past." [32]

Although André was viewed as an unfortunate victim of justice by many American officers, his espionage revealed the brutal reality that, thanks to Arnold's treachery, West Point had nearly been lost to the British. Gone was the naïve post-Saratoga sense of professional comradeship between US and British officers. Now, more than ever, the war was seen by the American officers as a true "life and death" struggle. The Arnold/André case also intensified the anti-espionage paranoia of ordinary American citizens by demonstrating that individuals such as André who managed and supported spies could be as dangerous as the spies themselves. In other words, people who harbored or facilitated the operations of British spies were "accessories" to hostile espionage activities, and hence, also guilty of spying. As a result, by the fall of 1780 Albany County's remaining Loyalists were viewed by their neighbors as a more serious potential security threat than ever.

In early 1781, John Graves Simcoe noted that his Queen's Rangers were now re-equipped with new uniforms which included '....light caps, neat and commodius [sic], in room of the miserable contract hats, which had been sent back to England.' "In those caps were worn black and white feathers, a sign of mourning for Major André, hanged by the rebels as a spy." [33] Loyalists throughout the colonies were outraged by General Washington's decision to approve the hanging of Major John André. A good example of this anger is provided by a poem written by Ann Seward in 1781:

> "Oh Washington! I thought thee great and good,
> Nor knew thy Nero thirst for guiltless blood:
> Severe to use the power that fortune gave.
> Remorseless Washington! The day shall come
> Of deep repentance for this barbarous doom:
> When injured André's mem'ry shall inspire
> A kindling army with restless fire,
> Each falchion sharpen that the Britons wield,
> And lead their fiercest lion to the field;
> Then, when each hope of thine shall end in night,
> When dubious dread and unavailing flight
> Impel your haste, thy guilt-upbraided soul
> Shall wish, untouched, the precious life you stole;
> And when thy heart, appalled and vanquished
> pride, Shall vainly ask the mercy you denied,
> With horror shalt thou meet the fate thou gave,
> Nor pity gild the darkness of thy grave" [34]

SETTLING SCORES—1781-1783

CHAPTER SIX

The Strategic Context

By 1781 the British were beginning to suffer reverses in the Carolinas (a stinging defeat at Cowpens on January 17th and a costly victory at Guilford Courthouse in mid-March). Loyalist support in the region had again proved disappointing, especially after the defeat of British-led Tory forces at King's Mountain. On the other hand, British leaders were encouraged by the successful raiding operations of sea-land forces under Benedict Arnold and General William Phillips against targets in Tidewater Virginia. In May the major focus of British combat operations shifted to the north, as Cornwallis' expeditionary force moved into Virginia, where he planned to link up with Phillips and destroy both Rebel supply bases and the small, but gradually-strengthening American army commanded by Lafayette.

After several minor victories (the burning of Richmond on January 7th and the Battle of Green Spring on July 6th), Cornwallis was ordered by General Clinton to withdraw to Portsmouth and prepare 3000 of his men for evacuation to help defend New York against the perceived threat of a combined French and American assault. Neither Cornwallis nor his superiors in New York City were aware that this threat was an elaborate deception ploy engineered by George Washington. During this period military tensions along the New York-Canada border remained high, and both sides watched each other for signs of large-scale military movements. In reality, neither force was in a position to mount a major offensive, but both wanted to keep their opponents guessing about their intentions. At the political level, the governments in Canada and New York were competing for the allegiance of the Republic of Vermont. At the humanitarian level, both sides were trying to retrieve their lost citizens (both military and civilian) through a series of prisoner exchanges.

The assignment of Brigadier General John Stark in late 1781 to his second tour as Commander of the Continental Army's Northern Department was a sign of George Washington's increased concern about potential British threats to the northern Hudson River Valley, and Albany in particular. Caleb Stark notes that his grandfather's new headquarters "…was established at Saratoga, on or near one of the estates of General Schuyler, whose lady and daughters came to the farm in the autumn to prepare their winter stores. At this time General Stark, with his son, Major Caleb Stark, frequently called upon them, and detached a sergeant, with a party of soldiers, for their protection…" [1]

From this remote garrison located at what is now the town of Schuylerville, Stark and his small contingent of Continentals, supported by local militia units, formed a kind of "trip wire" designed to detect and slow any major thrusts to the south by General Powell's forces. Washington did not want to lose Albany while he was in the process of trapping and destroying Cornwallis' expeditionary force at Yorktown. However, Washington had few Regular Army troops to spare for the defense of Albany and was reluctant to permanently increase the size of Stark's garrison. If the British came south in strength, Washington was prepared to use militia from as far away as New Hampshire to help defend the Northern Department's Headquarters and New York's capital city. Otherwise, he expected Stark and Schuyler to make do with the limited resources at their disposal.

The Declining Strength of New York Loyalist Military Units Based in Canada

After more than four years, attrition (due to age, illness, casualties or desertions), had drastically reduced the number of men serving in the Tory Provincial Corps units that had arrived in Canada in late 1777. In an effort to solve this problem, on November 12th, 1781 Haldimand issued a General Order which combined the remnants of Ebenezer Jessup's Kings Loyal Americans and John Peter's Queen's Loyal Americans into a single unit, to be known as "The Loyal Rangers."

Also known as "Jessup's Rangers," the new unit was commanded by Major Edward Jessup, and led by five Captains, eight Lieutenants, and four Ensigns. Dr. George Smyth was listed as the Corps' surgeon, and its list of "Pensioners" included both Ebenezer Jessup and his son Edward. "Invalids" belonging to the Loyal Rangers included veterans Lt. Colonel John Peters, Captain Gershom French, and Justus Sherwood's son Thomas. The total manpower of this combined force probably did not exceed three hundred men. Based at Sorel, it maintained detachments at Isle-aux-Noix, Rivier-du-Chine, and Yamaska.[2]

In the spring of 1781 the frontier region's remaining Loyalists were looking forward to another invasion from Canada, and there were rumors that the Tories were planning to hold a grand reception for their liberators in recaptured Albany. While still operating under his hospital staff cover in the capital, Dr. George Smyth was trying desperately to get General Haldimand to strike south, and "soonest." The following passages taken from Smyth's May 9th letter to the Governor-General make this clear:

"Now is the season to strike a blow on this place, when multitudes will join, provided a considerable force comes down. The sooner the attempt is made, the better...If a few handbills, intimating pardon, protection, &c. &c. were sent down, and distributed about this part of the country they would effect wonders; ...A few lines of comfort, in print, from your Excellency to those people [local Tories], would make them the more eager in Prosecuting their designs; and if the Vermonters lie still, as I have some hopes they will, there is no fear of success." [3]

Smyth's enthusiasm for another invasion was driven by the precarious nature of his situation—he was under increasing pressure from local Patriot authorities, and was eager to be exchanged. His May 9th letter ends with the plea: "There is a flag [of truce] from this place shortly to be sent; perhaps I may go with it; I expected before this time I would 'be removed from my present situation...' When his original letter was sent off on May 25th, Smyth attached a similar request: "For God's sake, send a flag for me. My life is miserable. I have fair promises, but delays are dangerous...A flag—a flag, and that immediately, is the sincere wish of..." (signed H. [Hudibras] Senior). [4]

Intensified Efforts to Counter Loyalist Support for British Intelligence Operations in Albany County

Although a majority of the Tory residents of New York's frontier areas had already left for Canada, the minutes of the Albany Board of the "Commissioners for Detecting and Defeating Conspiracies in the State of New York" provide a vivid picture of the kinds of hostility and countermeasures still being directed against Loyalists under their jurisdiction as late as 1780-1781:

--On September 18, 1780 Seth Perry informs on James Starks, Ephraim Knowlton and Philip Philips [probably Quakers or Shakers], charging that they are saying it is "contrary to Scripture" to take up arms in defense of the country.

On April 20, 1781 two local informers claimed that three other local men were "Disaffected Persons and that they have drank the King's Health, and that another man "...has advised many persons to accept of Sir Henry Clinton's Proclamations, telling them it contained Offers of Peace and that it would be the last time that any would be made..." Yet, on the same day an arrest warrant was made out for all the men so charged.[5]

By 1781, the Albany Board had begun to increase the investigative and coercive pressures being applied to the inhabitants of the county's few remaining Tory enclaves. In March of that year, the Board acted to "...more effectually punish adherence to the King of Great-Britain." Those who were found 'adhering to the enemies of this state' were declared to be guilty of high treason. Anyone who maliciously by preaching, teaching, speaking, writing, or printing maintained that the King of Great Britain had or of right ought to have authority or dominion in or over the State...or attempted to persuade or seduce any inhabitant to renounce his or her allegiance to the State...was guilty of a felony without benefit of clergy."[6] [The phrase "without benefit of clergy" meant that if the defendant was convicted of a capital offense, he would be put to death.]

In addition, during the summer of 1780 and the spring of 1781 the State Legislature and the Albany Board adopted more draconian measures to physically remove Tories from the frontiers of the Northern Department. In July, 1780 the Legislature passed an act approving the "removal" of the families of those former residents who had "joined the British." This was justified because "their habitations served to harbor secret emissaries [and] conceal members of their families who had come surreptitiously from the British lines…The deportation involved wives and, "at their [the Board's] discretion," all or any of their children not above the age of twelve years."[7] Children over the age of twelve were considered potential military recruits, and hence were not to be deported.

By March 22nd of the next year, the Commissioners were empowered to order the wives of Tories to leave New York State as well as the authority "to take and sell all the goods and chattels in the possession of the Wives of Persons who have voluntarily gone over to and joined, or shall hereafter go over to and join, the Enemy." The funds raised from the sale of these goods were to be used to defray the costs of removing the wives and children to "within the Lines of the Enemy."[8]

Ultimately, all Loyalists still living within the frontier areas of Albany County were vulnerable to deportation. The <u>Minutes</u> of the Board's proceedings of April 30, 1781 noted that "Whereas there are several Families remaining settled on the north side of the Hudson's River in an about Jessup's Patent, who are all disaffected," the Board resolved "…that it is necessary, for the safety of those frontiers, that all said families be ordered forthwith to remove from thence with all their effects down into the interior parts of the Country, without delay…and that all the males sixteen years old and upwards, be ordered to appear before this Board on or before the 20th day of May next at their peril."

Likewise, because the Board had "…received information that there are a number of Tory Women (whose husbands have joined the enemy) residing, and going from parts below to reside, above Saratoga, which this Board from manifest reasons disapprove of;" it resolved "...that the said women be all brought down below Saratoga and ordered there to remain as they will answer the contrary at their peril; until they receive further instructions from this Board or from some other proper authority."[9]

Disaffected persons living in the most remote areas were especially suspect during war scares. Having been warned by the Schenectady Commissioners of the presence in the Helleberg Hills of "a number of persons who have harbored [Tory Spies], and convinced of the necessity of removing such persons, "especially as the Enemy are daily expected upon the frontiers," on June 13, 1781 the Albany Board resolved to cooperate with "a party of men from Schenectady to apprehend some of those who are most notoriously disaffected in that Quarter." A day later, the Board noted that "As there are a number of disaffected persons in the Regiment at present commanded by Major Ezekiel Taylor, some of whom as they live upon the Frontiers," Resolved that such men should be removed, and that Major Taylor "be requested to furnish this Board as soon as possible with a List of his Regiment together with the Political Character of Each Man." [10]

The foregoing list of anti-Tory security measures employed in Albany County in 1781 provides ample evidence of how much more difficult and dangerous it was for the remaining Loyalists to support Canada-based British intelligence operations A year earlier, similar measures had been used to intimidate those Tories still living in New Jersey. As a result, New Jersey Loyalists had to take greater risks to support Tory provincial corps officers like James Moody when he was operating behind Rebel lines. Near the end of his subsequently published <u>Narrative</u> describing his exploits, Moody pays tribute to such men and women, as follows:

"...though Mr. Moody, in the course of his adventures, was often obliged to put his life into the hands of the Loyalists, in different parts of the country, he was never disappointed or deceived by any of them...They were men of such inflexible attachment to Government, that no temptations could induce them to betray their trust. Though many of them were reduced to indigence and distress, and they knew that almost any price might be obtained for giving up so obnoxious a person, yet they were so far from betraying him, that they often ran great hazards in giving him assistance."[11]

Rebel Arrests of Loyalists' Dependents Force the British to Kidnap Americans

British military leaders in Montreal had sought mutual exchanges of prisoners ever since early 1778. They were not just eager to recover deserters and captured British Regular or mercenary troops. After Bennington and Saratoga, it became obvious that captured Loyalist prisoners were likely to receive especially harsh treatment at the hands of their Patriot captors. Unlike the Hessians and other Germans, who were considered prisoners of war, Loyalists (and especially local ones) were treated as traitors. Public pressures on the British to obtain their release strengthened the Rebels' bargaining position.

Moreover, in addition to British and Tory military prisoners, in the course of the war the authorities in Albany arrested, interned, or placed under house arrest a large number of civilian Loyalists. As a result, the Commander of the American Northern Department always had more prisoners--especially officers and other "high-value" individuals--to exchange than did his British counterpart in

Quebec. This led the British command to sanction the kidnapping of Patriot leaders and the abduction of other Rebel civilians (including women and children) to balance the scales of prisoner exchanges.

This more aggressive policy had its risks. In March, 1781, New York Governor George Clinton wrote to General Haldimand listing the names of 159 women and children, "...taken by parties in the British service" and threatening retaliation: "It becomes...my duty to inform your Excellency that unless the inhuman and unmilitary Practice of capturing Women and Children ceases, I shall be reduced to the disagreeable necessity of detaining and treating the remaining families of those who have gone into the British lines as objects of Exchange, and thus involuntarily increase the distresses of many, whom the Fate of War has separated from their nearest connections." [12] However, since Patriot authorities in Albany County were already detaining Loyalist family members for exchange purposes by early 1781, the threat of additional such retaliation in the future probably had little impact upon Haldimand and his staff.

CHAPTER SEVEN

WHY THOMAS LOVELESS' SEPTEMBER 1781
INTELLIGENCE MISSION WAS DOOMED TO FAIL

The fate of Ensign Thomas Loveless and his companions was sealed long before they left the Loyal Blockhouse. During the previous year, American forces led by General Philip Schuyler had upgraded their CI and security capabilities in the Old Saratoga area. In contrast, the Tory Secret Service's leaders had failed to strengthen their own CI defenses, blinding them to growing Rebel threats to their operations behind American lines. Meanwhile, British military leaders in Canada continued to demand more recruits for Provincial Corps units and more Rebel hostages for use in prisoner exchanges. Finally, Sherwood and Smyth badly misjudged the likely impact upon their future operations of General John Stark's resumption of Command of the Northern Department.

General Schuyler's leadership was crucial to the increased effectiveness of the Patriot forces' campaign against British intelligence activities. After Congress removed him from command of the Northern Department in 1777 following the British capture of Fort Ticonderoga, Schuyler remained in Albany, serving in a variety of public bodies, including the Continental Congress and the New York Senate. He continued to support the war effort by providing tactical advice to field commanders in the region, and vital political support for the financial and logistical needs of George Washington and the Continental Army In addition to his large mansion ("The Pastures") overlooking the Hudson River east of Albany, Schuyler also maintained a summer house at Old Saratoga on the west bank of the Hudson twenty-five miles north of the capitol. Burned by Burgoyne's retreating forces in 1777, the summer house had been rebuilt by US military personnel following the victory at Saratoga.

Perhaps because of his friendship with George Washington, who created and skillfully managed his own agent networks, Schuyler also became an expert spymaster and counterintelligence officer. His best-known biographer has summarized these accomplishments as follows: "Schuyler...maintained private lines of intelligence reaching into Canada, and constantly aided Washington with supplies, plans, and information. Likewise, he had zealously assisted the Albany County commissioners for detecting and defeating conspiracies, providing them with information and moving them to arrest and interrogate suspected spies and persons otherwise aiding the enemy. The commissioners in turn had relied on Schuyler for assistance in prisoner exchange and for executing orders for arrests." [1]

Schuyler's informal agent network in Canada was based upon his pre-war business connections there, plus contacts which he established during his command of the Northern Department in 1775-1777. These linkages were augmented over time, and included spies reporting on British military plans from Crown Point, a "Monsieur L'Eglise" (or "Dominique L'Eclise) in Canada who was rewarded with Captain's pay and $600 compensation by the Continental Congress, and one Pierre Chapeton who was active during 1775-1781 but was later captured and imprisoned by the British.

Figure 8:
Engraving after Trumbull's Portrait of Major
General Philip Schuyler

In addition, William L. Stone claims that Schuyler "...had been specially charged by the Commander-in-Chief with the prosecution of all practicable measures for intercepting the communications of the enemy," and especially the vital packets being exchanged between Quebec and New York City. In April 1781, George Washington learned from a double agent that the dispatches of a British courier party were about to be seized by Continental troops. Sensing a rare "communications intercept" opportunity, Washington instead recommended that the double agent receive the packet of dispatches from the British couriers, and before passing it on, "...let him carry the letters and answers...to General Schuyler, who might contrive means of opening them without breaking the seals, take copies of the contents, and then let them go on. By these means we should become masters of the whole plot; whereas were we to seize [the double agent] on his first tour, we should break the chain of communication, which seems so providentially thrown into our hands."[2]

Schuyler's success in intercepting enemy couriers also gave him opportunities to deceive the British about American and French troop movements. One of Schuyler's most ambitious disinformation ploys took the form of a bogus letter from himself to George Washington dated July 15th, 1781, which he allowed to be "carried to the enemy." The primary purpose of the letter was to reinforce British fears (already heightened by deception ploys mounted by Washington himself) of an American assault against General Clinton's bastion in New York City. However, the opening sentence of Schuyler's letter went further, playing upon Haldimand's fears of French military intervention in Canada as well: "I cordially congratulate you, on the explicit reassurances you have, that a detachment of Count De Grasse's fleet will speedily join that under Monsieur De Destouches for the attack upon Quebec, but am [sorry that a] larger body of troops had [not been] ordered from the West Indies..." Later in the letter, he comments that "I am perfectly in sentiment with your Excellency that every demonstration of an attack upon New York should be given and [that] Count De Rochambeau with the [French] troops should not march from you, until the fleet sails from Boston." [3]

These security improvements were accompanied by better coordination between General Stark's Regular forces and the Albany County militia. In addition to Schuyler's leadership and the Albany Board's aggressive "Loyalist removal" activities, by 1781 the Continental Army's Headquarters at Old Saratoga had begun to coordinate its defensive CI operations with local Militia units, especially during periods of high military tension and other kinds of alerts. As a result, local Loyalists found themselves under increasing scrutiny, and more troops were available to detect and counter Tory-led courier runs, scouting teams, and kidnapping parties. In short, the operational environment facing the Tory Secret Service behind enemy lines was becoming increasingly dangerous.

Over time, General Schuyler's leadership and CI successes inevitably attracted the attention of the Tory Secret Service As a result, plans to kidnap him were under consideration as early as May, 1781, and a reward of 200 guineas was posted for his apprehension. Schuyler responded by evacuating his family from their summer house at Old Saratoga and requesting a guard detail from the Second New York Regiment stationed at Albany.

THE HIERARCHY OF PROTAGONISTS IN THE "SPY WARS" CONDUCTED IN ALBANY COUNTY, N.Y. DURING 1778-1783

BRITISH/TORY

General Sir Frederick Haldimand, Governor-General of Canada, 1778-1786. His Headquarters were at Quebec

General Watson Powell. Commander of British military forces in Canada. Based at Montreal.

Colonel Barry St. Leger. Commander of Tory Provincial Corps units and supporter of Tory Secret Service operations. Based at St. Johns.

Captain Justus Sherwood. Senior Director of the Tory Secret Service.

Dr. George Smyth. Deputy Director of the Tory Secret Service.

Private (later Ensign) Thomas Loveless. An Albany County farmer who joined The King's Loyal Americans in 1776 and conducted Secret Service operations in the Albany County area during 1779-1781.

AMERICAN

George Clinton, First Governor of the State of New York, 1777-1795.

General Philip Schuyler. Major General in the Continental Army, Member of The Continental Congress and the New York State Senate. Self-taught spymaster and counter-intelligence officer.

General William Heath. Continental Army Commander based in Albany, 1779-1783.

General John Stark. Served twice as Commander of the Continental Army's "Northern Department," based at "Old Saratoga" Fort near today's Schuylerville.

Colonel Cornelius Van Vetchen. Commander of the Albany Militia regiment based in Ballstown. Ran successful counterintelligence operations against the Tory Secret Service.

Captain Hezekia Dunham. Commander of a company in Colonel Van Vetchen's Militia regiment. Leader of the three-man team that captured Thomas Loveless and his party on September 25, 1781.

Figure 9:
The Opposing Chains of Command in the "Spy Wars" conducted in Albany County, New York during 1778-1783

In contrast to Schuyler's efforts to improve Rebel security, by early 1781 Sherwood and Smyth remained oblivious to the fact that their service was losing the counterintelligence battle with its American opponents. Driven by their need for Loyalist military recruits and American hostages for use in prisoner exchanges, the TSS was continuing to accept penetrations and double agents sent by its enemies in New York and Vermont. Although these individuals were routinely screened and interrogated, and many of them were identified as potential "CI risks," far too many were accepted as having changed sides and were then allowed to "escape" or return on parole to the United States. Once in place, such individuals posed a serious threat to future cross border operations by British and Tory spies.

By the summer of 1781, General Haldimand himself was pressuring Smyth and Sherwood on CI issues, demanding that they uncover more of the enemy agents operating in Canada, and especially near Montreal. According to Ian Pemberton, in July "...Smyth discovered that a Mrs. Cheshire in Montreal was supposedly providing information and lodging to enemy agents. Smyth subsequently dispatched a party of men whom he described as "three cunning fellows" to seek out Mrs. Cheshire, and to pretend to be recent arrivals from New England. These counterspies were suitably equipped with old clothes, Yankee firelocks, Vermont and Connecticut currency, and a forged letter from Jacob Bayley to add authenticity to their disguise." Three men under suspicion were eventually identified as "connected with Mrs. Cheshire," and they were arrested four months later. [4]

In the long run, however, Haldimand's Tory spies not only failed to protect themselves from American double agents and Rebel spies operating in Canada, they failed to penetrate or disrupt the US Intelligence leadership that was directing these hostile operations. Moreover, the Tory Secret Service's continued reliance upon a weakening Loyalist support network increased their vulnerabilities to American countermeasures. In short, by 1781, American CI defenses in Albany County had improved so greatly that the Northern Department area was becoming a "hard target" for the TSS. As a result, previous sources of intelligence information began to dry up, the number of active loyalist support cadres declined, and the pendulum of successful CI deception and control operations began to swing toward the American authorities.

Meanwhile, the escalation of Tory-sponsored kidnapping attempts was galvanizing Albany County leaders into more concerted action. The first exchanges of prisoners had been conducted at Fort Ticonderoga in 1778. Since many of the prisoners held on both sides were civilians, the New York authorities agreed from the outset that some categories of civilians could be exchanged for enlisted military personnel. However, because Haldimand's forces captured so few American soldiers and the Rebel authorities continued to arrest and detain local Tories for use in prisoner exchanges, the British Secret Service in Canada soon found itself in the business of kidnapping American civilians.

Although he approved raids designed to capture ordinary residents of New York State, General Haldimand initially resisted proposals to kidnap high-level Rebel leaders. In the summer of 1781, however, he ordered the Tory Secret Service to abduct those Rebels "most conspicuously aggressive" in persecuting Loyalists. The most ambitious of these raids took place between July 30th and August 7th, 1781, and targeted three key American leaders: Dr. Samuel Stringer of Ballstown, Mr. John Bleeker of Hoosic Falls, and General Philip Schuyler, as well as Saratoga garrison commander Colonel Vandyke and several prominent Rebels in Stillwater, Half Moon, and New City. Each of the eight kidnapping parties consisted of four to six men, some of whom were British Regulars whose cockney accents were so strong that they were ordered not to respond if accosted by the locals. Traveling by night, all the teams were in position by July 31st and ready to strike.

Due to bad luck, poor leadership, and security blunders, all of the planned kidnappings failed. As his team was poised to abduct Dr. Stringer, veteran Tory scout Joseph Bettis —who was married and the father of three children-- suddenly abandoned his mission to elope with the daughter of Loyalist tavern owner Jellis Lagrange, leaving the rest of his party to fend for themselves. Meanwhile, when Mathew Howard and his group were captured on July 31st, the Rebels obtained Howard's copy of Sherwood's instructions listing the membership and the assigned targets of each of the Tory kidnapping teams.

This revelation raised popular fears and intensified preparedness throughout the Albany-Saratoga area. As Mary Beacock Fryer described the situation: "The atmosphere around Albany was tense and people were in a panic. Reports arrived on other raids that had taken place, and while no one of any consequence had been kidnapped, every leading citizen fully expected to see his home attacked. Demands for protection poured in from every side which the Commissioners tried to turn down." [5] Angered by his daughter's escapade, Jellis Lagrange offered to help the Albany Board capture Bettis. Ironically, Lagrange was later arrested and jailed by the Board as a possible co-conspirator.

Tory spymaster Dr. George Smyth was furious when he learned about the Bettis debacle. From St. Johns he wrote Mathews that Bettis was ". . . now confined to the garrison for refusing to deliver up his Desdemona, who he has secreted. Should this Dame be sent back [to Albany], I think he will not be long after her." General Haldimand was also outraged by Joe Bettis' caper. Captain Mathews informed Dr. Smyth that "Mr. Bettis' conduct has met with His Excellency's highest displeasure, and prevents him from fulfilling His intention of putting him on the subsistence list, which would have been immediately done if he had acquitted himself properly on the late occasion…He may be made acquainted with the fact that the woman he brought from the Colonies will be returned when Captain Brownson is sent." [6] Yet, regardless of the uproar this incident caused the Secret Service's leadership, Bettis remained on active duty until he was captured at Ballston and executed eight months later.

The General was even more upset with the Secret Service team led by Captain John Walden Meyers that had stormed Philip Schuyler's home near Albany but failed to kidnap him, and in the process stole a quantity of the Schuyler household's silver plate and utensils. The August 7th attack, launched in the evening by a party of twelve men which included some local Tories and two British soldiers in civilian clothes, was violent, but brief. Schuyler's servants and guards exchanged fire with Meyer's men who had forced their way into the main hallway on the first floor. Schuyler escaped to the second floor and signaled for help, while members of his family (his wife and a dozen of their children and grandchildren were home at the time) cowered in the basement with their slaves and servants.

Unable to subdue the defenders, and fearing the arrival of reinforcements, the Tory kidnapping party withdrew, leaving one of its men dead and carrying two prisoners and the two wounded Redcoats back to St. Johns. Schuyler believed that the raiding party had been sent to kill, rather than kidnap him. Thus, he took additional steps to ensure his safety, declaring to Governor George Clinton that if "these kidnapping Gentry" made another attempt, "they will not be able to retire with impunity." [7]

Meanwhile, round-ups of the "usual [Tory] suspects" intensified. In mid-September the General's son, Colonel Stephen Schuyler, led a militia detachment to an isolated area known as the "beaver dams," where, according to William Stone, "From seventy to a hundred families 'of the most notoriously disaffected' were arrested and brought into the city, where they were placed under a more vigilant surveillance than could be exercised over them in their own township." [8]

Embarrassed by his underlings' theft of his pre-war acquaintance's silver, General Haldimand ordered the missing items returned, along with a personal letter of apology. Apparently General Schuyler did not regain all of his pilfered silver service, however. Nineteenth Century historian Benson Lossing later described a man who, after seeing a portrait of General Philip Schuyler in Washington, D.C. in 1841, reportedly exclaimed "Why, I ate soup not long since at Belleville in Canada, from a tureen that was carried off from his [Schuyler's] home by some spies in the Revolution." [9]

Back at St. Johns, Dr, Smyth continued to underestimate the counterintelligence dangers in the Old Saratoga area. The following passage is from a letter written to Smyth on August 20, 1781 by Lt. David Jones, the leader of the TSS team that had failed to kidnap Major John McKeinster, who had replaced Colonel Vandyke as commander at Saratoga. A careful reading of its contents reveals just how desperate and gullible the Tory Secret Service had become:

"Now in order to obtain the object of my attention, I sent for Mr. Cole who was father in law to Captain Dunham

133

[no first name is given, so it is impossible to know whether Jones was dealing with Hezikiah or Holton Dunham, both of whom were Captains in the Albany County Militia at the time] of a company belonging to the said Major McKeinster's regiment, they having been recommended to me as Faithful Subjects—the same Captain Dunham came to me and freely promised me all the assistance in his power to bring about some favorable opportunity whereby I might apprehend the said Major McKeinster, after which Capt. Dunham returned to the barracks at Saratoga, in order to carry into execution his promise to me. But it unfortunately happened that Capt. Dunham fell into some dispute with Capt. Gray of the said Major McKeinster's regiment which was carried so high that the said Capt. Dunham was sent to his farm at Stillwater under an arrest, which put it out of his power to fulfill his promise to me. After he sent Mr. Grant who is Lieutenant & Adjutant to said regiment, to inform me what had happened at the same time showing me his crime, by which I knew that nothing that had passed betwixt me and Capt. Dunham had been the cause of his confinement." [10]

"Now I applied to Mr. Crocker [probably Levi] , an inhabitant, a faithful subject who agreed with me to give me intelligence of the situation of the Rebels at Saratoga and let me know if the said McKeinster should go abroad, although I did not let Mr. Crocker know my intent. Crocker proved faithful in the evening of the 30th July: Crocker informed us that the Major was to lodge in a certain house at about 30 rods distance from the barracks. I being under a promise to the rest of the parties not to strike till the night of the 31st, I went to Lieutenant Tyler to advice with him, who would not consent that I should strike until the night agreed on, notwithstanding the favorable opportunity that they presented."

"Now on the 31st day of July Crocker came to me at about 10 O'clock in the forenoon, informed me that there was an alarm and that it was occasioned by one Gyles who said that he had discovered a party of Indians near the creek, near to Saratoga. The same day about 5 O'clock in the afternoon, Crocker came to me and informed me that Youngblood was killed and two more wounded. He also informed me their [sic] was a Party fired upon at Ballstown and that there was a deserter come in and had informed Colonel Pearce that their was a number of Parties out, and that he called a number of names that was at the head of the Parties, and that the country was all in armes." [11]

"Now I being adviced [sic] by some friends to apply to Vanvacten [Col. Cornelius Van Vetchen] which I did, and Vanvacten sent me word that his advice for me with my party to lay still in some secret place until the alarm was over. He said that he dare not see me at present, by reason that he was suspected and closely watched, but as soon as the alarm was a little abated he would assist me. Now in the evening of the 2nd day of August, I was informed that their was a large Party of Rebels, at least 150, surrounding the ground on which we lay, which I found to be the truth, although I found my way through them with my party, which gave me to believe that their had been some discovery made of me which proved to be so, for the man that supplied us with provisions had a daughter that was courted by a Rebel and she told him that I had a connection with Capt. Dunham, and he went and informed Major McKeinster, as I was informed by some friends." [12]

Sherwood later claimed to have advised Smyth against releasing or exchanging either the Crockers or the Bitelys (whom he did not trust), all of whom had been abducted to Canada the previous June by a party led by Ensign Thomas Sherwood (Justus Sherwood's cousin)

Contrary to Sherwood's warning, however, both the Crockers and Bitelys were finally allowed to "escape" after promising to serve as informants and supporters in the vicinity of Old Saratoga. [13]

The TSS Leadership's Failure to Recognize the Dangers Posed by John Stark's Resumption of Command in Albany

In addition, Smyth and Sherwood underestimated the operational implications of General John Stark's return to command of the Northern Department. John Stark was one of the true folk heroes of the American Revolution, a man whose reputation as a Patriot persisted in the public's memory long after his death. Stark's ancestors were Presbyterians who had been driven from Scotland by James the Second's persecution of the Scottish Kirk, settled for a time in northern Ireland, and then emigrated to New Hampshire in 1720. Raised on a frontier farm, John and his three brothers (William, Samuel, and Archibald) were trained as woodsmen and Indian fighters, and all of them held commissions in the British service during the French and Indian War. Between 1755 and 1759, John Stark took part in several major military campaigns and rose to the rank of Captain in "Roger's Rangers," the famous irregular Indian-fighting unit.

In April of 1775, he became a Colonel--first of New Hampshire militia, and later of the 1st New Hampshire regiment of the Continental Line--and took part in the battles of Bunker Hill, Trenton, and Princeton. His spectacular victory over a combined force of British, Hessian, and Loyalist troops at the Battle of Bennington on August 16, 1777 boosted his public reputation as an aggressive combat commander. Just before the battle of Saratoga (during which his forces blocked Burgoyne's escape route) he was promoted to the rank of Brigadier General, even though he had frequently been criticized by his peers for his chronic insubordination.

As a result of Bennington Stark became something of a celebrity, and patriotic Rebels began to name towns after him. His fame was also put to use in other ways. In 1780 David Pierce of Gloucester, Massachusetts built a heavily-armed privateer which he used to capture three large British merchant ships, the cargoes of which were valued at $400,000. In a personal letter written thirty-four years later, Pierce told a friend that "<u>The General Stark</u> was built under my direction. In one cruise, in three weeks, she sent me $300,000, I having sold some part of her. She was a ship of 350 tons; twenty guns on her lower deck, eight guns on her half deck, and two on her forecastle—a very fast sailer [sic] and very stiff. I named her in honor of John Stark." [14]

After Saratoga, Stark remained on active duty, serving in New York, Rhode Island and New Jersey. Perhaps because of his knowledge of the area, he was first given command of the Continental Army's Northern Department in 1778. It was during his second tour in this post (which began in the Spring of 1781) that he encountered Thomas Loveless. Because of his French and Indian War service, General Haldimand may have remembered John Stark as a senior officer in Roger's Rangers. On the other hand, Captain Mathews was apparently ignorant of General Stark's political background, i.e. whether he was a "Yorker" or a Vermont "Yankee." In a letter to Sherwood from Quebec dated 20 September, 1781, Mathews mentions that General Haldimand has recently received a letter from "a B. General Stark, commanding the Northern District." Mathews then asks "Who is this Stark belonging to--Vermont or the United States?" [15]

Stark harbored an intense personal hatred for Tories. The previously described harsh treatment of the Tory prisoners captured at the Battle of Bennington could only have taken place with the approval of the American commander in charge. At Bennington Stark clearly refused to treat captured Loyalists as POWs. Caleb Stark described the aftermath of the battle as follows:

"Lieutenant Colonel Baum, who was mortally wounded, died soon after the action, and was buried with military honors. The Hessians and English were treated as prisoners of war, and marched from the field in their ranks; but the tories, 152 in number, were tied in pairs; to each pair a horse was attached by traces with, in some cases, a negro for his rider; they were led away amid the jeers and scoffs of the victors—the good housewives of Bennington taking down beds to furnish cords for the occasion." [16]

After burying thirteen Tories, "...mostly shot through the head," an American veteran of the Bennington battle later witnessed the formal surrender ceremonies, which he described as follows: "Afterward we went to Bennington and saw the prisoners paraded. They were drawn up in one long line; the British foremost, then the Waldeckers [Hessians], next the Indians, and hindmost the tories."[17] As early as the Fall of 1777, General Stark had apparently decided that, in keeping with his experiences as an officer in Rogers' Rangers, not all captured enemy combatants deserved to be treated equally.

During his first tour of duty as Northern Department Commander in 1778 John Stark sent the following letter to the President of the New Hampshire Congress in which he summarized the military situation in the vicinity of Albany and commented on the hanging of Loyalists:

Figure 10:
Alonzo Chappel's Painting of Brigadier John Stark

"They (the people) [sic] do very well in the hanging way. They hanged nine on the 16th of May, and on the fifth of June nine; and have one hundred and twenty in jail, of which, I believe, more than half will go the same way. Murder and robberies are committed every day in this neighborhood. So you may judge of my situation, with the enemy on my front, and the devil in my rear." [18]

Stark's military correspondence during the war is full of comments which reveal his intense hatred of Tories and their British and Indian allies. In an August 15, 1778 letter to Colonel Alden, Stark congratulates him on a successful scout, during which the Americans captured some Tories disguised as Indians, and comments "As to the tories you sent, I shall take care that they are properly treated." In the same message. Stark declares "If your scouts should be fortunate enough to fall in with more of those painted scoundrels, I think it not worth while to trouble themselves to send them to me. Your wisdom and your scouts may direct you in that matter." [19] Clearly, John Stark did not see Tories caught "out of uniform" as prisoners of war, and he was encouraging his subordinates to execute such persons if they encountered them in the future.

Another incident three years later also reveals General Stark's free-wheeling attitude toward hanging Tory intelligence officers. In August, 1781 Mathew Howard, a Lieutenant in the King's Loyal Rangers who had earlier helped Dr. Smyth escape to Canada, was captured while attempting to kidnap prominent Patriot John Bleeker. Howard was imprisoned near Bennington, and General Stark, then the local commander, sentenced him to be hanged. In a March 1, 1783 deposition, Howard claimed that the noose was placed around his neck three times and that he was once raised off the ground "…because he would not inform them of the Royal Army." [20] Howard was later exchanged, much to the satisfaction of Dr. Smyth.

John Stark's hatred of Loyalists was undoubtedly intensified by the revelation that Benedict Arnold-- one of his most famous military colleagues—had ultimately betrayed the American cause. Arnold was the man with whom Stark had shared the glory of the October 7th victory at Saratoga. Stark served on the Review Panel of thirteen generals that decided the fate of Major John André, so he was privy to the full extent of Arnold's betrayal of both his country and his fellow officers in the Continental Army.

Like Benedict Arnold, John Stark was a brilliant field commander who led his troops from the Front, rather than from the Rear. Both his speech and his actions were colorful, and designed to inspire the confidence of his men, as evidenced by the famous comment he reportedly made prior to the Battle of Bennington, one version of which goes as follows: "Now, my men, over there are the Hessians. They were bought for seven pounds, ten pence a man. Tonight the American flag floats over yonder hill or Molly Stark sleeps a widow." [21]

Stark was also endowed with an extreme sense of personal honor, coupled with an independent streak which sometimes irked his superiors. Like Arnold, he had no respect for the inexperienced, but politically well-connected generals who were often raised to their rank by the Continental Congress. When, after two years of successful duty as a Colonel, Stark was passed over for promotion to Brigadier General in favor of Col. Enoch Poor, he resigned his commission and went home to his farm. As one historian has observed, "It was not the first time he had been passed over for lesser men with less experience but with more social graces and more tactful tongues."[22]

Stark's insubordinate tendencies were probably strengthened by his years of service with Roger's Rangers, where initiative and independent action were rewarded, and this trait continued throughout his Revolutionary War career. When, after four months of private life, he accepted his commission as a Brigadier General of New Hampshire militia, he refused orders to deploy his troops to Saratoga, and sent them to Bennington instead. Like Arnold before him, he was first reprimanded by the Continental Congress for his insubordination, and then rewarded with a promotion. The Bennington victory "made" Stark's career, but one of the authors of the Stark's biography in the Encyclopedia of the American Revolution notes that: "To Stark's discredit it must be said that except at Bunker Hill he showed a consistently insubordinate character; but for incredible luck he would not be the national hero he remains today." [23]

From the start of his service in the War of Independence, John Stark primarily saw himself as a military representative of the State of New Hampshire. He was willing to subordinate his militia units to the Continental Army, as required, but (like many other State Militia commanders) he insisted upon recruiting and leading men from his own state. After his stunning victories at Bennington and Saratoga, he came to see himself as an independent regional field commander who, like the officers who fought under Robert Rogers in the French and Indian War, was expected to exercise the maximum possible personal freedom in tactical decision-making. This would be especially true in times of peril when facing both an enemy to his front and the possibility of fifth column attacks upon his rear.

CHAPTER EIGHT

THOMAS LOVELESS' LAST OPERATION: ITS OBJECTIVES AND BETRAYAL

David Jones' August 20th letter to Dr. Smyth describing the unsuccessful July 25th –August 2nd attempt to kidnap Major McKeinster makes it clear that Van Vechten and the Dunhams were baiting a trap which they hoped would trick the TSS into making some major operational mistakes. Indeed, the narrow escape of Jones' party showed that the enemy's security and counterintelligence defenses in the Saratoga area were on high alert. Why Jones' report raised no "CI flags" (i.e. concerns that the enemy officers who negotiated with Jones at Old Saratoga might be only pretending to defect) in the minds of Smyth and Sherwood is difficult to explain.

Apparently undaunted by the Jones Party's experience, the Tory spymasters decided in early September to send another Secret Service team to determine the true allegiance of the mysterious Colonel Van Vechten. By August 26th, Smyth was informing Captain Mathews that "he had no doubt of the fidelity of Loveless," and had chosen him to deliver a letter to "Van Vactin" [sic]. In reality, Thomas Loveless and his men would be conducting a very risky "CI bona fides" mission. In a letter of September 3rd Smyth told Mathews that "From what you say of Mr. Loveless, there is little doubt that if he should not succeed with Van Vacten [sic], he will discover his real sentiments & prevent [presumably by kidnapping him] any evils that might arise from design." [1] Thomas Loveless was probably chosen to lead the team because of his intimate knowledge of the geography of the Old Saratoga area and its people—possibly including Colonel Van Vechten and Captain Dunham as well.

The exact nature of Thomas Loveless's mission is revealed by the formal instructions which he was given prior to the departure of his party. These instructions, addressed to "Mr. Loveless" and signed by Captain David Forbes of the 34th Regiment, who was in command at St. Johns at the time, have been preserved for our examination, thanks to their October 4th publication in a newspaper at Fishkill, in Dutchess County (See photocopy on page 159). The following is taken from this document, which was apparently given to the press after Loveless' capture and which subsequently appeared in the The Pennsylvania Evening Post and The Continental Journal in Massachusetts:

"Sir---You will proceed with your party to Saratoga, and bring me from thence one or more intelligent persons. You must be necessarily aware of the address, activity, and courage required to conduct an enterprise of this nature, with honor to yourself and advantage to your cause. You will carry in your mind, that the weaker your force, the stronger must be the shew [sic] and vigorous exertions of your courage; this will deceive the enemy, who will naturally multiply numbers, when they see an attack with confidence. I have dwelt upon this point, as I have, for good reasons, given you are but a small party."

"In case of being observed, before you have executed your business, and by the disposition of the enemy precluded from the possibility of a retreat, you may show them these orders, to evince that you are come openly and avowedly in arms, to do the duty you are commanded on; and not like lurking spies, or secret assassins, as such are too often for the honor of war, sent from the enemy into this province.

"Avoid even the shadow of cruelty, and every kind of mischief unauthorized by the laws of war. The distressing of individuals is but partial evil, and avails nothing. No destruction must be levied that will not affect the collective body of the enemy."---D. Forbes, capt. 34th regt. Commandant, St. Johns." [2]

  This remarkable document is of vital importance to our understanding of the ambiguities surrounding General Stark's decision to execute Thomas Loveless. It clearly states that the members of the Loveless party are on a kidnapping mission, that they are to conduct themselves as soldiers, not "spies, or secret assassins," and that they are to operate openly and "in arms." These instructions must have been read (but ignored) by both Stark and Loveless' Court Martial panel. More significantly, the fact that the instructions were publicly disseminated indicates that the Commander of the Saratoga Garrison must have assumed that his execution decision would have broad public support. This support would have been bolstered by the discovery on Loveless' person of a letter addressed to Colonel "Van Vactin" from Smyth or Haldimand asking for his support and possible defection to Canada.

  The several competing versions of the betrayal and capture of the Loveless party all mention the involvement of two Patriot officers: Colonel Cornelius Van Vechten and Captain Hezikiah Dunham of the 13th Regiment of the Albany County Militia.

FISHKILL, October 4.

Captain Forbes, of the 34th regiment, who commands at St. John's, lately sent a party towards Saratoga to take a prisoner or two, for the purpose of obtaining intelligence; but notwithstanding his very particular instructions, a copy of which is transmitted, on the morning of the 25th ult. a Capt Dunham of the militia, and two men only, took five of the party, and conducted them safe to Saratoga, in a manner which does this little party much honor. Scouts are out in search of the remainder.

The following is a copy of the Instructions.

"SIR,

"You will proceed with your party to Saratoga, and bring me from thence one or more intelligent persons. You must be necessarily aware of the address, activity and courage, required to conduct an enterprize of this nature, with honor to yourself and advantage to your cause.---You will carry in your mind, that the weaker your force, the stronger must be the shew and vigorous exertions of your courage: This will deceive your enemy, who will naturally multiply numbers when they see a party attack with confidence:---I have dwelt upon this point, as I have for good reasons, given you but a small party.

"In case of being observed, before you have executed your business, and by the disposition of the enemy precluded from a possibility of retreat, you may shew them these orders, to evince that you are come openly and avowedly in arms, to do the duty you are commanded on; and not like lurking spies or secret assassins, as such are, but too often, for the honor of war, sent from the enemy into this province.

"Avoid even the shadow of cruelty, and every kind of mischief unauthorised by the laws of war. The distressing of individuals is but partial evil, and avails nothing. No destruction must be levied that will not affect the collective body of the enemy."

D. FORBES, Captain 34th regt.
Commandant St. John's.
To Mr. Loveless.

Figure 11:
A newspaper article dated October 4, 1781 containing the orders captured with Thomas Loveless

Of Dutch extraction, Cornelius Van Vechten's family had lived on a farm near the town of Old Saratoga since the late 17th century. With the coming of the war, he was offered, but declined, a First Lieutenant's commission in Captain Jacobus Rosekrans' company in the 4th New York Regiment commanded by Philip Van Cortland. He later served in the Albany militia, and became one of its senior officers, eventually rising to the rank of Colonel. He was a member of General Gates' staff during the battles of Saratoga. The numerous references to him in Tory Secret Service records suggest that Van Vechten was a wily opponent. As commander of the Saratoga District's militia company, he would have been in close contact with the commander of the Continental Army garrison at Old Saratoga, and may have served as Stark's adjutant for Intelligence.

Hezikiah Dunham came from a family of early settlers of New York Colony that had lived in the Saratoga area for several generations. In 1778 he is listed as a Second Lieutenant in the 6th Company (commanded by Captain Joseph Palmer) of the 13th Regiment (Saratoga District) of the Albany County militia. Military records indicate that two other members of his family—Jonathan Dunham and Holton Dunham—were serving as Lieutenants in two other companies of the same regiment. By 1781, Hezikiah Dunham had been promoted to Captain of his company, which included Lieutenants John Davis and Richard Hilton, and Ensign William Green.

Interestingly, various records reveal that Hezikiah's brother Holton Dunham may not have remained a loyal supporter of the American cause. In August, 1779 a voucher signed by "Ezra Buell" shows that he was paid by the Albany Board to serve a warrant upon Holtham Dunham to facilitate his investigation by that body. Two years later,

Holton was arrested and charged with having supported the August, 1781 attempt by David Jones' party to kidnap Colonel "McKinstrey," Commander of the Old Saratoga garrison. By November 19th of the same year, Captain Holton Dunham had been "dismissed, as guilty of treasonable practices and desertion to the enemy." [3] Whether Holton Dunham's dismissal was real (suggesting that he had been bargaining in good faith with the Jones party in August), or simply a double agent used by Colonel Van Vechten to entrap more teams of Canada-based spies, is hard to determine.

The following is mid-19th Century historian Benson Lossing's brief description of the role of Captain Dunham in the Loveless Party's capture:

"Intimations of his intentions and of his place of concealment were given to Captain Dunham, who commanded a company of militia in the neighborhood, and he at once summoned his lieutenant, ensign, orderly, and one private to his house. At dark they proceeded to the "Big Swamp," three miles distant, where two Tory families resided. They separated to reconnoiter, but two of them, Green and Guiles, were lost. The other three kept together, and at dawn discovered Lovelace and his party in a hut covered with boughs, just drawing on their stockings. The three Americans crawled cautiously forward till near the hut, when they sprang upon a log with a shout, leveled their muskets, and Dunham exclaimed "Surrender, or you are all dead men!" There was no time for parley, and believing that the Americans were upon them in force, they came out one by one <u>without arms</u>, and were marched by their captors to General Stark at the barracks." [4]

Another version of the capture is provided by local historian Simeon Bloodgood, who claimed that his father was a secondary kidnapping target of the Loveless team. He says that Colonel Van Vechten and Captain Dunham were tipped off to the likely presence of the Tory party by a young boy's attempt to buy some rum at a local tavern. Dunham immediately recruited a blacksmith named Green and three others to begin a search. At daybreak Dunham and two of his men found a path leading from a Loyalist's house to a large thicket. The author then goes on to paint the location and circumstances of the Tories' capture in great detail, including snatches of Rebel dialogue to enhance the story:

"Dunham paused, and turning to his companions said, 'Here they are, will you follow me?' They instantly agreed to accompany him, and the party moved on in single file, with light and cautious steps. As they got nearly to the center, Dunham in advance, a log stopped up the path, and seemed to prevent any further approach. With a motion that indicated the necessity of their remaining still, he mounted the log, and looking over, discovered, sure enough, at once a desired and yet imposing sight. Round the remains of a watch fire, which day break rendered less necessary, sat a group of five fierce looking men, with countenances relaxed from their usual fixedness, but yet betokening boldness, if not savageness of purpose. They were dressing themselves and putting on their shoes and stockings, which stood by the side of their rude couches."

"Their clothes were much worn, but had a military cut, which made their stout and muscular forms more apparent, had a peculiar snug fit, and distinguished them from the loose, slovenly, scare crow figures which the homely character of our country seamstresses imposed upon every thing rural or rusticated among our people. Their hats or caps were set carelessly on their heads, with the air of regulars; and what made them still more observable was, that every man of them had his musket at his side on the ground, ready to be used at an instant's notice."

"Dunham surveyed this scene a few moments, and then drew back cautiously to his companions. In a tone not above a whisper, he said, "Shall we take'em?" A nod from his companions decided him. Each now examined his musket and re-primed it. The Captain took the right of his little band, and they moved forward to the log. They mounted it at the same instant, and, as they did so, Dunham cried out "Surrender, or you are all dead men!" The group thus found themselves almost under the muzzles of their enemies' guns and were indeed astonished."

"All but their leader, Lovelass, seemed petrified and motionless. This resolute man seemed disposed to make an effort for their lives. Twice amid the silence and stillness of the perilous moment he stretched out his hand to seize his gun. Each time he was prevented by the nearer approach of the muzzle that pointed at his head, and beyond which he saw an unflinching eye steadfastly fixed upon him, at the same instant he was told, that if he touched it he was dead. At this critical period of the rencontre [sic] Dunham peremptorily ordered the party to come out, one by one, which they reluctantly did, fearing, perhaps, that they were surrounded by and in contact with a superior force." [None of the accounts of the capture of the Loveless party offer a fully credible explanation of how three Rebel militiamen were able to intimidate and overpower five well-armed TSS veterans.]

"In this way they were secured, and were marched out of the thicket to the adjoining house. The inmates of the dwelling were thunderstruck at perceiving the prisoners. Some young women, who proved to be sisters of some of the party, gave way to the most violent grief. Well aware of the danger they were in, and of the speedy vengeance inflicted upon Tories and spies, they anticipated the most dreadful consequences to their unhappy brothers, and no words can express the frantic sorrow to which they abandoned themselves." [5] If this account is true, then Thomas Loveless was clearly not the only Loyalist soldier in the team who was operating in his old neighborhood.

General Stark was aware of the presence in his area of a larger British scouting force that may have included Thomas Loveless' party. A September 24, 1781 letter to General Heath contains Stark's description of the increased tempo of Tory Secret Service operations in his command area as of that date:

"There are in this neighborhood about thirty persons, who lately came from Canada, as I suppose to bring dispatches to Albany, and to find out the situation of the country. I have taken every possible method to trepan them, and hope to succeed…One of the parties [could this have been Loveless' group?] employed for the purpose, shot one man through the arm, as he was endeavoring to pass them last evening. He is likely to suffer amputation." [6]

Stark's description of the capture of Thomas Loveless and his party is contained in the same letter, but dated the following day: "September 25th. This moment are brought in five of the party I mentioned, supposed to be in this neighborhood, but they will give no satisfactory account of the remainder of the party. They were taken by Captain Dunham and two more persons this morning. Too much honor or praise can not be bestowed on these three brave militia men, for this special and meritorious conduct." [7]

The news of the Loveless party's capture was apparently leaked to the local press, and a Dutchess County newspaper's account published on October 4th subsequently appeared in at least two other papers in Pennsylvania and Massachusetts stating that:

"...Capt. Forbes, of the 34th regt. who commands at St. Johns, recently sent a party towards Saratoga, to take a prisoner or two, for the purpose of obtaining intelligence. But notwithstanding his very particular instructions, on the morning of the 25th ult. a capt. Dunham of the militia, and two men only, took five of the party, and conducted them to Saratoga, in a manner which does this little party much honor. Scouts are out in search of the remainder." [8]

The Trial and Execution of Thomas Loveless

Because no transcript of the trial by court martial of Thomas Loveless has survived, we do not know the names of the officers who served as members of the court. The identity of the Judge Advocate remains unknown, but a Colonel Weissenfels apparently served as President of the body. However, the few comments made by witnesses suggest that the trial was probably conducted in accordance with the usual regulations. Under these, the warrant for a General Court Martial was issued by the district, brigade, or regimental commander, who also decided the membership (by name or regiment) of the court. The Judge Advocate usually functioned as the prosecutor and managed the court proceedings.

The Continental Army used court martial proceedings to try its own personnel, as well as those civilians whose activities might jeopardize its security or operations. Unlike military courts held at the regimental or garrison level, a "General" Court Martial was empowered to try officers, as well as lesser ranks, and could issue sentences of death. General Court Martial panels were usually made up of thirteen officers, and in Capital cases (such as those involving espionage) guilty votes by nine jury members were required to obtain a conviction. However, the opinion of the Commanding Officer of the regiment or garrison usually had a determining influence upon a jury's opinion.

In a typical General Court Martial trial, the prisoner was formally charged, asked to plead guilty or not guilty, and allowed to make challenges to the jury for peremptory or cause reasons. He was allowed to speak in his own defense and to call character witnesses and others to testify on his behalf. Sworn depositions and official documents could be submitted as evidence. The jury's deliberations and voting were kept secret, and it was responsible for determining both the verdict and the punishment. The following comments by eyewitnesses and historians suggest that Thomas Loveless tried his best to defend himself by arguing that he was a prisoner of war, rather than a spy.

A man named John Becker (1765-1837), who claimed that his father had been a potential target of Tory raiders, later compiled a memoir of the events that took place in the Saratoga area during his boyhood. A professionally-edited version of the Becker manuscript was published, minus the author's name, by an Albany press in 1866. Becker describes Thomas Loveless' trial and its verdict as follows:

"The poor wretches were tried and condemned at a court martial, of which the celebrated Stark was President. Lovelass [sic] alone suffered death. He was considered too dangerous a man to be permitted to escape. He complained that being found with arms in his hands, he was only a prisoner, and many thought, that being the fact, he was scarcely punishable as a spy. Indeed he even bewailed his hard fate, and the injustice done him, but found he had nothing to expect from the judges." [9]

Historian Benson Lossing described the trial and execution as follows: "They were tried by a court-martial as spies, traitors, and robbers, and Lovelace, who was considered too dangerous to be allowed to escape, was sentenced to be hung. He complained of injustice, and claimed the leniency due to a prisoner of war; but his plea was disallowed, and three days afterward he was hung upon the brow of the hill at the place delineated, during a tremendous storm of rain and wind, accompanied by lightning and clashing thunder-peals." [10]

The official announcement of the court martial verdict and sentence is contained in a document entitled <u>Death Warrant of Thomas Loveless. By John Stark, Esq., Brigadier General in the Army of the United States, and Commander of the Northern Department, &c.</u> and reads as follows:

"At a general court-martial, held at Saratoga, October 2nd, 1781, whereof Colonel Weissenfels was President, Thomas Loveless, of the tory forces in the British army, was brought before the court, charged with being a spy; and the court, after hearing the examinations, and other testimony, have pronounced their opinion that he was a spy, and, by the usages of war, he be hanged by the neck until he be dead; which sentence being approved by me, you will remove him from the main guard to-morrow, the 8th instant, at half-past ten o'clock A.M., and exactly at eleven o'clock cause him to be hanged until he be dead—for which this is your sufficient warrant.

Given under my hand and seal, at my head quarters, at Saratoga, this 7th day of October, in the year of our Lord one thousand seven hundred and eighty-one.

By the General's command---

JOHN STARK
Brigadier General Commanding

Caleb Stark, Brigade Major
To the Adjutant of the day. "[11]

In addition to the detailed description of the hanging provided by Jacob Bitely, a number of other local residents published their own comments on the event, or provided them to early historians. An article in the <u>Sexagenary</u> volume told the tale in the following words:

"In two or three days (Loveless) was brought out upon the hill, on the south side of General Schuyler's house, and suffered death upon the gallows. Nothing could have been more quiet and unaffected that his manner; the spectators themselves were touched with compassion, but public policy seemed to require an unbending sternness on the part of the court, and his punishment certainly put an end for that time to all marauding expeditions by the Tories [this was not to be the case]. Lovelass's [sic] companions were sent down the river the same day to a depot for prisoners." [12]

It is difficult to guess what was going on in Thomas Loveless' mind as he approached his execution. Like Nathan Hale, he was not a professionally-trained spy, and he probably had no understanding of the legal risks he was taking. Perhaps he felt betrayed by the orders that he had been given by Major Forbes which suggested that his activities would not be interpreted by his enemies as espionage. Perhaps he realized that he had unfortunately crossed paths with the notoriously hostile John Stark, who may have remembered him as a veteran of the French & Indian War. Perhaps he discovered that he had been betrayed by some of his former friends and neighbors. As the first TSS officer to be hanged after being captured, he must have realized that the "rules of the game" in the Intelligence War along the New York frontier had suddenly changed.

Loveless's hanging came as a shock to his Tory colleagues. On October 18th, Justus Sherwood, who was aboard the T<u>rumble</u> (an eight-gun row galley captured from the Americans in 1776) near Crown Point anticipating the prisoner exchange, reacted bitterly to the news in a letter to Governor-General Haldimand in Montreal:

"While [Tory officer Andrew] Rikely was at Saratoga he saw Mr. Loveless Hang'd before General Stark's door & by his order. This barbarous Murder of my worthy friend (& as true and brave a subject as ever left the Colonies) stings me to the heart! I hope in God His Excellency will permit us to retalliate [sic] either by hanging up some of the rascals we have prisoners from that State, or by taking and hanging on their own ground some of those inhuman butchers, which I know we can do. I have inform'd the Captain of their Flag, on board the T<u>rumble</u>, of Loveless's death, & told him at the same time, that we might with as much propriety & much more Justice hang him on the bow sprit of the Vessel…I entreat His Excellency to Consider Mr. Loveless's poor widow & family as he was sent on secret service in which he has always been Exceedingly useful . . ."[13]

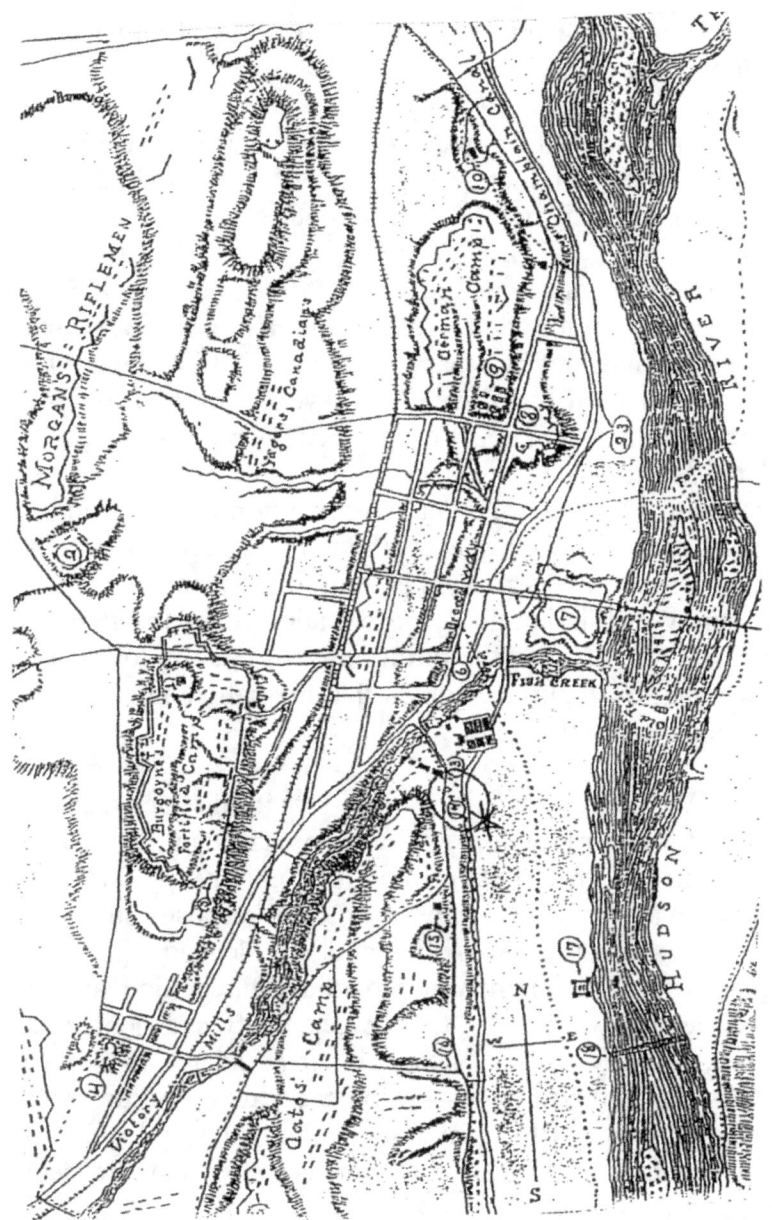

Map #5:
A 19th Century map of Old Saratoga/Schuylerville, showing the locations of Burgoyne's surrender and Loveless' hanging

The Reactions of Tory, American and British Leaders to Thomas Loveless' Execution

The British Command's perspective is revealed in Captain Mathews' Letter of 1 November, 1781 to Dr. Smyth concerning the hanging of Thomas Loveless:

"I am favored with your letter of the 18th ultimo—I have partially communicated its contents to His Excellency the Commander in Chief, but that painful part of it intimating the melancholy fate of Mr. Loveless, I have not yet had courage to impart to him, on appeal to my feelings on this occasion, and my advice---uninfluenced by sudden impulse or rash resentment which just indignation at so horrid an act might create, I refer you to a conversation we had upon a similar occasion---you may remember our reflection upon the inhumanity of this infamous system adopted by the Rebels, and while we lamented the futility of self-defense, following the working example, we agreed that retaliation alone could put a stop to it on their part."

"We were likewise satisfied that this destructive, unnatural war, originating with the populace in ignorance and confusion, has been supported entirely by acts of oppression and violence, many loyal, well-disposed subjects, the fates of whose wives and children depend upon the mandate of a Stark, are driven into arms and rebellion, and of course become victims to it. That generosity and nobleness of soul, primary to this Nation, but particularly so of her soldiers, has hitherto trespassed on the Law of Nature, and forbid retaliation—these are sentiments that unfit us to contend with the illiberal, cruel parricides we have to deal with, and while we impatiently observe them, we must ever be the dupes of their barbarity—I told you these murders, if not taken notice of, would become frequent, and I told you very plainly that had I upon a scout an opportunity of retaliating, I would without hesitation take upon myself the painful duty I should owe to humanity, and the name of my sacrificed friend, or fellow soldier."

"In the present instance, I would go myself, or with some active officer, with as many resolute men as might be necessary, to the ground, or as near it as I could penetrate, where the unhappy Loveless suffered. To meet the vile perpetrator is not to be expected, murderers are cowards, but I would seize three or four of his servants and hang them up with labels signifying "These in Fourfold Retaliation for Mr. Loveless, immorally executed by General Stark of the Continental Army" No law on earth could call the equity of this in question—our laws, not the orders of our Commanders, nor those of any civilized nation cannot authorize these cruel necessities, and under the circumstances we labor, they are bound to justify them."

"…As the putting an end to this inhuman practice is more the just than to gratify revenge—it would be painful, and might have a good effect to hang up the bodies of three or four who died in action, with labels to the foregoing purpose. I am not singular in my opinion—I have heard the same declared by many old officers of much humanity and feeling as any in the Army. It is assumed your conduct, if it be directed by this opinion, will meet with <u>general</u> (underlined) support."[14]

In the final paragraph of a letter dated October 8[th,] General Starks's son, Major Caleb Stark, informed General Schuyler of Thomas Loveless' execution:

"Yesterday [actually on October 8th] Thomas Lovelace the commander of the last party that fell into our hands, was hanged. He was tried by a court martial, and by them condemned and was executed at twelve o'clock. He

159

made no essential discoveries [i.e., he provided his captors with no useful intelligence data]."[15]

General Schuyler's reaction to this news is unknown, but the Continental Army Commander in Albany, General William Heath, was clearly unhappy about the decision to hang the Tory officer. A letter that he wrote to Governor George Clinton of New York on October 11th concluded with the following paragraph, which reflects his doubts about the legality of Stark's action, and his own concern about possible British reprisals: "I am exceedingly sorry to find by General Stark's letter that he has tried at a courtmartial [sic] and executed Loveless, who came with very particular written instructions to seize a prisoner from the neighborhood of Saratoga, in which attempt he and his party were taken…<u>He having written instructions, the tenor of them, and the party being armed, I think clearly barred the idea of his being considered a spy, and upon what principle he was executed I am at a loss to determine</u>—and am apprehensive it will make some difficulty. It may be best to say as little about it, at present, as possible." [16]

General Heath probably had no idea of how effectively the Loveless party had been deceived and betrayed by the Crockers, Captain Dunham and Colonel Van Vechten. However, when he published his memoirs in 1798, he had the following to say concerning the importance of deception in military operations: "The stratagems of war are almost infinite, but all have the same object, namely to deceive—to hold up an appearance of something which is not intended, while under this mask some important object is secured; and be a General never so brave, if he is unskilled in the arts and stratagems of war, he is really to be pitied; for his bravery will but serve to lead him into those wily snares which are laid for him."[17]

CHAPTER NINE

THE FINAL YEARS OF THE "TORY SECRET SERVICE"

For two weeks after Loveless' hanging, the American military leaders in the region remained in a "crisis" mode, preparing to counter a British thrust to the south. According to an 8 October, 1781 letter to Major General Heath from Stark: "By every appearance, it is plain that the enemy in Canada are either meditating an attack on this place, or that they are very anxious for intelligence from the westward. Their small parties are continually among us. Last night I sent a party who took two more of them prisoners, who are now safe in my guard-house. They say that they came over the lake with three more in company, who parted with them about five miles above my garrison; I am in hopes to take them, but can not insure success." [1]

On the evening of 11 October, 1781, a message from General Stark to Brig. General Peter Gansevoort, commander of the Albany Militia: "Dear Sir, By information this moment received, I am informed that the Enemy are now in reality on this side of Lake George. For God's sake hurry on with all the force you can collect as perhaps this may be the Last Information I can give you until they are in reality here. I can give no Information of their force but we must be prepared for the Worst.[2]

On October 12th, Philip Schuyler (in Albany) informed Stark that: "The night before last I intercepted a letter going to the enemy. It acknowledges the receipt of dispatches from Canada, and clearly points that this place is their object...The writer says we are ready to execute the business as soon as the party that is to conduct it arrives.

161

This business a former intercepted letter affords me the means of knowing: and it is to burn the city." [3]

However, by 21 October, General Heath had concluded that the enemy threat to Albany had not materialized, and was ordering the recently called out militia units to return home. Five days later, General Stark informed Governor Clinton of his intention to establish a winter garrison for his troops at Saratoga, and by 29 November, he was requesting permission to return to New Hampshire on leave:

"When I have finished the blockhouses, and got the barracks repaired...I shall retire to Albany, after which, as there can be little business for a general officer in this district, and the number of men will be so greatly diminished, and those scattered on the frontiers, I must beg leave to make a visit to New Hampshire. I hope this request will meet your approbation, and that you will be pleased to signify it as soon as convenient." I shall be ready to take the field whenever my services are required, but at present my domestic affairs strongly press my attendance." [4] The cause of this sudden turn-about in the perception of British threats from Canada can only be explained by the arrival of news concerning a crucial event which had recently taken place at Yorktown, Virginia.

The Impact of the News of Cornwallis' Surrender at Yorktown

In early October, 1781, neither the British nor the American commanders of forces along the New York-Canadian border knew anything about the failure of the Royal Navy to evacuate General Cornwallis's besieged army from Yorktown. The first reports (unconfirmed) of the British defeat in Virginia reached John Stark's desk on

October 25th, via a letter from Headquarters signed by General William Heath: "P.S. We have a report that Lord Cornwallis, with his army, surrendered on the 17th instant.(the surrender actually took place on the 19th). We impatiently wait a confirmation."[5]

General Stark's Headquarters did not receive such confirmation until November 3rd. In a 5 November letter to Vermont's Governor Chittenden, Stark exalted: "I congratulate you, with the most heartfelt satisfaction, on the glorious event which has placed another British army in our power, which was announced on the third instant by a discharge of fourteen cannon [Vermont was not yet a state, but the fourteenth cannon was fired in hopes that she might soon join the Union], and yesterday by that of a like number of platoons, in honor of the United States of America." [6]

In a 21 December, 1781 letter to General George Washington, Stark congratulated his commander-in-chief on his victory at Yorktown and summarized (to considerable personal advantage) his recent operations in northern New York as follows: "My exile here has not been attended with any interesting events. The enemy, to be sure, came as far as Ticonderoga; but when they learned the alacrity with which the militia turned out to defend their country, they returned, with shame and disgrace, without striking a blow at the northern frontiers." [7]

The news of Yorktown took even longer to reach the British in Canada. On September 27th William Lawson, a soldier in Jessup's Corps, reported that the army of Cornwallis had been cut off by Lafayette on the James River, but for some reason his report was countermanded and ignored. Quebec also remained unaware of the September 3rd defeat of the British fleet by Admiral De Grasse's fleet off the Virginia Capes. As a result, Haldimand's command did not learn of the Yorktown surrender until three weeks after the execution of Thomas Loveless. The last paragraph of a November 1st, 1781 letter from Continental Army Major General Sterling at his Saratoga Headquarters to Colonel Barry St. Leger informed him that : "I have the honor to communicate to you Intelligence I have received, that Lord Cornwallis with the Army under his command consisting of 5500 Regulars and 4000 Refugees, sailors, and negroes, with all the shipping of force and transport attending them surrendered on the 18th Ultimo to His Excellency General Washington—His Lordship and many of his officers are to go to England on Parole." [8]

Confirmation of the disaster at Yorktown caused the British administration in Quebec to revise its intelligence collection priorities and intensify its tasking of the TSS. In a February 2, 1782 letter to Sherwood, Mathews declared that there could be "...no further doubt of Lord Cornwallis' fate being as reported by the Rebels;" and passed on his superior's concern that "...the indispensable necessity of procuring authentic intelligence of the enemy's preparations and motions in every quarter is such that no pains, no trouble or expense must be spared to effect it. There is every reason to think that an attempt will be made upon this Province...Mr. Stevens' report of 2,000 French being assembled at Albany for that purpose points to it;" Haldimand also feared an attack via the "new road" built in the Connecticut River Valley by Moses Hazen, and directed Sherwood to "send messengers to all persons in that quarter from whom you can expect information." [9]

Meanwhile, the news of the British defeat at Yorktown made the TSS's operations in Rebel territory much more dangerous. As Haldimand awaited for guidance from London concerning "...the turn of public affairs [that] are likely to take the ensuing campaign," Sherwood and

Smyth faced the reality that (as one of their New York agents reported in April, 1782), "The disposition of the Rebels is greatly altered since the capture of Lord Cornwallis...the Rebels are in Great Spirits and the staunch friends to Government does [sic] not know what to say. . .Friends that might be trusted last summer will betray us first now by the incouragement [sic] of the taking of Lord Cornwallis." [10]

By August of the same year, the new wave of arrests and attacks upon the Tories remaining in northern New York had begun to take their toll. In a letter to Dr. Smyth, Captain Mathews described the arrival in Quebec of an agent named Davis as follows: "Davis is arrived—no news. Nothing going on to the southward—in anxious expectation of the packet from England, which it is thought would decide something— The Congress very still. Since Washington's tour (he had visited Albany, Saratoga, and Schenectady in July), all our friends on the route to [New] York have been served [with arrest warrants] or obliged to abandon their settlements, in so much that Davis missed six friends who used to protect him, & he was obliged to live in the woods & was three days without provisions." [11]

The Thomas Loveless incident did not put an end to British-American prisoner exchange efforts. Less than a month after the Tory Spy's hanging, General William Alexander (a.k.a. Lord Sterling), who had just replaced General Stark as Northern Department Commander, sent a letter to Colonel Barry St. Leger at St. Johns proposing an exchange of the remaining Americans imprisoned in Canada in exchange for ". . . the whole of them, rank for rank, of the troops lately under the Command of Major Ross and captured in Tryon County." He also held out the prospect of obtaining the release from prison of "other persons in the civil line" including Dr. Smyth's son, Terence, who had been captured in 1780. Alexander noted that "If you assure me that our prisoners in Canada shall be immediately sent for to be delivered up at Skenesborough I will have the like number of yours ready to be sent to the same place on the first notice of your approach."[12]

Such exchanges continued until September, 1782, when General Haldimand's Government announced a new British policy concerning the release of American prisoners. A note from Captain Mathews. explained the change to Dr. Smyth as follows: "In consequence of Instructions His Excellency has Received, He proposes ere long to send all Prisoners in this Province into the Colonies for Exchange, but if there are any so notoriously violent, whom you have had occasion to know, and whom you think are not to be restrained by Parole, the General desires you will mention their names and characters to me in order if possible that they may be detained."[13]

Tory Secret Service Operations During 1782

The year 1782 began with another war scare along the New York-Canada border. After the surrender of British forces at Yorktown the French fleet returned to the Caribbean, but the French troops in Virginia commanded by General Rochambeau were not evacuated until March of 1783. Lacking the requisite sea power to mount an attack upon New York City, and eager to keep the British off balance, Washington decided to disseminate rumors of a Franco-American invasion of Canada. In response, Haldimand once again ordered the Tory Secret Service to learn more about the possibility of another US offensive. Unfortunately for the TSS, this new intelligence-gathering campaign was soon awash in Rebel disinformation. According to intelligence historian G.J.A. O'Toole:

"This carte blanche approach to the problem boomeranged...tempting informers and subagents to furnish prodigious quantities of that which Sherwood was apparently prepared to pay handsomely to hear. By the end of February, the Secret Service had reports of eight thousand stand of arms and as many suits of military clothing deposited at Claverack on the east bank of the Hudson south of Albany; British cannon captured at Yorktown transported to Hartford, Connecticut; seven thousand French troops with some support marching northward through the Mohawk and Connecticut valleys; a Franco-American force of ten thousand gathering in Albany; and news of De Grasse's imminent return to northern waters from the Caribbean. One may imagine the distress such intelligence caused Haldimand, who had estimated a few months earlier that he could muster no more than twenty-five hundred troops to defend Canada against an invasion." [14] In point of fact, the entire "war scare of 1782" was the outgrowth of Washington's and Schuyler's deception ploys, and none of the alarmist intelligence reports listed above turned out to have any validity.

There were other reasons why 1782 was a busy year for the Tory spymasters and their men. In addition to gathering "indications and warning" information about enemy troop movements, they were still supporting Haldimand's covert diplomacy with pro-British elements in Vermont, and were also expected to assist the growing number of Loyalist refugees fleeing from New York State to Canada. As a result, by early summer as many as forty-seven members of the TSS were still operating behind American lines on a wide variety of missions, including ambushes, courier runs, kidnappings (in Vermont), and sabotage (spiking cannon at Fort Ticonderoga).

In late February, Sherwood had identified a tempting target for a Secret Service sabotage raid. As part of a larger message, he wrote Mathews that "I think it my duty to inform you that the Vermonters have got about 40 good gun carriages at Crown Point ready to draw away; if you judge it essential to the service to have them sunk under the ice, Lt. Sunderland thinks it may easily be done." Four days later, Major Mathews replied that "As the ice is reported so fine, the General wishes no time to be lost in destroying the gun carriages collected by the Rebels at Crown Point but thinks a small scout not only unequal to the labour it will require but subject to be cut off while employed at it, he proposes sending a party that can effectively execute it, and he desires you will communicate his commands to Lieut. Sunderland to repair immediately to St. Johns to give Col. St.Leger every information in regard to their situation and the easiest and most effectual means to destroy them."[15]

The desire for four-fold retaliation expressed in Mathews' outraged letter of November 11, 1781 did not lead to any retaliatory measures. in response to Thomas Loveless' hanging. Instead, Haldimand approved a temporary suspension of scouting missions "until the general alarm has subsided" and ordered Smyth to send fewer scouts in future. He also directed that "...those persons chosen for messengers (should) have the fewest family connections in the country, which often induce them to discover [reveal] themselves with too much freedom & remain too long inactive, amongst them, as it will now be more than ever necessary to hear what goes on in the country..." The General also noted that "...the indiscriminate permission to recruit has had...a bad effect, not only disturbing to Loyal subjects, but tending to a total prevention of obtaining authoritative intelligence of the enemy's motions and intentions." [16]

But by the end of the year, Haldimand had renewed the tasking of his Tory Spies, demanding greater attention to communications and operations security, more aggressive procurement of Rebel newspapers, and the limited resumption of scouting missions. Moreover, Dr. Smyth had begun to propose a return to selective kidnapping operations aimed at "seditious persons." Suffering from another attack of the gout, Smyth argued in support of his proposal in a brief December message to Captain Mathews, as follows:

"If the enclosed meets with the Genl's approbation, and if it is his pleasure it should be put into execution, I will, by having the choice of particular men, well acquainted with the different places, engage to have these seditious persons brought in.---I wish the intention may be kept a profound secret---My leg is much inflame'd." [17]

Slowly returning to its former tempo of operations, within five months of the Loveless hanging the TSS was faced with yet another "execution crisis." In late March, 1782 a three-man Tory courier party led by Joseph Bettis was captured at Ballstown. One of the party (Jonathan Miller) managed to escape, but Bettis and John Parker were taken to the Albany jail and charged with espionage. Refusing to provide vital information to their captors, the two men were sentenced to be hanged.

Haldimand ordered Sherwood to intervene on Bettis' and Parker's behalf, offering the promise of an exchange of high-level prisoners combined with threats of retaliation: Haldimand's message to the Americans (dated May 7th and passed to Sherwood via a letter from Mathews) noted that "…if the threats against their lives which have been reported to be made, should be put in execution, or any other punishment inflicted upon them, the unavailing examples of Humanity hitherto practiced by us shall cease, and ample retaliation shall be made, not only for them, but for all others who have inhumanely and unprecedented'ly [sic] suffered death in the like predicament."

Captain Mathews' letter observed that: "The war has not furnished a <u>single instance</u> [sic] where a prisoner has suffered death in this Province, tho' we have now in confinement, several who are notorious for having carried on an intercourse between our enemies and their emissaries in the Province, some of who have actually been taken with letters of advise, proposing plans against it—such has been the lenience practiced by Government in return for the cruelties committed on our scouts in many instances…but should this effort prove ineffectual, [Sherwood] knows what orders to give his scouts, and he knows the blood that has been shed in that way by the Rebels." [18]

Once again, Haldimand and the leaders of the Secret Service were faced with the decision of whether to retaliate for the execution of their comrades, and there are indications that this time the British came very close to making good on their retaliation threats. On the 18th of May, Mathews informed Smyth that "Reakley's report of Betis [sic] and Parker gives the General much pain—there is now no alternative but that determined upon with you and Capt. Sherwood—Sutherland will call on you in a very few days—his going out must be kept profoundly secret, and his party will pass St. Johns on the other side of the river in the night, and push on to the Block House. You will have your orders for W. C. ready, that no time may be lost on his arrival with you, as he must, during that time, be absent from his party."[19] Clearly a kidnapping mission was underway designed to obtain a retaliation victim.

But because Bettis was so notorious a foe, his captors moved quickly and Haldimand's letter arrived too late to prevent the two Tory prisoners' executions. Three days later, Mathews was informing Sherwood as follows: "The flag for Parker and Betis is now unfortunately needless—you did right not to execute the man brought in by Crowfoot, the example would not have had sufficient time...a scout will soon be sent, who may have an opportunity of retaliating properly." [20] Yet, contrary to these plans, the available records provide no evidence of "revenge" executions of American intelligence personnel by the Tory Secret Service in retaliation for the hangings of Bettis and Parker.

The TSS continued to suffer from failure to improve its counterintelligence capabilities. The capture of Joseph Bettis and his party was proof of this weakness, and the following testimony (dated April 3, 1782) by an eye-witness to this event reveals that informers and double agents continued to plague the Service's effectiveness six months after the death of Thomas Loveless:

"I have the disagreeable nuse [sic] to inform you my brother tells me he saw Mr. Bettes and two men with him from Canady brought prisoners in Albany and put in gale. The two men is turned states evidence and informed on the inhabitants that is friends [of government]. One Cooke betrayed them at Boloston (Ballstown). The packet is taken & it has prevented the friends from giving their assistance at this time, but I shall take every opertunety to execute my orders. Mr. Bettes is to be hung without jury or clergey." [21]

A brief article concerning the arrest of Bettis (but not his execution) appeared in no less than five New England newspapers between April 18th and 26th. Originally datelined "Fishkill," the article noted that: "Joseph Bettis, a spy, was taken near Balls'town the 31st of last month, and committed to Albany gaol, a letter was found on him wrote in ciphers." The article also stated that "Three men were carried to Albany last Saturday, supposed to be employed as spies from Canada."

Bettis' execution could hardly have come as a surprise to his Patriot enemies, or for that matter, to his Secret Service colleagues. Described by early Revolutionary War biographer Lorenzo Sabine as "a shrewd, intelligent, daring and bad man" whose British Intelligence exploits included "almost every enormity that can disgrace a human being," Joseph Bettis (or Bettys) was probably the most colorful character in Sherwood & Smyth's stable of Tory "scouts." A native of Ballstown, Bettis had begun the war as a sergeant in the Rebel army, and briefly served under Benedict Arnold. Captured at the Battle of Valcour Island in October, 1776 he was "turned" and became a courier for the British, delivering to Sir Henry Clinton on October 20, 1777 the news of Burgoyne's surrender at Saratoga.

Bettis combined his courier runs with other Secret Service missions, which included recruiting Whites for military service and Blacks for "freedom" and honest employment in Canada. Evidence of the effectiveness of his operations in the Northern Department during his five-year career is provided by the fact that the Index of the three volumes of the <u>Minutes of the Albany Board</u> contains thirty separate page citations dealing with Bettis' activities and the Board's efforts to kill or capture him. These included rewarding informers who reported the names of individuals who "harbored or concealed" Bettis, incarcerating John and Teunis Van Alstyne for doing the same, and ordering Militia and Ranger parties to hunt Bettis down. In June, 1781 the Board released a prisoner named Robert Bohannah when he promised to obtain information about Bettis' whereabouts, and two months later the Board extradited Bettis' brother-in-law from Schenectady in order to interrogate him. [22]

Based in the Helderberg Mountains along the Hudson River below Albany, Bettis made use of an elaborate network of safe houses owned by friends and family, including his father's Inn and a tavern in Ballstown owned by fellow Loyalist Jellis Legrange. Over the years, Bettis' exploits gained him an "outlaw" reputation, in which (according to Willliam Stone) he "…recruited soldiers for the King in the midst of the settlements, he captured and carried off the most zealous and efficient Whigs, and subjected them to the severest sufferings…No fatigue weakened his resolution—no distance was an obstacle to his purpose—and no danger appalled his courage. No one of the borders felt secure." Of course, Bettis' enemies realized that he was not acting alone: "…what added to the apprehension of the people, was the well-known fact, that he had always at his beck, openly or in concealment, according to the nature of the purpose at hand, a band of refugees [i.e. the Tory Secret Service] partaking of his own desperate character." [23]

He was captured several times, but managed to escape and elude his pursuers. However, Betty's luck ran out in March, 1782, when his courier party was detected and surprised by three men (named Cory, Perkins, and Fulmer) who broke down the door of a Ballston home owned by a Tory named Hawkins. William Stone described the circumstances as follows: "[Bettys] was seated at dinner when they entered, his pistols lying on the table and his rifle resting on his arm. He made an effort to discharge the latter; but forgetting to remove the deer-skin cover of the lock, did not succeed. Powerful and muscular as he was, the three were an over-match for him, and he was immediately pinioned as to render resistance useless and escape morally [sic] impossible." [4]

Stone goes on to describe other details of Betty's capture as follows: "Apparently resigning himself to his fate, Bettys now requested permission to smoke, which was readily granted. While taking the tobacco from his box, and making the usual preparations, he was observed…to cast something into the fire. It was instantly snatched from thence with a handful of coals, and proved to be a small leaden box, about the eighth of an inch in thickness, and contained a paper in cipher, which the captors could not read; but it was subsequently ascertained to be a dispatch addressed to the British in New York. It also contained an order for thirty guineas, provided the dispatch should be safely delivered. Bettys pleaded hard for permission to burn the paper, and offered a hundred guineas, for the privilege. But they refused his gold, and all his proffered bribes for the means of escape, with the most unyielding firmness. He then exclaimed "I am a dead man" It was even so."[25]

Bettis' capture is also referenced briefly in a 19th Century poem entitled "Rime of the Ancient Traveler" written by Jean H. Higby, a descendant of John Higby, who had been captured by a British party and taken to Canada in October of 1780. The relevant parts of the Higby poem go as follows:

> One day, while Jacob Fulmer worked,
>   Out 'sugaring' a tree,
> He saw a stranger passing near;
>   He wondered who could be.
>
> His son did gather up three friends,
>   And followed thru the snow.
> The trail did double back and forth,
>   For he was lost, you know.

> At Hawkins' house, a Tory spy,
>   The trail did fail away.
> They rushed the door and caught their man
>   Without too much delay.
>
> They marched him off to Albany,
>   And there put him on trial,
> And then he was condemned a spy,
>   And hung, which closed his file. [26]

Chronic CI shortfalls such as the Bettis incident led to leadership friction and morale problems within the TSS. The mounting evidence of inadequate CI management eventually ruptured the close working relationship between Dr. Smyth and Justus Sherwood. Unable to solve their service's CI problems and under increased pressure from Haldimand, the two veterans sometimes seemed to work at cross-purposes, blaming each other for the situation. In early 1782 Mathews informed Smyth that in future all scouts would be sent from Sherwood's Loyal Blockhouse, rather than from St. John's--an arrangement which benefited internal security, but which antagonized the already cranky Smyth. Although Captain Mathews lobbied both parties to put aside their differences, his hortatory memos seem to have had little effect.

Secret Service morale declined as casualties and "blown" operations continued to mount, and disciplinary action often involved issues of security or counter-intelligence. The example of veteran scout John Platt described as "an incendiary" who had "behaved extremely ill to Dr. Smyth in the line of his duty" is a case in point. In early 1782 Platt was ordered by General Haldimand to leave St. Johns for Montreal, where he was placed under the observation of Abraham Cuyler, who was "...to have an eye to his conduct fearing, from his character, that resentment may induce him to do something hurtful to the Secret Service ." But the sensitivity of Platt's situation also caused Haldimand "...NOT to strike his name from the Pension List for a muster or two longer." It appears that John Platt knew something of value to the enemy in New York, and the British were unwilling to risk the compromise of such information, at least not in the short run. [27]

Because he was only belatedly informed of the progress of peace negotiations then underway in Paris, Haldimand became increasingly cautious about recruiting New York Loyalists. An inquiry on the subject of recruiting submitted by Sherwood and Smyth in January, 1782 received the following reply from Haldimand: "I am directed to acquaint you that in the present uncertain state of affairs, without intelligence or any knowledge of what is passing to the southward or in the Colonies, His Excellency does not choose to risk recruiting parties in the enemy's country. The Gentlemen in your return must therefore wait a more favorable time for that undertaking." [28]

This caution was still evident in October of the same year, when Major Edward Jessup was warned that "His Excellency is pleased to permit you to send out a few of the most prudent and true men you have, but he expects you will be answerable for their conduct, the Friends of Government having already suffered so materially by the imprudence of recruiting parties, every caution is likewise necessary to avoid discovery, on account of the critical situation of public affairs." [29]

By 1782, many Loyalist soldiers were being shifted to the Provincial Corps' pension rolls. After nearly seven years of service, a growing number of the older New York Loyalists still serving at Sorel and Fort St. John had become eligible for pensions. According to a March 1, 1782 "General

List of Loyalists Having Pensions" prepared by Major John Nairne, the average age of the fifty-seven pensioners at St. John was forty-four years, with several men in their sixties and seventies. Only thirty-four of them were married, and less than half had any children. All but two of the pensioners were receiving eleven pounds per muster. Interestingly, this document lists the widow Loveless' new husband, Andrew Naughton (age 55) as "married," and entitled to eleven pounds, and (on the same page) lists Thomas Loveless (age 42) also as "married" and "Lately executed by the Rebels," as receiving seven pounds per muster, which must have gone to his widow. [30]

For the British forces in Canada, the campaign against the American Rebellion ended with a whimper, rather than a bang. The British Government did not officially proclaim a cessation of hostilities until February 4th, 1783, and the treaty of peace between England and America and its French and Spanish allies was not signed in Paris until seven months later. The preliminary articles of peace were not published in the Quebec Gazette until April 27, 1783. After enduring a period of frustrating uncertainty, Haldimand finally ordered the dissolution of the Tory Secret Service and began to plan for the resettlement of its veterans in various parts of Canada.

On April 27th, Captain Justus Sherwood was the senior officer on duty at the Loyal Blockhouse at the northern end of Lake Champlain. His letter to Mathews on that day reflects his growing impatience with the arrogant behavior of the Americans passing through his post:

"...I never was at any time so much embarrassed as I have been since the declaration of peace. Not a day passes but the Country [New York] people are coming in. Some of them are Loyalists who come to ask advice & seek a safe

177

settlement and others are Rebels, who come (under pretence of trading or to procure the discharge of their brothers in our Army or prisons, &c.) but apparently to insult us, for many of them are so very Naughty & provoking that my soldiers would certainly cut them to pieces if I did not keep a cautious look out. They Naughtily boast that they are Independent, that this is their Ground & that they shall have possession of it by the middle of May, &c...I considered those expressions as the mad sallies of Vulgar fools, which would soon subside, until I saw the Act Against the Loyalists in the Inclosed [sic] paper. But that fully convinces me that it is the General Spirit of the Whigs throughout America." [31]

A biographic summary of the service of Private Israel Tompkins claims that he was honorably discharged following the "reduction" of Jessup's Corps on January 21, 1783, but the majority of the Loyal Rangers were not discharged until December 24th of that year. A copy of a typical Provincial Corps discharge certificate used by the Loyal Rangers—that of Private Daniel Colton from Connecticut, aged thirty-four, who had served for four years and five months—is located on pg. 195. The officers of the Loyal Rangers and the King's Royal Regiment of New York went on half pay, and the men of these units were ordered to remain in their quarters, receiving provisions, near Montreal, Sorel and Lake Champlain until they could be resettled further up the St. Lawrence River in the spring.

A Muster Roll dated January 1, 1783 lists fifty-four remaining "Privates and Non-Commissioned Officers of the Loyal Rangers." At the time of its dissolution, the unit was made up of six Sergeants, a Drummer, three Corporals, and forty-four Privates, only five of whom had been born England, Ireland, or Scotland. These troops were much younger (most were between 20 and 30 years of age) than their officers, and the majority had seen five or six years of service. Five of those listed were teen-agers, most of them children of the unit's officers or pensioned personnel.[32]

The final lists of the officers of three New York Loyalist Provincial Corps units that were demobilized in 1783—The Loyal Rangers (34 men), and the two battalions of The King's Royal Regiment of New York (69 men)--have survived, thanks to the Haldimand Papers. Of the 103 officers in these units, fifty-four were born in America, and the rest originated in Scotland, Ireland, England, or were listed as "foreigners." Most of the Americans had come from New York and Connecticut, and the majority of the foreign-born officers had come from Scotland or Ireland. The length of service of these men ranged from two to twenty-six years, but the vast majority had seen between six and seven years of service.[33]

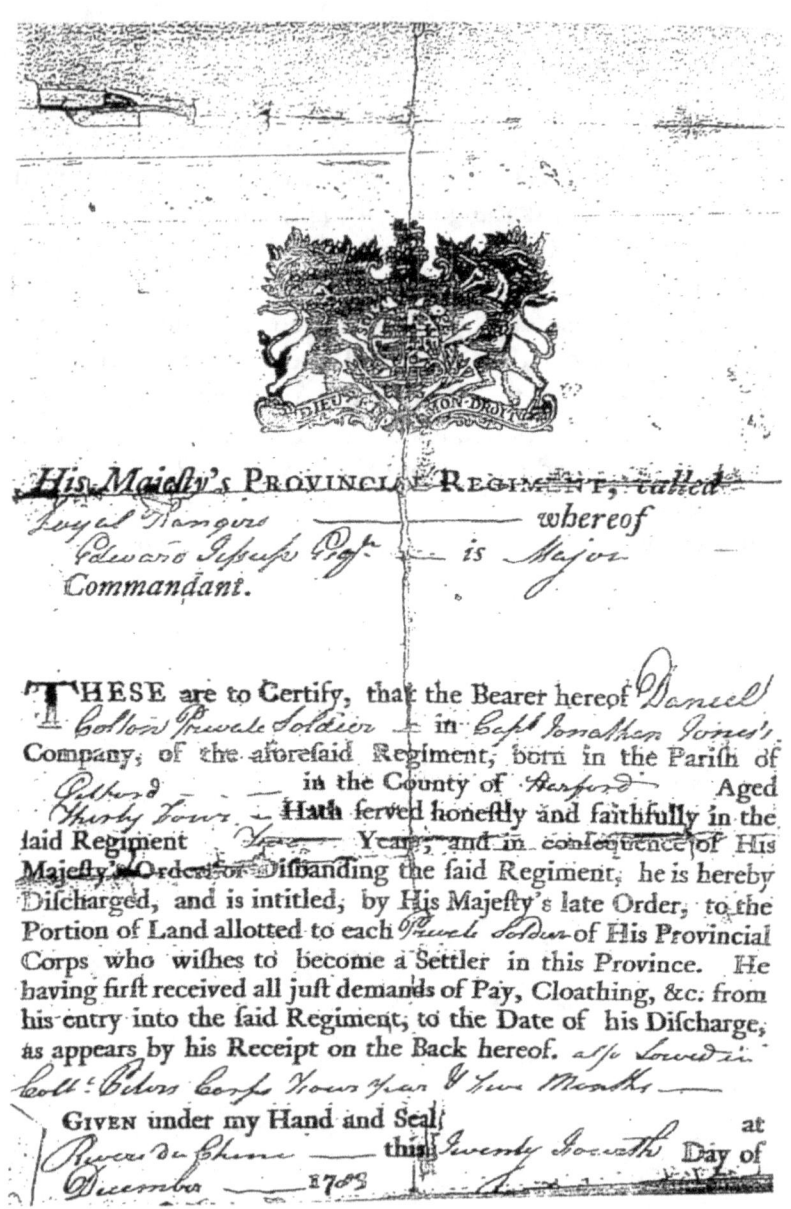

Figure 12:
A copy of Private Daniel Colton's Certificate of Discharge from Edward Jessup's Loyal Rangers (Haldimand Papers)

CHAPTER TEN

A GARBLED STORY: THE CAPTURE, TRIAL, EXECUTION, AND BURIAL OF THOMAS LOVELESS

As Remembered by Eye-Witnesses

In the 1840s, amateur historian Dr. Asa Fitch began to collect information about the history of Washington County, New York, which had been formed from parts of Charlotte County. During his research he encountered a Revolutionary War veteran named Jacob Bitely, who told him a story about "Lovett, the spy." Jacob's brothers (John and Henry) had been captured by the Tory Secret Service and taken to Canada in June, 1782. In addition to providing the most detailed description of the Tory Spy's execution (See page 1), Bitely offers the following version of the background to that event:

"That Lovett had lived (near Old Saratoga) was well-known to several. He had gone in among the garrison to spy it out and learn what the plans of the Whigs were. He was taken prisoner. Papers were found on him that showed he was commissioned to enlist men among the Tories in this quarter, to form a company and go to Canada."

Fitch also included an account of the Thomas Loveless incident by Mary Gillespie Bain of Argyle, whose father was a Tory active in the British cause. According to Mary: "Lovett [Loveless] was at our house, and stayed in our barn overnight the third day before he was hung on a tree at Schuylerville. Two other men were in company with him at the same time. <u>He was as fine a looking man as I ever saw</u>."[1]

Apparently Thomas Loveless' hanging was an event remembered by several of the Patriot soldiers who served in the Albany area during the war. A cursory review of the warrants submitted by Revolutionary War veterans in search of pensions and bounty land revealed the following references to the "Tory Spy's" demise:

As part of his application, militiaman Samuel Chase recalled that "On Sunday, October the 6th [actually the 8th] was executed on the gallows one Thomas Loveless. He was taken on the morning of the 23rd of Sept.[actually the 25th] with a party of men with him as spies at Saratoga. The rest was sent to Albany."

Private William Pattison of New York served in a unit that "was involved in keeping peace and scouting" claimed that "one of our scouting parties took Thomas Loveless and seven others who had left these parts and trained in Canada were Tories. I heard Ensign Palmer say to one of them "I expect you were after me." He made no reply. Loveless was tried by a court martial and found guilt as a spy and was hung on the hill south of Fish Creek near Schuylers Mills."

1836 pension applicant John Brewer of New York certified that as a militiaman from Stillwater who enlisted in 1777, he was "…called out more frequently during the year 1780, on alarms by reasons of one Thomas Lovelace and one Harris and one Mornell [sic] who were leaders of the Tories and caused considerable alarm among the people. That during all these alarms the said Brewer lived in the town of Stillwater in the County of Saratoga. In addition, Brewer claimed that he had served for nine months in 1781 in a militia unit commanded by Captain Holton Dunham, and "That in the said year (1781), the said Thomas Loveless was taken as a spy and hung."

In August of 1781, New York native Abiel Harding had begun his second three-month militia enlistment, this time as Orderly Sergeant under Captain Oliver Shaddock and Colonel Mckeinster. He was stationed at "a block house about six miles below Saratoga Meadows." During this tour of duty, Harding was responsible for "guarding the lines and watching the "cowboys" as they called the Tories. While there they [his men] took four men prisoners, three of whom were Canadians and one a Tory by the name of Thomas Loveless who had a Lieutenant's commission from the British." Brewer stated that "Thomas Loveless was there executed as a spy."

Two of the aging veterans who recalled Thomas Loveless as part of their wartime service history garbled the facts in especially colorful ways. John Vanderbrugh of New York was so eager to include the capture of Thomas Loveless in his warrant application that he moved the event to the year 1777. He claimed that, while serving under Captain Andrew White, his regiment "...went to West Point and thence to Saratoga—He was one of the detachment sent out to destroy the bridges between Fort Edward and Saratoga to prevent the approach of General Burgoyne and his army—and [that] this detachment took a spy from Burgoyne's army by the name of Thomas Loveless who was afterwards tried, condemned, and hung."

Massachusetts soldier Jesse Shippee was also on a three-month militia assignment with Captain Oliver "Chaddock" in the Saratoga area during the summer of 1781. Private Shippee recalled that while General Schuyler was in Albany and General Stark had command, "...a Tory who was said to be a Lieutenant in the British service and six men under him were captured as spies near the American camp. The name of the said Lieutenant was Thomas Loveless. General Stark called a court martial and sentenced the said

Loveless to be hung & <u>he was hung accordingly near Gen. Schuyler's house by an Indian who was under sentence of whipping for enlisting and taking the bounty twice for the same service."</u> ²

Within seventeen years of the event, a former critic of the Loveless hanging had apparently changed his mind. Published in 1798, the memoirs of Major-General William Heath provide an interesting example of how the recollections of a key participant in the follow-up to the execution of Thomas Loveless changed over time. As previously noted, General Heath's October 11th, 1781 letter to Governor George Clinton expressed outrage at the fact that the Tory Spy had been hanged at the order of John Stark for "espionage" while armed and on a kidnapping mission. Yet seventeen years later, the published version of his daily record for September 29th noted that:

"Intelligence was received from the northward that a small party had been sent from St. John's to Saratoga, to take a prisoner or two, for the purpose of obtaining information, but that five of the party, with the instructions of the British commandant at St. John's were taken and brought in by captain Dunham." But on October 10th, Heath's logbook recorded only that "Our General [James Clinton] ordered the 2nd New Hampshire regiment and a detachment of artillery to the northward. Gen. Stark has executed a Mr. Loveless, sent in by Capt. Dunham as a spy." ³

Something must have happened in the immediate post-war period that made it impossible for General Heath to include a copy of his October 11th letter to Governor Clinton in his <u>Memoirs</u>. Perhaps his understanding of the legal definition of "espionage" had changed since his wartime service, or perhaps in 1798 it was not "politically correct" to point out the random nature of American espionage executions during the War of Independence.

The Strange Travels of the Tory Spy's Skull

For more than two centuries following his execution, the Tory Spy's remains were the object of a strange sort of "historical necrophilia," and oral and written accounts of the burial position of his body have differed over time. According to local legend, following Thomas Loveless' hanging, the attending crowd buried his corpse <u>"head downward"</u> in an unmarked grave. In the mid-19th Century a Schuylerville road crew digging for gravel discovered the Tory Spy's skeleton, and his skull and a few other bones were distributed to residents as souvenirs. As a result, Loveless' skull remained an object of public curiosity, and disagreements over his skeleton's exact burial position continued among local historians for more than ninety years.

In 1878 Nathaniel Bartlett Sylvester noted that "…George Strover, about 1839 or 1840 bought the old Schuyler place, and is still living there at an advanced age. He had heard his father say that he was present at the execution of Lovelace the traitor. He was hung on the Gravel hill, near the Schuyler place, and buried <u>in a standing position</u> by an oak tree. George Strover himself saw the oak stump dug out when the Gravel hill was cut away, and the bones were found in accordance with the statement of the father. [4]

In his late 19th Century account of the event, William Stone described the interior of the Schuyler mansion--then owned by the Strover family—as follows: "(Here) The veritable skull of Thomas Loveless is to be seen, who was hung on a gallows during a terrific rain storm, and afterwards <u>perpendicularly buried</u> in the gravel bank opposite the

185

Strover mansion. When the bank was dug into for the purpose of procuring gravel the body was disinterred and the skull was taken into keeping by the late Colonel Strover, who was wont to show it to curiosity seekers." [5]

On the other hand, in his <u>The Story of Old Saratoga</u>, (1900) John Henry Brandow described a slightly different burial position: "On the eastern brink of that hill, as it then was, the noted spy Lovelass was hung, on the limb of an oak tree. He was buried beneath it <u>in a sitting posture</u>; John Strover saw him hung and buried, and told his son all about it. When the Waterford and Whitehall turnpike was built this gravel hill was partially dug away. George Strover was present and waited until Lovelass's remains were unearthed, when he appropriated the skull. This gruesome relic is still kept in the Schuyler mansion."[6]

What happened to the Tory Spy's excavated skull and other bones reveals a post-war Patriot fascination with Loyalist human remains associated with espionage. Because of his economic losses during "The Panic of 1837," Phillip Schuyler II had been forced to sell his Schuylerville house to Colonel George Strover, who put the newly discovered skull of the Tory Spy on display in his new home. The Lowber family who purchased the mansion some fifty years later, did the same. In the summer of 1943 the US National Park Service began the process of acquiring the Schuylerville mansion for eventual inclusion in the Saratoga National Historical Park (SNHP). In its final years, the house had been occupied by one of the Lowber sisters, a Mrs. Jessie Marshall. When Francis Ronalds, Coordinating Superintendent of the Morristown National Historical Park, inspected the mansion just prior to its being vacated by Mrs. Marshall, he noted that: "Mrs. Marshall, fortunately an eccentric, has as a table decoration the skull of a spy hung at

Saratoga in 1777 [sic]. The poor Tory's chaps are bound up with red, white, and blue ribbon." [7]

Apparently the NPS was never entirely comfortable with its newly-acquired war relic. In a letter of September 20, 1946, an official of Saratoga Park informed one of his colleagues at Morristown that "Mr. Lovelace now guards the office [as opposed to a public space] with some guns, swords, and other odds and ends." When an NPS historian proposed in the following year that the Lovelace skull be placed in the Park's Block House Museum, Superintendent Ronalds warned his Saratoga Park counterpart that "It would be against Service policy to display a human skull in this manner. I agreed with Warren that we might as well take the skull from the Marshall house when it was offered, but I believe that it should be kept in hiding."

The Park Service's ban on the public display of the Tory Spy's skull remained in force until June 18, 1987, when, in the words of one of the four SNHP staff who participated, "[the skull] was placed in the yellow plastic crypt with the other unknown burials that had been recovered and buried in the back of the visitor center." The official document, or "Case Incident Record" describes the event as a "Pre-planned burial carried out for human remains in collection catalogue numbers 3710—3711—3712. Remains placed in canisters one day earlier were put in fiberglass vault and buried 6' deep grave with about 3'-4' fill above." It lists the location of the burial as "Visitor Center Lawn" and states that "Grave is located 64' south of the V.C. [Visitor Center] southernmost corner." [8] On September 19, 1987 (the 210th anniversary of the First Battle of Saratoga), a stone monument with a brass plaque containing the words "In Memory of Unknown Soldiers Re-interred Here" was dedicated at the collective gravesite.

To this day the Tory Spy's ghost may still haunt the archives of the Saratoga National Historical Park. Indeed, it is possible that not all of Thomas Loveless' bones have been returned to the soil of the Saratoga-Schuylerville area. When the author visited the SNHP headquarters in 1995, the glass and mahogany case (along with the red, white, and blue ribbons used to hold the skull's jaw in place) was still to be found in the research room where the Park's files on Thomas Loveless were kept. With the permission of the NPS officer then on duty, the author photographed the case with its door wide open, so as to reveal the ribbons used to hold the skull's jaw in place (See photo on page 209).

Of even greater interest, in 1995 the archives' "accordion" files on the Tory Spy contained a seven-inch-long corset batten, upon which was inscribed (in ink) the phrase "Made from the rib of Lovelace the Spy." This startling discovery set the author to wondering how many more parts of Thomas Loveless' unearthed skeleton had been parceled out to other Schuylerville residents as war trophies. Could there be other "Lovelace the spy" corset battens hiding in the attics of older houses in the Saratoga/Schuylerville area that remained undiscovered?

Thomas Loveless was not the only "Tory Spy" whose bones became war trophies. The skeleton of another young Loyalist soldier, twenty-three-year-old David Redding (or Redden), of Hoosick Falls, New York, met a similar fate. Reportedly an early volunteer with the Queen's Loyal Rangers, Redding returned home after the Battle of Bennington and remained in touch with the Loyalist support network in his area. In 1778 he was accused of selling arms and horses to the British, and of being a spy. After several escapes and recaptures he was tried in Bennington, Vermont and hanged on July 11, 1778.

What followed was even more bizarre than the events associated with Thomas Loveless' burial, resurrection, and skeletal dispersal. According to Canadian historian Dr. H.C. Burleigh, "After the hanging, the body was given to the brother of the Sheriff, Dr. Jonas Fay. By the use of lye and quicklime, the flesh was removed and the re-assembled bones were used for anatomical research at the Williamstown Medical School [today's Williams College]."[9] From time to time, children of Judge Clarence M. Smith of Williamstown were allowed to play with the Redding skeleton "as if it were a toy." The skeleton remained at Williams College until 1927, when it was transferred to the Bennington Museum where it was put on public display. In 1976 David Redding's bones were finally removed from the Museum and buried in the cemetery of Bennington's "Old' First Church. [10]

Thomas Loveless' Career As Described by Historians

The most widely-read 19th Century account of the Thomas Loveless incident is the one contained in Benson J. Lossing's popular two-volume Pictorial Field Book of the Revolution, which was first published in 1846 and remained in print for more than a decade. Born in Beekman, New York, Lossing was a self-taught editor and historian who published well-written, but notoriously ill-documented, histories of the American War of Independence, the War of 1812, and the Civil War. In Volume One of his Revolutionary War book, Lossing devotes two pages to the "Lovelace" story, including a small sketch of "The Place where Lovelace was Executed." He lists only one source ("the son of Colonel Van Vechten") for his account of the Tory Spy's career and fate.[11]

Figure 13:
The display case in which Thomas Loveless' skull was privately exhibited for more than fifty years

In Lossing's words, "We next visited the Headquarters of General Gates, south of Fish Creek...On our way we passed the spot, a few rods south of the creek, where Lovelace, a prominent Tory was hung...Lovelace was a fair type of his class, the bitterest and most implacable foes of the republicans." He goes on to applaud those Loyalists who "shouldered no musket, girded on no sword, piloted [sic] no secret expedition against the republicans." However, according to Lossing, "There was another class of Tories, governed by the footpad's axiom that "might makes right." They were Whigs when royal power was weak, and Tories when royal power was strong. Their god was mammon, and they offered up human sacrifices upon its altars. Cupidity and its concomitant vices governed all their acts, and the bonds of consanguinity and affection were too weak to restrain all their fostered barbarism. Those born in the same neighborhood; educated (if at all) in the same school; admonished, it may be by the same pastor, seemed to have their hearts suddenly closed to every feeling of friendship or love, and became as relentless robbers and murderers of neighbors as the savages of the wilderness. Of this class was Thomas Lovelace, who, for a time, became a terror to his old neighbors and friends in Saratoga, his native district."

Without mentioning any dates, Lossing then describes Thomas Loveless's brief career with the British Army: "At the commencement of the war Lovelace went to Canada, and there confederated with five other persons from his own county to come down into Saratoga and abduct, plunder, or betray their former neighbors. He was brave, expert, and cautious. His quarters were in a large swamp about five miles from the residence of Colonel Van Vetchen at Do-ve-gat, but his place of rendezvous was cunningly concealed. Robberies were frequent, and several inhabitants were carried off. General Schuyler's house was robbed, and an attempt was made by Lovelace and his companions to carry off Colonel Van Vechten; but the active vigilance of General Stark, then in command of the barracks north of Fish Creek, in furnishing the colonel with a guard, frustrated the maurauder's plans."

Based upon local reminiscences and lacking vital information contained in official American and British documents from the period, Lossing's summary of Thomas Loveless's Loyalist career is both naïve and highly misleading. Writing for the grandchildren of Revolutionary War veterans, Lossing perpetuated the myth that Loyalists were primarily motivated by economic interests (i.e. "their God was Mammon"), and (unlike the Patriots) dominated by the axiom that "might makes right."

Lossing's bits and pieces of local lore paint a confusing picture of Loveless' military career with the British in Canada, describing the failed September, 1781 kidnapping operation against Colonel Van Vechten as part of a larger effort to terrorize his former neighbors in Old Saratoga. Contrary to the account in Bloodgood's Reminiscences, which repeatedly refers to the presence of "muskets" or "guns" in the hands of the Loveless party during their capture, Lossing's description of the event states that: "There was no time for parley, and believing that the Americans were upon them in force, they came out one by one, without arms, and were marched by their captors to General Stark at the barracks."

Lorenzo Sabine's 1864 Biographical Sketches of Loyalists of the American Revolution with an Historical Essay described the Tory Spy's capture as follows: "In 1781 (Thomas Lovelace) was found within the American lines, with a British commission in his possession; and by order of General Stark, who had established his headquarters at

Saratoga, was brought before a court-martial, tried, condemned, and executed, as a spy. He had family connections in the neighborhood who sought to avert his fate, by addressing a remonstrance to the Commander-in-Chief, but Washington refused to interfere. The country included in Stark's command was, at this time, overrun with spies and traitors. Of a band of these miscreants, Lovelace was the commander." [12]

Sabine appears to have based his summary largely upon Lossing's description of the incident, having accepted the same incorrect spelling of the spy's name (i.e. "Lovelace"), the reference to Albany County's being at the time "overrun with spies and traitors," and the myth of the failed clemency appeal to George Washington.

The description contained in Dr. A.W. Holden's A History of the Town of Queensbury [now Glens Falls] in the State of New York seems to be derived partially from the Lossing account, but does not mention the spy's first name: "Scattered through this region lived a number of Tories, among whom may be enumerated the following. John Howell who dwelt up the Sacandaga River, in the direction of Johnstown. Six brothers of the name of Lovelace, descendents of [New York Colonial] Gov. Lovelace, who resided at different points on the opposite side of the river, and one of whom, who lived near the Stiles place in the town of Wilton was in one of the last years of the war, executed at Schuylerville, as a spy, by order of General Stark, after due trial by drum head court martial. Another was Jacob (Henry) Salsbury, who was shortly afterward captured in a cave known to this day as the Tory House, situated among the Helderbergs" [13]

Written and compiled by General Stark's grandson, Caleb Stark and published in 1877, The Memoir and Official

Correspondence of Gen. John Stark was another widely-disseminated source of information (and disinformation) concerning the Thomas Loveless incident. After describing Stark's resumption of command of the Northern Department in the spring of 1781, grandson Caleb Stark notes that the frontier area was lightly defended and "...overrun with spies and traitors." He then mentions the failed kidnapping attempt against General Schuyler and describes the arrest of the Thomas Loveless party as follows: "Soon after the establishment of the military post at Saratoga, a party of these brigands was discovered within the lines, unarmed, and a British commission found upon their leader, a refugee from the States. A board of officers examined the case, pronounced him a spy, and condemned him to he hanged; which sentence was executed on the next day." [14]

The assertion that the Loveless party was unarmed contradicts the testimony of all the early first-hand accounts, including that of militia Captain Hezikiah Dunham, who led the team that captured Loveless and his companions. This claim also goes against the information contained in General Heath's October 11th letter to Governor Clinton, which cites Loveless's having written orders and his being armed as evidence that he was not engaged in espionage, and therefore should not have been executed. Perhaps ninety-six years later, Caleb Stark felt that he had to alter the evidence a bit in order to justify his grandfather's actions. Perhaps he simply did not recognize the significance of the matter, and passed on a garbled version of the story. And perhaps, at the age of ninety-one, General John Stark had begun to believe that an "unarmed" version of the event was a more convenient reality.

The younger Stark's account of the Loveless incident goes on to claim that "One of the prisoners" (presumably one of Loveless's accomplices) under promise of quarter, informed that he belonged to a party of fifteen, who had come down from Canada as spies; that his companions were then variously disguised and scattered through the country to ascertain its defensive condition for the benefit of the British officers in Canada, who were planning an inroad..." After helping the American forces to set a trap for his fellow spies, the prisoner escapes, but is recaptured. When the Patriots fail to ambush the Tory invaders, however, the informer [although previously promised "quarter"] is hanged, even though "The relatives of the spy, residing in the vicinity, complained to the commander-in-chief [General Washington], and said much about retaliation." As Caleb Stark puts the matter, "The cure of the body politic was radical." If this execution of a second member of Thomas Loveless's party did, in fact, take place, there is no mention of it in the <u>Haldimand Papers</u>. Even if false, its inclusion in the Stark papers Memoir reveals that nearly a century after the event, few Americans would have questioned the legitimacy of a hanging under such circumstances.

In a footnote on the same page, the junior Stark further claims that in 1777 John Stark had acted to <u>prevent</u> a mob from executing some captured Loyalist "scouts":

"A party of the same character [as Loveless's] was captured at Bennington, soon after General Stark assumed the command of the troops there concentrated. <u>On this occasion all his address was necessarily employed to prevent the sovereign people from exercising summary justice upon the culprits.</u> They were sentenced to Symsbury Mines. Lynch Law was often the most potent authority in those days...During the years 1778 and 1781, many such persons, arrested as spies or traitors to the continent, were condemned by courts-martial, ordered by General and sentenced to be confined in prison, or be compelled to serve on board public American ships [prison ships] for the remainder of the war."
[15]

Some late 19th Century historians managed to misread the "Lovelace" story as it appeared in Lossing's two volumes. Writing in 1895, William Stone offered the following fanciful account of the Loveless capture in his book entitled <u>Visits to the Saratoga Battle-Grounds, 1780-1880</u>: "During the campaign Burgoyne employed Lovelace [sic] and other tories as spies, and they were generally secreted in the woods between old Saratoga and Saratoga Lake. One day Capt. Dunham, then residing near the lake, in company with Daniel Spike and a colored man, was scouring the woods, and while crossing upon a tree which had fallen over the brook east of the Wagman farm, <u>discovered five guns stacked in the hiding place of the spies</u>. With a sudden rush, Dunham and his associates seized the guns and captured all five of the spies, bound and brought them into the American camp." [16]

As 20th Century Canadians, the writings of both Hazel Mathews and Mary Beacock Fryer reflected their own unique national perspectives on the Tory Secret Service. Fryer, for example, treated both Justus Sherwood and John Walden Meyers as essentially heroic figures, and on one occasion describes the ruthless Joseph Bettys as "a loveable scamp." While both Canadian authors used the <u>Haldimand Papers</u> and other original documents to describe the purposes of Loveless' final mission and the circumstances of his betrayal and capture, neither of them seems to have been fully aware of the serious counterintelligence weaknesses that plagued the Tory Secret Service. As a result, both Canadian authors missed many of the CI warning "flags" indicating that the Loveless party was doomed from the outset.

Because Hazel Mathews' book was privately published in Florida in small quantities and Ms. Fryer's books were published in Canada, these books did not enjoy wide circulation in the United States. The result has been wide-spread ignorance among Americans about the "Tory Secret Service" and its operations. As late as 1999, the authors of a volume subtitled "A Biographic Dictionary of Espionage in the American Revolutionary War" were still regurgitating some of the mythological information contained in Lossing's 1851 volume: "Lovelace apparently knew many influential Americans who attempted to intercede for him with General. In addition, his family, otherwise loyal Americans, sought to avert his fate and addressed their pleas to George Washington. General Washington refused to intervene, concluding "Stark's command at this time was overcome with spies and traitors and Lovelace was their commander."[17]

CHAPTER ELEVEN

WHAT HAPPENED TO THOMAS LOVELESS' WIFE AND CHILDREN FOLLOWING HIS DEATH?

Within less than a year Thomas Loveless's widow (her first name is spelled either "Lois" or "Loes" in the British Claims Commission documents) married another Loyalist Provincial Corps veteran, Andrew Naughton. A native of Connecticut, in 1763 Naughton had purchased 100 acres of land near Windsor, New York which had originally been part of the "New Hampshire Grants." By 1775 he had cleared twenty acres and built a house and several outbuildings. In addition to farming, he also managed a small tavern. In his 1786 Claims Commission petition Naughton declared that at the war's outbreak he was jailed for five months for refusing to take up arms against Great Britain. He joined Burgoyne's army in 1777, signed "the Convention" at the Saratoga surrender, and was evacuated to Canada, where he joined Jessup's Corps. It is probable that the Loveless family and Naughton had been friends or neighbors for several years prior to the Tory Spy's death.

In January, 1783 Lois Loveless petitioned the Governor-General for the continuance of her husband's pension to her children in the event of her marriage to Naughton. After the war, the couple moved to Chaleur Bay, New Brunswick. On March 16, 1786 "Loes Naughten" filed a deposition on behalf of a claim submitted by fellow Loyalist Perry Samuel. In this document she was described as "(a) relict of Thomas Lovelass [sic], late of Palmer Town, [Albany County] New York." [1]

In a December 5, 1781 letter to Captain Mathews, Sherwood first brought up the subject of compensation for Thomas Loveless' widow: "I hope you will be so good as to represent to His Excellency the situation of Mrs. Loveless, who is left here [at Verchere] in great distress and poverty with four children, three of whom are very young, her husband being lately on Secret Service and taken prisoner by the Rebels and hanged at Saratoga."[2] In a 10 December, 1781 letter Mathews replied that: "His Excellency the Commander in Chief, feeling sensibly for the misfortune of Mrs. Loveless, is pleased to continue to her, until the end of the muster, her husband's pension, and afterwards, subsistence at the rate of 20 Pounds per annum, upon the list, together with provisions for herself and children as before." [3]

The British Command's correspondence of the period 1781-1783 reveals that several British and Provincial Corps officers were active on behalf of Mrs. Loveless and her younger children. In an attachment to a January 27, 1782 document sent to Capt. Mathews, Major John Nairne, the Regular officer (Royal Highland Emigrant/84th Regiment of Foot) responsible for loyalist units' logistics and finance, asked permission of Haldimand: "…to allow Mrs. Loveless a small pension, for the relief of herself and family. Mr. Thomas Loveless, her husband, was always remarkably zealous and active in the Secret Service, he enjoyed a pension of 7 pds. Per muster…I beg to know…whither the subsistence of the late Thomas Loveless may be continued for this muster, to be given to his widow." [4]

Writing from Rivier Duchene on April 12, 1783 Edward Jessup noted that: "The widow Loveless is married to Andrew Norton [sic] who is a pensioner at 7 [pds.] per muster, but as Mr. Loveless left a number of children, three of which are small and will be much distressed if she is not continued on the subsistence for a time longer. I think it my duty to mention these circumstances for His Excellency's consideration." Official documents from as late as December 24, 1783 show that Colonel Jessup was continuing to approve pensions, at a rate of 20 pds per annum each, for five widows (Mrs. Crothers, McLaren, Loveless, Bettis, and O'Hare) of men killed while serving in his unit.[5]

In addition, there is evidence that British Army Headquarters sought to keep Thomas Loveless's children on the military payroll during 1782-1783. In a 6 June 1782 letter to Capt. Mathews concerning "Officers for the next two companies proposed to be added to the Loyal Rangers," Edward Jessup added a "post script" as follows: "Should any vancancys [sic] happen otherways then by the means of raising new companies, I think it my duty to mention to His Excellency Mr. Thomas Freeman whose mournfull story is well known, and Mr. James Loveless, son of the unfortunate Mr. Thomas Loveless."[6]

Although Thomas the Spy's two eldest sons (James and Ebenezer) were old enough to have joined provincial corps units at some point during the period 1780-1783, the evidence to prove this remains circumstantial and conflicting. According to Hazel Mathews, James Loveless eventually became a Subaltern in the Loyal Rangers. If James obtained a junior commission in the Loyal Rangers, it must have happened <u>after</u> Edward Jessup's letter of June 6, 1782, and his name is missing from the unit's final return.[7]

Mathews also claims that two of Thomas' other sons joined the King's Loyal Americans—Thomas Junior as an Ensign, and Ebenezer as an enlisted man. However, Mathews probably confused the identity of "Ensign" Thomas Loveless senior (he became an officer late in his career) with that of his third son Thomas, who would have been only thirteen in 1781. Because Ebenezer would have been no more than seventeen years old when the KLA was combined with the Queen's Loyal Rangers in late 1781, the probability of his having served with the KLA before that date is remote.

A United Empire Loyalist list published in 1884 claims that Ebenezer Loveless "served in Burgoyne's expedition," but because he was most likely born in 1764, Ebenezer would have been thirteen during 1777—much too young to have fought alongside his father in Burgoyne's army.

A Corporal William Loveless is listed on the October 10, 1783 Mustering-out roll of the 2nd Company (commanded by Capt. Alexander McDonalds) of the 1st Battalion, 84th Regiment (the only Canadian provincial corps unit to be placed on the British Army's "regular establishment" during the war), dated at Windsor, Nova Scotia. Given the siblings' birth order submitted by James Loveless in his July, 1786 compensation claim, it is unlikely that this soldier was the Tory Spy's son William, who was probably no more than 10-11 years old in 1783.

Thomas Loveless had two daughters, the youngest of whom was named Elizabeth. The name "Elie" Loveless appears on the January 1, 1783 muster roll of "Privates and Non-Commissioned officers, Loyal Rangers, Major Edward Jessup's Company. This soldier is aged 14 years, is only 5 feet, 2 inches tall, and had seen only eight months of service.[8] It is possible that this daughter, who had earlier signed for her mother's pension payments, may have been left on the Loyal Rangers' muster roll for financial hardship reasons.

The Loveless Family's Permanent Resettlement in Canada

The resettlement throughout eastern Canada of more than 40,000 thousand military and civilian Loyalists after 1783 was a complicated and expensive task which took more than two years to complete. An estimated 7,000 American Loyalists were already living in Canada by the time the

Treaty of Paris was signed on September 3, 1783. Some 2500 of these were assigned to Provincial Corps units, and the rest were their dependents. The Provincial Corps units, including the men of the Tory Secret Service, were some of the first Loyalist groups to be resettled. Indeed, Haldimand had sent out Justus Sherwood to seek out appropriate resettlement areas as early as May 5th, with instructions to find suitable areas for Loyalist resettlement.

Whenever possible, the men and families of each Loyalist military unit were re-located in specified townships and remote settlement areas, so that cohesive communities could be quickly established. Although they were given generous grants of land as well as logistics and financial support by the British authorities, resettlement of the lower ranks of Provincial Corps veterans was an arduous and protracted experience. According to a Return of Loyalists and Disbanded Troops found in the <u>Haldimand Papers,</u> 5,628 men, women and children had been settled on "the King's Lands" in 'The Province of Quebec" during 1784. Ultimately, a total of more than 25,000 Loyalists would come to live in the Province of Upper Canada.[9]

Most of Major Jessup's Loyal Rangers were given land in the "upper St. Lawrence" and along the north shore of Lake Ontario in the townships of Edwardsburg, Augusta, Elizabethtown, and Ernestown. A 1904 Report of The Ontario Bureau of archives indicates that many of the families associated with "Jessup's Corps" were settled in townships numbered six to eight above Lake St. Francis and the second township at Cataraqui. This land was to be given to them as permanent settlers only, and in accordance with the following guidelines:

- 100 acres for heads of families, plus 50 acres for each family member.

- 50 acres for each single man.

- 300-1000 acres for officers.

- 200 acres for non-commissioned officers, plus 200 acres for their wives.

- 100 acres for a private soldier or his widow, plus 50 acres for each family member.

In 1789 these conditions were amended to allow the sons of Loyalist veterans to receive 200 acres when they reached the age of twenty-one years. Daughters were to receive the same number of acres upon their marriage, or when they became twenty-one. Locations of the lots were drawn by lot, and the owners received a deed at the end of one year's occupancy. The Tory spy's five sons survived the war and were eventually granted sizeable parcels of land in Canada for settlement, and in the case of the elder son James, land and money in compensation for his father's lost property in New York. The following information is derived from James Loveless's 1786 Claims Commission application, as well as various Canadian Government documents:

James—Settled first at Fort St. Johns, Quebec, and later at Dartmouth, near Halifax, Nova Scotia.

Ebenezer—Moved to the Detroit River area near Niagara (then called Newark) on the Canada-US border.

Thomas—Also settled in the Newark/Niagara area.

William--Relocated first to Edwardsburg Township in Johnstown settlement on the St. Lawrence River, and then to the "Bay of Chaleur" in New Brunswick.

Archibald--Settled at Ernestown in Cataraqui settlement on the north shore of Lake Ontario, and later at Bay Chaleur, Nova Scotia, (which had become part of New Brunswick in 1784). [9]

There is no evidence that Thomas Loveless' two daughters (Elizabeth and Lucy) obtained land from the British authorities, although each would have been eligible to receive 200 acres after turning twenty-one. Lucy Loveless reportedly married and moved to "Chedabucto" (later called New Manchester, then Guysborough, and now Milford, Nova Scotia), and Elizabeth settled near her mother and step-father on Chaleur Bay in New Brunswick.

Two of Thomas Loveless' children eventually settled on the shores of the Detroit River near Niagara. The rest, along with Thomas' remarried widow, scattered to various parts of Canada, from Cataraqui (modern Kingston) on the northeast shore of Lake Ontario and along the north shore of the upper St. Lawrence River, (near today's Brockville), to settlements along the Bay of Chaleur (along the northeast coast of New Brunswick), and at Dartmouth, Nova Scotia.

The rapids of the St. Lawrence River made the transport of supplies to the townships at Cataraqui and the northeast lakeshore uncertain and irregular. As a result, like many of their fellow Tories, some of the Loveless siblings who started out in the province of Upper Canada later moved to Lower Canada and the Maritime Provinces, where Loyalist settlements could be more easily re-supplied by sea.

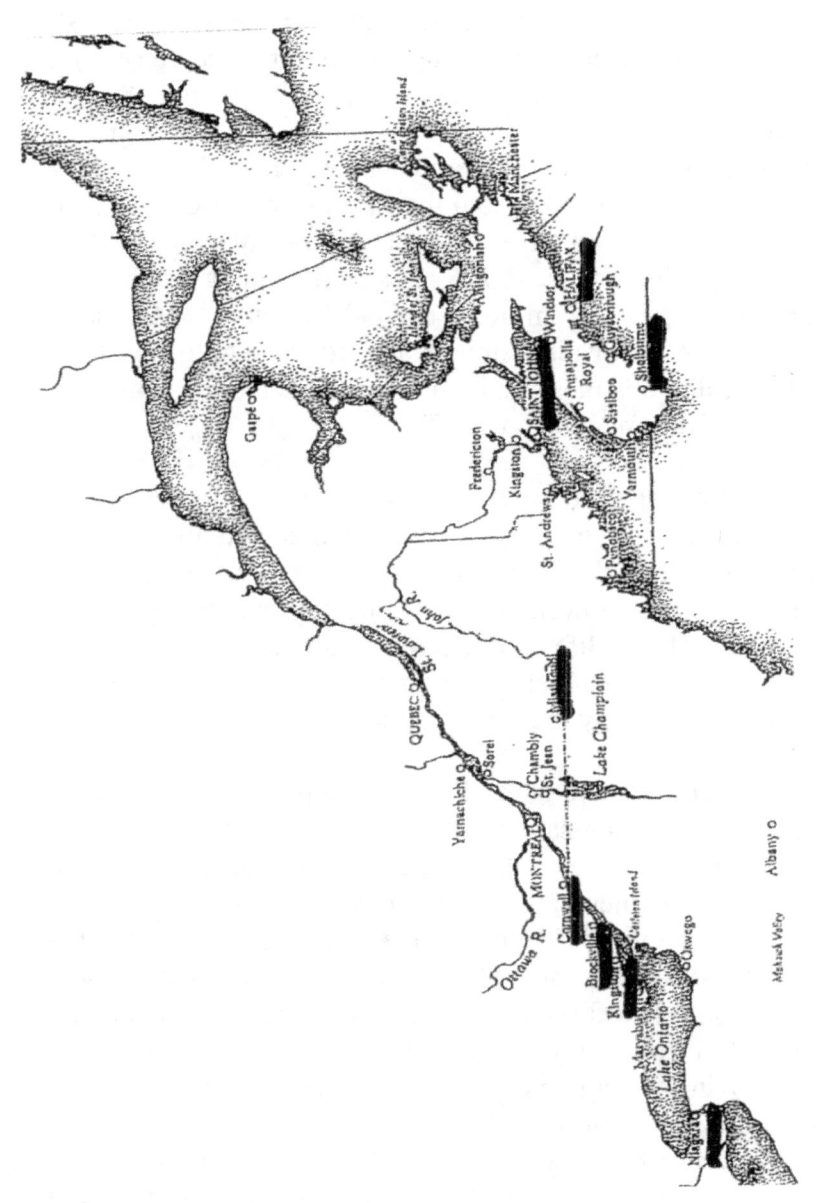

Map #6:
The principal areas of Loyalist resettlement in Canada

Following the news of the Treaty of Paris, the British Government issued a proclamation inviting the remaining Loyalists in the United States to assemble at several entry points (including at Isle aux Noix in northern New York) preparatory to their emigration to Canada. Many Tory families now hastened to join their heads of household in the townships at Cataraqui and on the St. Lawrence. This first wave of settlers totaled 3,776 persons, including 1,568 men, 626 women, 1,492 children, and 90 servants.[10] Although some of these Loyalist families arrived too late to sow their fall wheat crop, most had established themselves on their new properties by the end of 1784.

Although we have no detailed information about the lifestyles lived by the Loveless family members in their new domiciles, it is likely that their early years of resettlement were far from comfortable. The following passage from the summary of the life of General Haldimand found in the <u>Dictionary of Canadian Biography</u> gives some idea of the challenges faced by the former Americans:

"But if the refugees had a place to settle, they lacked many of the necessary items that would enable them to create homes in the wilderness. All required seeds, tools, clothing, and other supplies, which were often insufficient or simply unattainable. Moreover, the Loyalists demands" often took no account of scarcities. Fortunately, the government stores could still dispense provisions, which Haldimand had decided to continue for a year after the official disbanding of the provincial regiments, although these rations too were sometimes in short supply. The Governor had to employ agents to purchase seed and provisions surreptitiously in the United States. ..When in the summer of 1784 he received orders from London to reduce the rations to two-thirds allowance, to one-third the following year, the united protests of the Loyalists that the step would cause great difficulty persuaded him to continue full rations on his own cognizance." The Dictionary article concludes that "Any examination of the founding of what was to become Ontario must therefore conclude that without the generous and unwavering support of Haldimand the original settlers would have faced much greater hardships."[11]

In 1914 Canadian historian W. Stewart Wallace described the life of the early Loyalist settlers of the Upper St. Lawrence as follows: "They did not receive lumber for building purposes…they had to wait until saw-mills were constructed; instead of ploughs they had at first to use hoes and spades, and there were not quite enough hoes and spades to go around. Still, they did not fare badly. When the difficulty of transporting things up the St. Lawrence is remembered, it is remarkable that they obtained as much as they did…Tools for building were given them: to each family were given an axe and a handsaw, though unfortunately the axes were short-handled ship's axes, ill-adapted to cutting in the forest; to each group of two families were allotted a whip-saw and a cross-cut saw, and to each group of five families was supplied a set of tools, containing chisels, augers, draw-knives, etc. To each of five families was also allocated 'one fire-lock [a musket or fowling piece] intended for the messes, the pigeon and wildfowl season'; but later on a fire-lock was supplied to every head of a family." [12]

Thomas Loveless's sons were among the estimated 3,000 Tories from New York who served in Canada-based Provincial Corps units during the war. They and their sisters joined the more than 40,000 refugees from the American Revolution who fled to Canada after 1783. The majority of these (some 30,000) went to Nova Scotia, with about 10,000 going to Quebec, which at that time included the eastern Great Lakes. This influx of American refugees to western

Quebec led to the creation in 1791 of the separate province of "Upper Canada," which became "Canada West" in 1841 and "Ontario" in 1867.

Later known as "The United Empire Loyalists," the descendants of these families produced many of the "Founding Fathers" of an independent Canada. As defined by a government decree on November 9, 1789, a United Empire Loyalist was someone who had joined the British cause against the Americans prior to the signing of the peace treaty of 1783. Eventually, any child or descendant of such a person was allowed to use the honorific "U.E." after his or her name.

According to historian Maya Jasanoff, the impact of the Loyalists' migration to Canada had both short-term demographic and long-term political consequences. She notes that "Americans and Britons easily forget that the loss of America was actually the making of Anglophone Canada, a demographic and cultural shift clearly expressed in the 1791 Canada Constitutional Act, which divided formerly French-majority Quebec into two parts and extended the reach of English Law and Protestantism." Jasanoff also notes that, ironically, that the Loyalist diaspora (and especially those in Canada) "…explicitly challenged imperial authority in terms uncannily like those of their rebel peers," citing clashes between Loyalists and British authorities in New Brunswick and Nova Scotia. She concludes that "[The] templates for home rule and decolonization as well as for the idea of a federal greater Britain were established not in Ireland or India but in Canada, the American loyalist stronghold." [13]

In addition to receiving land for their resettlement, many of the Tory veterans applied for compensation from the British Crown for their property left behind in the former

Colonies. According to James Whisker, New York Loyalists submitted over 1100 claims for their lost property—the highest percentage of claims (relative to a 1776 population of 203,700) of any of the rebellious colonies. In his groundbreaking study of the "composition and motives of the American Loyalist claimants," Wallace Brown discovered that "about sixty-seven per cent" of the claimants from New York indicated that they had served in some form of British-related military unit during the war. Nearly seventy-five percent of these claimants were farmers, and seventy-seven percent of them submitted claims for less than 1000 Pounds.[14]

Alexander Flick's research found that New Yorkers' claims for lost property amounted to about one-fourth of the total figure for such claims, which he estimated to be the equivalent of US$10,000,000. He also estimated that at least one-third of the estimated total of $30,000,000 that England spent on the Loyalists, both during and after the war, was paid to Loyalists from New York or spent on their behalf.[15]

In July, 1786 at Halifax, Nova Scotia James Loveless submitted a memorial to John Parr, the Governor of Nova Scotia, on behalf of "the whole family," asking for £444 pounds in compensation for the value of the Loveless family's farm and other lost property in New York. He was one of the sixty-four percent of the New York claimants whose claims amounted to less than £500 Pounds. James also asked that he be granted land near Dartmouth, Nova Scotia "to enable him to become a settler in this province and for his future support."

James' claim document contains a wealth of personal and family data, including his age in 1781 (nineteen years) and the fact that he was living in Canada at the time of his father's death. In addition to identifying the Canadian places of residence of himself, his mother, and his siblings as of July, 1786, James Loveless' petition provides the most credible example of the probable "birth order" (and hence, approximate age in 1781) of Thomas the Spy's children:

James	Age 19	(Probably born in 1762)
Ebenezer	Estimated age: 17	(Probably born in 1764)
Lucy	Estimated age: 15	(Probably born in 1766)
Thomas	Estimated age: 13	(Probably born in 1768)
Elizabeth	Estimated age: 11	(Probably born in 1770)
William	Estimated age: 9	(Probably born in 1772)
Archibald	Estimated age: 7	(Probably born in 1774)

In his memorial, James claimed that on February 3, 1775, his father had purchased 101 acres of land in Palmertown, New York from one Cornelius Tabout for "40pds, 12 sh. 6d N. York Cury [currency]." As recorded by a clerk, James' deposition describes the claimed land as follows: "This was wild land when he bought it. He cleared 30 acres & built a log house & barn. He thinks it was worth 150pds N. York Cury in 1775 as he was offered that sum for it." Son James' deposition also mentions Thomas Loveless' purchase of another parcel of land--"One hundred acres of wild land in Jessup's Patent purchased in 1775. He cannot say what he gave for it. He cannot value it. Says he knows nothing of the present state of the property." The 1786 Deposition then goes on to list the following possessions as belonging to Thomas Loveless' farm:

```
Pr. Oxen..........................pds. 14.0.0
4 Milch Cows....................     17.10.0
5 Hogs............................      5.0.0
Furniture.........................     36.0.0
Wheat............................      20.0.0
Corn..............................     15.0.0
[Total]                          pds. 107.10
```

The petition concludes with the statement "All this was plundered by a party of Rebels when his father was with the British." In 1791 the British granted James Loveless and his siblings £130 pounds (a little more than £18 pounds each if all the children survived until 1791)—a small part of the £3,300,000 pounds which London paid to settle the 4,118 Loyalist claims (estimated at eight to nine million pounds) that had been submitted after 1783. In addition, James was granted 500 acres of land in Preston Township, east of Dartmouth, Nova Scotia.[16]

What Happened to Other Players in this Drama?

Other Albany County Loyalists. It is difficult to accurately determine the number of Canada-based former Loyalists who returned to their homes in Albany County in the years after the war. Whatever their numbers, they would most probably have been small land-owners like Thomas Loveless. Unlike him, however, they would not have actively participated in the more violent aspects of the seven-year conflict. Although reason and moderation prevailed at the State level in the long run, in the immediate post-war period considerable hostility toward Tories remained at the local level. According to a newspaper account of a May 6, 1783, a meeting of Saratoga District residents passed the following resolutions:

- Any Loyalist attempting to return to the District would be treated with severity.

- Any who returned would be allowed until June 10th to depart, or face the consequences.

- Militia officers should enquire about such persons so that the inhabitants could expel them.

- Anyone helping a Loyalist would be held in contempt.[17]

Although the majority of New York's Tories did not leave the state following the war, their treatment by their Patriot neighbors and the New York authorities ranged from the benevolent to the outrageous. According to historian E. Wilder Spaulding, "For years after the evacuation, the New York Loyalist who remained was despised and persecuted. He was treated as an enemy alien. The Governor favored a law, vetoed by the Council of Revision, which would have disfranchised all those who had voluntarily remained within British lines during the war. The Whig county of Ulster forbade Tories to return to their homes, and instructed Ulster legislators to urge legislation that would keep the exiled Tories out of the state. The freemen of Dutchess County, in a series of meetings, adopted the same policy." [18] Loyalists were disenfranchised, and a New York law cancelled debts owed to Loyalists, on the condition that one-fortieth of the amount be paid to the State treasury. Even after the signing and ratification of the Peace Treaty, Spaulding claims that Tories were occasionally tarred and feathered, beaten, mutilated, or subjected to hamstringing.

John Stark and his Family. Caleb Stark claimed that his grandfather was suffering from rheumatism during 1782, and did not return to the army until ordered to headquarters by General Washington in April, 1783. In later life he avoided politics and concentrated instead upon the needs of his New

Hampshire farm and his large family. He died at age 94 on May 8th, 1822, having been for some years the last surviving Continental Army general.

General Stark's fear and loathing of the British and their political supporters within the United States remained with him for the rest of his life. While he avoided direct involvement in national politics during his retirement, he consistently warned those in power of the continuing threat posed by Great Britain. For example, in an October, 1805 letter to Thomas Jefferson, Stark mentioned his transient fears that the young republic might fall victim to a resurgent British Imperialism: "I will confess to you, sir that I once began to think that the labors of the revolution were in vain, and that I should live to see the system restored which I had assisted in destroying. But my fears are at an end..." [19]

Likewise, in a January 21, 1810 letter to President James Madison, Stark argued against forming an alliance with the British against the French: "If the enmity of the British is to feared, their alliance is still more dangerous. I have fought by their side, as well as against them, and have found them to be treacherous and ungenerous as friends, and dishonorable as enemies." Stark also warned against the influence of "pro-British" elements in the American population: "But of all the dangers from which I apprehend the most serious evil to my country, and our republican institutions, none requires a more watchful eye than our internal British faction." [20]

Stark was not the only American who feared a resurgence of Loyalists threats to the United States. Historian Roger Brown has pointed out that during the early phases of the War of 1812 "The northern Connecticut Valley was wide open to attack from Canada, and settlers in Coos County,

New Hampshire, feared raids by exiled Revolutionary War Loyalists and St. Francis Indians near the border. Settlers living on the frontiers of New York State near the Niagara and St. Lawrence lines were defenseless and feared British-inspired Indian attacks before they could obtain protection."[21]

Governor George Clinton. Violently anti-Tory, New York State's first Governor remained in office and dominated New York's populist politics, at the expense of traditional leaders such as Philip Schuyler and John Jay, until 1795. He served as Vice President under Presidents Thomas Jefferson and James Madison, and died in 1812.

Cornelius Van Vetchen/Vechten remained politically active after the war, eventually serving Albany County as a member of the New York State Assembly in 1789-1790. That he remained a local "Hero of the Revolution" is revealed in a colorful, if unsubstantiated, story about him contained in a book of Revolutionary War "Reminiscences" published in 1866: "One of our neighbors, a Colonel Van Vechten, who lived three miles below the barracks, had a narrow escape...He was in the habit of riding from his own house up to General Schuyler's and to the barracks, in order to receive and communicate intelligence. ...In a ravine, concealed behind the trees, a Tory placed himself to shoot Van Vechten as he passed, who had rendered himself obnoxious to the partisans of the English, by his constant assiduity in the service of his country. As he approached, mounted on his favorite grey, the assassin raised his gun to fire. His finger was on the trigger when, as he afterwards confessed, the bold and manly air which Van Vechten possessed, joined with his unsuspecting manner, unnerved his arm. The weapon of death fell from its position, and Colonel Van Vechten rode by unharmed."[22]

Hezikiah Dunham was revered as a local hero of the Revolution and died at age sixty-five on April 27, 1810. He was buried in the cemetery of The Old Baptist Church at Cramers Corners, south of Victory Mills, on Moe Farm, Town of Saratoga, Saratoga County, New York. Legends have persisted to this day that on occasion, Loveless rides up the hill by the church as a headless horseman calling out the name of his captor.

Philip Schuyler died at his Albany mansion in 1804 at the age of seventy-three. After retiring from the Continental Army, Schuyler remained a major figure in the New York state politics. He did not become Governor, but served several terms in the US Senate, and briefly as a US diplomat. He was a strong advocate of New York's Western Canal Project, and remained a strong Federalist. His daughter Elizabeth married Alexander Hamilton, who (legend has it) drafted key sections of the US Constitution while visiting the Schuyler mansion near Albany.

Frederick Haldimand spent his last years as Governor-General planning and managing the resettlement of Loyalist American and Mohawk Indian refugees throughout Canada. He was knighted during a visit to England in 1784, and replaced as Governor-General by Sir Guy Carleton in 1786. The General remained a bachelor, retired to a comfortable life in England, and died at the age of seventy-three in 1791 while on vacation in Switzerland.

Robert Mathews. In the summer of 1782 Captain Mathews had begun courting sixteen-year-old Miss Mary Simpson, the socially ambitious daughter of the Quebec garrison's provost-marshal, Colonel Saunders Simpson. However, according to Mary Beacock Fryer, "...Mathews had a rival, the captain of the Royal Navy ship Abermarle, which was docked in Quebec City for a month. When ordered to sail for

New York City, the impetuous captain jumped ship rather than be parted from his love. Fortunately for British history (and Robert Mathews) some friends forcibly dragged the young captain back aboard and weighed anchor. Mathews won the hand of the lady and his rival won the Battle of Trafalgar, for his name was Horatio Nelson." [23] Twenty-four-year old Captain Nelson may have been smitten, but according to most sources, he did not get a lot of encouragement from young Ms. Simpson at the time.

After his duties on General Haldimand's staff ended in 1784, Major Mathews remained in the British Army and was later promoted to the rank of Colonel. His last command was that of London's Chelsea Hospital, which was responsible for the care of the British military's invalided veterans. In his book "Nelson's Women," Tom Pocock notes that, many years later, "Nelson continued to call at the Royal hospital in Chelsea to see Dr. Benjamin Moseley about his eyesight…It was there that another reminder of his past materialized, for Mrs. Mathews, the wife of [former] Major Mathews, the staff officer in charge of the pensioners there, was the once haughty Mary Simpson, who had rejected him in Quebec." [24]

Justus Sherwood and his wife were resettled on three lots in Augusta Township of the Johnstown Settlement in what is now the Province of Ontario, and he was also granted 1000 acres of additional land. He served as a Justice of the Peace and was an early member of his county's Legislative Assembly. A hard-driving farmer and early entrepreneur, he died in a logging accident at age fifty-one in 1798.

Dr. George Smyth's health continued to deteriorate following the war, and he and his wife remained at Sorel after 1783. Smyth's pension and his squabbles with Sherwood remained on his mind in the post-war period. In

September, 1784, he wrote a letter to Captain Mathews in which he insisted "...if it was not for me, not three out of the numbers that corresponded with us [i.e. the "Tory Secret Service"] would afford or assist us with intelligence. This is notoriously known to him who has the merit of my indefatigable endeavours [sic]. I wish no man ill; nor do I envy any man for his happiness, but lament myself for not being taken a little more notice of at a time when I most need it; and, when, I think, my past services deserve it." [25] Dr. Smyth died at Sorel in 1789.

The Crockers. According to Hazel Mathews, the brothers survived both the war and their role in the Thomas Loveless incident. She claims that they "...were evidently never suspected of any double dealing, and upon returning home from Canada lived out their lives as respectable Patriots...Upon their return from Canada the brothers, according to Ephraim's confession, carried dispatches and Levi junior kept Rebel troops at Saratoga informed of the advent to his neighborhood of British scouts."[26]

The Jessup Brothers. The Jessups lost all of their holdings in New York, and spent the rest of their lives in Canada and other parts of the British Empire. Shortly before the Battle of Saratoga, the newly-appointed Commander of the Northern Department, General Horatio Gates, ordered a raid by New York militia against what was known as "The Jessup Colony" along the upper Hudson River. The Jessup's previously-looted dwellings were burned, along with grain crops, lumber yards and mills, and the abandoned property soon reverted to wilderness.

After the war, the Jessup brothers were forced to flee to Canada and the West Indies. In 1791 the British government granted Ebenezer Jessup [the equivalent of] $18,000 out of a claimed loss of $110,000, while Edward

Jessup received $20,000 in compensation for losses which he had claimed amounted to $54,000.[27] Ebenezer moved first to England, then became an official in Calcutta India, where he died in 1818. Edward Jessup's petition for land in Canada was supported by a personal letter from General Burgoyne. Edward was granted 3800 acres of "unimproved" land in Quebec, and settled upon 1200 acres of land in Augusta Township in the District of Luneburg, where he died in 1816.[28] The Jessup brothers' properties in northern New York were confiscated by the State Government and sold to land speculators who then sub-divided them for re-sale.

Captain John Peters. Peters spent his early postwar years unsuccessfully trying to get General Haldimand to approve increased compensation for himself and his family for their wartime service and property losses. Sabine claims that he died in England in 1788 of "gout in the head and stomach," leaving his wife and eight children as settlers on Cape Breton Island.

Philip Skene's name was on the list of Tories who were legally "attainted" by New York authorities in 1779, and all of his properties were therefore confiscated. The property claims of both Philip and his son Andrew eventually received some compensation from the Crown. Both men left Canada for England, where Philip Skene died in 1810 and the son sixteen years later.

CHAPTER TWELVE

WHY GENERAL STARK DECIDED TO EXECUTE
THOMAS LOVELESS: SOME ENABLING
AND PRECIPITATING FACTORS

By 1781 New York State authorities had enacted a variety of laws and statutes designed to counter British-sponsored Intelligence threats. In addition to expanding the list of activities the State defined as espionage, special legislation had been drafted to deal with the challenges posed by British or Tory recruiting and kidnapping operations conducted in close proximity to Patriot army and militia garrisons and other military base areas. These strictures, as well the heightened public sensitivity to the dangers posed by British Intelligence penetrations that followed the Arnold/André case, provided General Stark with both the legal justification and the public support required to execute an enemy prisoner like Thomas Loveless

Fears of Potential British Military Threats to Albany

Moreover, in the fall of 1781, there was a major war scare underway in the territories to the north and west of Albany. Rumors of a British offensive had persisted during the previous summer (strengthened by the discovery in the river near Saratoga falls of a small howitzer and a barrel of hams left over from Burgoyne's expedition in 1777), and the report of a Tory sniper's unsuccessful attempt to assassinate Colonel Van Vechten. These fears were not unfounded, for by mid-October General Haldimand had ordered his forces (including a contingent led by Major Edward Jessup) to make a feint towards Saratoga in order to prevent General Stark from sending reinforcements to the Mohawk Valley. Jessup followed his orders, and on November 2nd a mixed

219

force under Colonel Barry St. Leger temporarily occupied Crown Point.[1]

Albany's leaders--Schuyler, Major General William Heath, and Governor George Clinton--were aware that in order to credibly threaten the British garrison in New York City while most of his army was heading for Virginia, George Washington could spare few troops for the defense of the State's northern frontiers. In short, they would have to face any British drive down the Champlain corridor with the 200 Continentals at Old Saratoga, plus three companies of Albany militia and whatever militia reinforcements could be obtained from New Hampshire and Massachusetts.

The growing concern about regional security is reflected in the following series of messages exchanged between American military and political leaders in the area during mid-September:

In a 16 September, 1781 letter to General Schuyler, Stark argued that Albany was capable of defending itself against the low probability of a Loyalist attack, and that, although his forces in Saratoga remained under threat, he was not counting upon assistance from the Albany militia: "In case of an attack here (which I am in daily expectation of), I can assure you, Sir, that I have no hopes of any assistance from Albany;...as the delays that attended their late march to Schoharie...are still fresh in my memory, and affords convincing proof that it is not their inclination to fight away from their own castle." [2] The next day Major General Heath warned Stark that intelligence information indicated that "the enemy have been building canoes and small bateaux for some time at St. Johns, and sending hard

Figure 14:
A portrait of Major General John Stark

bread from Montreal to that place; and it is now said that a number of troops have arrived there. Whether their design is to cross the lakes and advance toward you, or toward the towns on the Connecticut River . . . is uncertain."[3]

On September 20th, Stark complained in a letter to General Heath that his command ". . . is destitute of ammunition, there not being ten rounds to a man at his post; and none at Albany, subject to my order. There are no horses for expresses, or to convey provisions to the several posts, and if there were, they would starve for want of forage. We have not even paper to transact our business with, nor can we obtain it." He went on to describe the tactical threats faced by his department: "Intelligence from Canada, through sound sources, leads us to conclude that an attack is designed, either upon this post or the Mohawk River. From the situation of the country I think the attempt will be made upon this post, as the enemy can come here with twenty-five miles of land carriage; while on the other quarter, the distance is six times that number."

Finally, he described the situation in Albany: "The people of Albany are greatly alarmed for their city. They require all the troops of this district, or a major part of them, to prevent about fifty tories from burning them, their sloops, wives and houses; for it appears these turbulent sons of rapine have given out most fearful threats against that sacred place. However, Sir, unless you order to the contrary, I shall venture, in case I feel confident of the enemy's approach, to order all the troops at Albany to this post, or to the Mohawk." [4] In late September, Stark mentioned the following in a letter to General Washington: "The bearer of this, Major Guather, has found fifty-five shells, twelve boxes of musket balls, one vise, and one pair hand-screws in the river near Saratoga. It is reported that the enemy sunk some cannon in the river. I should think a farther search would be necessary, but, by reason of the scarcity of men, it has been neglected." [5]

Philip Schuyler's intelligence sources were of great value during the monitoring of this military crisis. On October 4th he informed General Heath that, according to one of his agents in Canada, the British were continuing to prepare for a southern "excursion," and that, as summarized by Don Gerlach, "…bateaux were being repaired and built at St. Johns, stores accumulated, and troops moved from Montreal. About 1,000 soldiers and seventy Indians were being assembled, and another 800 sent up the St. Lawrence to relieve the western posts." Eight days later, Schuyler received a message from Stark at Saratoga that the British were on the march from Lake George, and Schuyler replied that, according to an intercepted enemy letter, the British planned to attack Albany.[6]

In addition to countering another British attack, Stark was also eager to intercept enemy communications. Knowing that TSS scouting parties usually carried courier pouches between Quebec and Albany, Stark hoped to intercept one. On September 23rd he informed General Philip Schuyler that: "By my last scout from the northward I am apprised of about thirty of the Enemy coming from South Bay with a packet for Albany---they were yesterday very nigh this place, & by what I can learn they expect the return from Albany today." Two weeks later, Stark wrote Schuyler that British scouting parties were still active in his area, and "…Every possible means are taken to intercept them, the account of which I hope to have the pleasure of announcing to you in a few days; if they are taken, I am convinced we shall get the Albany packet."[7]

In retrospect, it appears that the Americans were confused by conflicting intelligence reports of the military activities underway in Canada in the fall of 1781. As it turned out, the real target of the British preparations was not Albany, but the Mohawk Valley and Schenectady. Although Governor Clinton sent token Army and militia reinforcements north, the British forces thrust west, rather than south, and the crisis over the defense of Albany quickly subsided. Nonetheless, the episode helps demonstrate the legitimacy of General Stark's fears that he was preparing to fight a two front war, with the enemy before him, and Tory-led fifth column operations in his rear.

In his biography of Philip Schuyler Don R. Gerlach offers the following summation of the military uncertainties facing the American leaders in the region during this crisis: "No one should underestimate the terrific strain that Schuyler, Governor Clinton, Col. Marinus Willett, and Maj. General William Heath were under in the late summer and early fall of 1781. Enemy forces at New York City were over sixteen thousand strong and ready to move. It is difficult to say what kept Sir Henry Clinton in the city (except for his attempt to relieve Cornwallis), when he might have offset the Yorktown disaster by seizing West Point from Heath's twenty-five hundred Continentals, or even Albany. Perhaps too irresolute, except for his determination to hold New York City at all costs, he was preoccupied with the events in Virginia."[8]

Stark was aware of the multiple (if unsuccessful) TSS kidnapping operations attempted against American targets in July and August, and he realized that the Tory abduction teams were being led by individuals with detailed local knowledge, including the housing and habits of their intended victims. For this reason alone, he would have seen Thomas Loveless as an especially dangerous threat to Patriot leaders (such as Van Vetchen and himself) in the Saratoga-Palmerstown area.

At the same time, General Stark was unquestionably aware of preparations for the next exchange of prisoners with the British, as demonstrated by the following documents, beginning with a 28 August, 1781 Letter to Stark from Governor George Clinton:

"Dear Sir—Your letter of the 11th instant is this moment received. I can have no objections against your sending a flag to Canada, to negotiate an exchange of the inhabitants who are prisoners of the enemy, as their liberation is an object I have frequently attempted, although in vain, and most ardently wish...I enclose you a list of the persons transmitted to me by the commissioners of Albany, to be offered in exchange, and against which I have no objection...If the enemy should consent to an exchange, due attention must be paid to give preference to those of our friends who have been longest in captivity, as this is consonant with justice, and the contrary would occasion discontent." [9]

Clinton replied to John Stark a few days later: "Dear Sir—When in Albany last winter, I addressed a letter to Governor Haldimand, respecting the exchange and liberation of a number of women and children, captured by the enemy on the frontiers of this State, which was to be forwarded by a flag. Brig. Gen. Clinton intended sending to Canada to effect the exchange of Dr. Smith and others, but it seems the situation of our affairs, while he had the command, rendered such communication inexpedient, and he has returned me the letter and papers; but the forwarding of them at this day might be deemed improper. I now take the liberty of inclosing them to you, and to request that the letter be forwarded by the first flag." [10].

To that end, Stark sent the following letter to Haldimand later that month: "Sir—The British military prisoners in this department are as anxious to be released from captivity as I suppose are the Americans in your power. Wishing to alleviate, as far as in me lies, the calamities incident on captivity, I have to propose to your excellency the exchange of all prisoners within my power, either agreeably to the mode settled between his excellency, General Washington, and his excellency, General Sir Henry Clinton, or on any other we can agree upon…Should your excellency deem it more eligible to settle the terms of exchange between us, I conceive it would tend to expedite the business, if commissioners were appointed to both sides, to meet either on this or the other side of Lake George, and settle the terms…"[11]

On September 26th, the day after Loveless' capture, Stark sent instructions to a Captain Hickoks concerning the latest flag of truce: "Sir—You will proceed with the flag under your direction to the British shipping on Lake Champlain [the Trumble]. On your arrival, you will tarry until you find out whether Captain […] will have it in his power to negotiate his business there; if so, I have no objection to your tarrying a few days, until that can be transacted; but, should he be under the necessity of going to Canada, it is by no means probable that you will be permitted to attend him, for which reason you will return by the route you go, and make report of your proceedings."[12]

The Influence of Divided Family Allegiances

It is a cliché among Anglo-American historians that the roots of the American War of Independence can be found in the French and Indian War. Likewise, a review of the personal and family histories of Thomas Loveless and John Stark strongly suggests that military service in the French and Indian War was a shared experience which influenced the outcome of their encounter in 1781. The intelligence operations conducted by the British and their Tory allies along the border between New York and Canada during 1778-1782 in many ways duplicated those conducted in the same geographical area twenty years earlier. While the allies and enemies of the two principal warring coalitions in the two conflicts were different, the technology, strategies, and tactics employed were remarkably similar. In both cases, the British deployed relatively small numbers of Regular and Provincial Corps troops, and relied heavily upon irregular, or Ranger units for raiding and Intelligence-gathering.

The most famous of these British-sponsored irregular units, known collectively as Rogers' Rangers, was commanded by Major (later Lieutenant Colonel) Robert Rogers. Although their combined force levels seldom exceeded 500 men, nine companies of Roger's Rangers were recruited and fielded by Lord Amherst's Military Headquarters during the period 1755-1760. Allowing for high levels of attrition, in five years as many as 1500 men may have served in Rogers' Rangers. Recruits were obtained from all over New England, and included Native Americans from Stockbridge, Massachusetts, "frontiersmen" from New York and Pennsylvania, and volunteers from Connecticut, Rhode Island, and Delaware. Under Rogers' direction, the Rangers were trained to fight "Indian style," in a type of small unit warfare best summarized by Colonel Rogers' famous nineteen Standing Orders, the first of which was "Don't Forget Nothing.."

Operating principally in a 600-square mile area between Fort Edward and Crown Point, during six years various detachments from Rogers' Battalion engaged in twenty-seven battles and reconnaissance operations against the French and their Indian allies. Casualties on both sides were high, and a steady flow of new recruits was required to maintain adequate manpower levels for British-sponsored Ranger units. By May of 1761, however, all of the Rogers'

Rangers companies on active duty had been paid off and disbanded, and their personnel had begun to return home. Within the next ten years, many of these veterans would acquire land in the vicinity of the New York-Canada frontier.

The leadership of Rogers' Rangers units was highly nepotistic. In addition to Lt. Colonel Robert Rogers (1727-1795), two of the Colonel's brothers also served as officers in the Rangers: Major James Rogers (1726-1792), and Captain Richard Rogers (born 1734), who died of smallpox at Fort William Henry in 1757. Likewise, Robert Rogers' second-in-command Major John Stark (1728-1822), had three brothers who also served as Ranger officers: Captain William Stark (1724-1781), who served from 1756 to 1759, First Lieutenant Archibald Stark (1730-1819) who entered the Rangers' as a Sergeant in 1756 and later obtained a commission, and Ensign Samuel Stark (1726-1809), enlisted as a Private in 1756, was made an Ensign in 1759, and served until 1760.

Several accounts of the Tory Spy's execution claim that he was "too dangerous to be allowed to live." If this was true, then where could he have learned such lethal combat skills? We know from British military records of the period that Thomas Lovelace was 42 years old at the time of his execution, so he would have been born in 1739/1740. By 1760, he would have been between nineteen and twenty years of age. During the same year, Colonel Robert Rogers would have been twenty-eight years old and his trusted subordinate Captain John Stark would have been twenty-seven.

Thomas Loveless' name does not appear in the few surviving "returns" or rosters listing the names of the Privates who served in Roger's Rangers units over time, or in the "Journals" kept by Robert Rogers. However, other documents prove that Rogers regularly recruited men from Rhode Island, Connecticut, and New York. Thomas Loveless was born in Rhode Island and raised in New York. If the Tory Spy had joined a company of Rogers' Rangers during 1759-1760, he could have served in a company commanded by then-Major John Stark or one of his brothers. Even if he served in another Rogers' Ranger's company, Loveless could have been well known to the man who was later to sign his death warrant.

The divisive "civil war" aspects of the American Revolution are vividly highlighted by the following summary of the schisms of allegiance produced by that conflict. Given the previously listed enabling causes, it is likely that the precipitating cause of John Stark's decision to execute Thomas Loveless was driven by the conflicting political loyalties which had been festering within the Stark, Rogers, and Loveless families since the start of the American Revolution

The Stark Family

Although he and his three brothers had all held commissions in the British service during the French and Indian War, at the outbreak of the Revolution John Stark jointed New Hampshire's 1st Militia Regiment and led it during the Battle of Bunker Hill in June of 1775. During the rest of the war, he and his two sons, Caleb and Archibald, served with distinction in the Continental army, and all three men were present at the execution of Major John André. However, like many other Yankee families, some of John Stark's other relatives sided with The Crown. His elder brother William defected to the British when the Americans would not give him command of a regiment. Sabine claims that William ". . . endeavored to persuade (his brother) to adopt the same course; but John was not to be moved."

William Stark died in a fall from his horse shortly after his decision to fight for the British. Several relatives from John Stark's mother's family also refused to support the Rebel cause, and were among those formally condemned as "Enemies of The Revolution" by the New Hampshire legislature after the war.

The Rogers Family:

All the members of Colonel Robert Rogers immediate family sided with the British during the Revolutionary War. The Colonel himself had spent most of the decade 1765-1775 in command of an isolated British garrison on the Great Lakes or in London unsuccessfully seeking appointments and commissions from The Crown. When he returned to America in 1775, he tried to obtain a commission in the Continental Army, but was so deeply distrusted by George Washington that he was arrested and imprisoned. Rogers shortly escaped and betrayed Nathan Hale to the British, thereby gaining the favor of General William Howe and the command he was seeking.

General Stark may also have been aware of Robert Rogers' role in the death of Hale, who had been executed more than five years before the hanging of Ensign Thomas Loveless. The son of a prosperous Connecticut farmer, Nathan Hale was born in Coventry on June 6, 1755. The sixth of ten surviving children, and of Massachusetts Puritan stock, he graduated from Yale in 1773 and became a teacher at a grammar school in New London. An early and enthusiastic Patriot, Hale was commissioned a Lieutenant in the Connecticut militia in July of 1775, and became a Captain in the 19th Continental Regiment six months later.

After his unit moved to New York City, he led a group of seamen from his company in a raid that captured a

British supply ship. This led to his selection as commander of a company of "Knowlton's Rangers" (commanded by Lt. Col. Thomas Knowlton), America's first Military Intelligence organization. It was during his service with Knowlton's unit that he volunteered for his fatal espionage mission, which began when he infiltrated Long Island on September 12th, 1776 and ended with his execution ten days later. He was hanged at a British artillery park located near what is today 66th Street and Third Avenue in Manhattan.

Hale was a courageous, but poorly trained spy who made the fatal mistake of openly admitting his guilt. Although for over two centuries a legend persisted that he had been betrayed by his cousin Samuel Hale, who was a both a Tory and a graduate of Harvard College, newly discovered evidence has proved that this was not the case. A privately-held manuscript donated to the Library of Congress in the year 2000 identified Major Robert Rogers as the person who turned Nathan Hale over to British Commander Sir William Howe.

By September of 1776 the opportunistic Rogers was busy recruiting troops on Long Island in hopes of forming his own Tory "Ranger" unit. Rogers apparently met Hale by accident, and tricked him into believing that he, too, was a Rebel Spy. He then turned Hale over to the British in hopes of proving his own bona fides for a future command. Confronted with Hale's open confession, General Howe had little choice but to order his execution, which was carried out by hanging within a day of his capture.

Figure 15:
The Execution of Nathan Hale as Conceived by Felix Darley

Robert Rogers was eventually given command of a Provincial Corps unit called the "Queen's American Rangers," later known as the "Queen's Rangers." However, new recruits were hard to find and few Rogers' Rangers veterans rallied to his flag. After leading his unit in a series of unsuccessful skirmishes, Colonel Rogers was relieved of his command and was replaced by a series of younger officers, the most successful of whom was Major John Graves Simcoe.

Colonel Rogers' brother James also allied himself with the British. He received a Major's commission from General Clinton in 1779, and commanded a small Canada-based provincial corps unit known as the "King's Rangers" until the end of the war. He and his family settled in Upper Canada in 1784, and his property in Vermont was subsequently confiscated by the American authorities.

The Lovelace/Loveless Family:

It is unknown whether Thomas Loveless' younger brother James remained alive at the outbreak of the Revolution, and if so, which side he chose to support. However, the majority of Lovelesses/Lovelaces living in New York State during the American Revolution clearly sided with the Rebels. At least eleven members of the family (even allowing for the possibility of multiple enlistments, mis-spelled surnames, and identical names given to multiple generations of male children), joined New York military formations for various lengths of time, serving in either Continental Line or Militia units. At least five of them applied for Federal pensions on the basis of their "War of Independence" service. According to the "Roster of the State troops" in Berthold Fernow's book <u>New York in the Revolution</u> and a variety of other sources, the following

Lovelace/Loveless family members supported the Patriot cause in New York while in uniform: [13]

- John Loveless—Served in the 14th Regiment of the Albany County Militia

- George and Jeremiah Lovelis [sic]—Served in the 4th Regiment of the New York Continental Line

- Elisha Lovelace—Albany County Militia, Yates' Regiment, Hadlock's Company.

- William Lovelass [sic]—Served in the 7th Regiment of the Dutchess County Militia

- Benjamin Loveless—Served in the 14th Regiment of the Albany County Militia during 1779-1780.

- Elisha Loveles [sic]—Albany County Militia, Van Rensselaer's Regiment, De Garmo's Company.

- Jeremiah Loveles [sic]—Albany County Militia, Van Rensselaer's Regiment, De Garmo's Company

- Joshua and Elisha Loveless—Served in the 6th Regiment of the Dutchess County Militia during 1777

- Joseph Loveless—Served in the "Minuteman" Regiment of the Dutchess County Militia

In addition to Thomas the Spy, at least two other Lovelesses also served with British-sponsored units that originated in or were eventually assigned to duty in New York State:

A Private George Loveless is listed twice (October 24, 1780 and June 18, 1781) on the muster rolls of "Captain William Fowler's Company, The Loyal American Regiment" at New York City and Flushing, Long Island. A March 1, 1782 muster roll lists him as a prisoner of war.

Private Peter Loveless is listed on three muster rolls (November 24, 1777, February, 1778, and June 24, 1778) of "Captain Stair Agnew's Company of the Queen's Rangers" by then commanded by John Graves Simcoe. Originally known as "The Queen's Loyal Virginia Regiment," this unit was raised in Virginia in November of 1775 by Royal Governor John Murray, Lord Dunmore. After its defeat at the Battle of Great Bridge in 1776, it was moved to New York and merged with other units to become the "Queen's Rangers." After fighting at Brandywine, Germantown, and Monmouth, the unit was transferred to Virginia in 1781 to support Cornwallis' expeditionary force, and, like Tarleton's British Legion, surrendered at Yorktown.

The Crucial Role of the Commanding Officer's Judgment in Espionage Executions

In the course of the war American authorities employed several definitions of espionage, and conviction of the crime could result in widely varied penalties. Under these circumstances, the decision to charge, convict, and execute a captured Loyalist as a "spy" remained highly subjective, and much depended upon the temperament and prior experience of the Commanding Officer in charge. Given John Stark's well-documented personal hatred of Tories, his role in helping to decide Major André's fate, and the painful memories of the disloyalty of many of his closest friends, family members, and military colleagues during the war, his decision to hang Thomas Loveless was probably inevitable.

A cursory review of the leadership, organization, missions, resources, and effectiveness of the British/Tory Secret Service and the American Intelligence apparatus reveals some striking differences. There is no question that the Americans were the less aggressive, more defensively oriented service. Schuyler, Van Vechten and Dunham were primarily concerned with developing counterintelligence capabilities that would confuse the British about US military intentions and blunt hostile intelligence attacks emanating from Canada. To a lesser extent, the Americans sought tactical intelligence concerning the capabilities and intentions of British forces. To accomplish this, they were willing to send small numbers of agents, and occasional military reconnaissance parties into Canada.

The British leaders in Quebec and Montreal, on the other hand, were more desperate for military information, and were willing to take greater risks to obtain it. In addition to maintaining the Quebec to New York City military courier route, the British (and later, the Tory-led) Secret Service had residual responsibilities for military recruiting, defending those Loyalists still behind American lines, and supporting covert British negotiations with the Allen faction in Vermont. As a result, the Tory Secret Service's operations were both varied and aggressive, and hence, likely to incur more casualties. Although the British-sponsored and American Intelligence establishments employed similar tradecraft and technologies, they did not apply these in identical ways, as evidenced by their divergent policies regarding espionage executions.

One can only guess at what made General Stark decide to send the Tory Spy's colleagues to Albany jail where they could expect to be eventually exchanged as POWs. From Stark's perspective, these men were probably not seen as major future threats. On the other hand, Loveless was both the "officer in charge" of an enemy scouting party and a highly experienced and dangerous opponent. In addition, the papers which Loveless carried proved his status as a formally commissioned officer (either an Ensign or a Lieutenant) and revealed his intent to recruit men for service in the Loyal Rangers or some other Canada-based Provincial Corps unit. Moreover, he was a locally-known Loyalist who had been chosen to lead this team on what was clearly his "home turf." In Stark's view, Loveless probably posed so many potentially serious threats to Rebel security equities in Albany County that he had to be eliminated.

An episode from the career of notorious New Jersey Loyalist Provincial Corps officer James Moody provides another dramatic example of how a captured Tory officer's reputation could result in his death sentence. During his 1779 imprisonment by the Continental Army he was told that instead of being exchanged he would be tried by Court Martial for "assassinating" two New Jersey militia officers in a firefight the year before. When Moody reminded his accusers that he had shot the two officers in open combat, an American Colonel told him to forget mounting such a defense, saying: "All this will be of little avail: you are so obnoxious, so mischievous to us, that, be assured, we are resolved to get rid of you at any rate. Besides, you cannot deny, and it can be proved by incontestable evidence, that you have enlisted men, in this state, for the King's service, and this, by our laws, is death." As it turned out, Moody managed to get free of his irons and escaped before his carefully-rigged trial (New Jersey Governor William Livingston was to be his prosecutor, and he was assured that the members of the Court Martial had been "carefully picked for the purpose") could be convened.[14]

CHAPTER THIRTEEN

WHY WAS THE TORY-PATRIOT CONFLICT IN NORTHERN NEW YORK SO UNUSUAL, AND WHAT CAN THIS TEACH US ABOUT THE AMERICAN REVOLUTION?

Regardless of the public executions of Tory Secret Service officers captured by Patriot forces in northern New York, none of the Rebel spies apprehended by the British in Canada during the war were executed. General Haldimand. may have held back because of the continued vulnerability of New York's Loyalists to reprisals. Perhaps it was because, unlike Philip Schuyler, he did not have to cope with an active (in his case, French) fifth column. Perhaps, after receiving the news of the Yorktown surrender he realized that the end of the war was drawing near, and decided that "the less additional bloodshed, the better." In any case, Haldimand's restraint in punishing captured spies was never shared by his enemies to the south. How can the circumstances and motivations associated with Thomas Loveless' hanging help us better comprehend this aspect of America's first civil war?

There were several reasons why the American authorities in New York State executed so many Tories as "spies." First of all, the presence of sizeable numbers (at least twenty percent of the state's population) of Loyalists presented the American authorities with a potentially dangerous fifth column. Secondly, in areas such as the border with Canada and in the vicinity of New York City, Tories could be easily recruited as supporters of British-sponsored Intelligence operations. Thirdly, as the conflict progressed, American counterintelligence capabilities improved faster than those of their British counterparts, who made costly mistakes. Fourth, because the British made extensive use of Loyalists in their intelligence-gathering programs, both official and unofficial Patriots tended to over-estimate Tory security threats, especially in the wake of the Arnold/André case. Such fears frequently caused Rebels to perceive Loyalist espionage capabilities and activities which did not, in fact, exist. Finally, charges of spying were sometimes a convenient means of settling personal scores or, in the case of criminal activities, diverting suspicion away from one's self.

Yet until late 1775, neither the Continental Congress nor the Continental Army possessed a comprehensive definition of what constituted "espionage," or the penalties to be imposed upon those found guilty of spying. These weaknesses were only discovered when Dr. Benjamin Church, the Harvard-trained Surgeon-General of the Continental Army who had been passing information to General Gage, was betrayed by accident and charged with espionage in November, 1775. Apparently the Articles of War in force at the time did not cover the possibility of espionage conducted by civilians or foreigners. John Bakeless has offered the following description of this bizarre omission:

"The indignant generals turned to the Army regulations that Congress had adopted in the previous June. There it was! Congress had foreseen such cases. Article XXVIII provided that anyone communicating with the enemy should suffer such punishment as a court-martial might direct. That seemed to fit the situation. Try the man and string him up!" At this point, someone searched a little further and made an embarrassing discovery. Article LI limited the punishment a court-martial could inflict. It could give penalties of thirty-nine lashes or a fine of two months' pay and it could cashier the offender—and that was all! No one had been thinking about British spies when that article had been adopted...Congress hastily authorized the death penalty for espionage, November 7, 1775. [1]

As the threat of a British invasion from Canada loomed in early 1777, New York again addressed espionage issues with some urgency. According to New York State's "Journal of the Provincial Convention," on March 31, 1777 the Convention, led by a Brigadier General and with representatives from New York City, Albany, and nine New York counties, met to discuss recent Tory depredations in Westchester County. This session led to the following resolutions:

"Whereas, from the want of courts properly instituted for the trial of treasons and other offences against this State, the resolutions heretofore passed for the punishment of the same have not been executed, whereby divers persons in this State, who have been employed by the enemy as spies, or for the purpose of enlisting men into their service, or furnishing them with supplies or intelligence, many of whom were not punishable by the Continental articles of war, have escaped with impunity:

Resolved, That all such persons as have been or shall be apprehended in this State, without the enemy's lines, by Continental or other American troops, as spies from the enemy, or for enlisting men for their service, or for furnishing supplies or intelligence to them, be tried for the said offenses by martial law, and if found guilty, suffer death or other punishment at the discretion of a general court martial of the Continental Army or the militia of this State; provided that where any person shall have been convicted by a court martial by virtue of this resolution, that the sentence shall not be executed until approved by this Convention or a future Legislature of this State."

Whereas, a form of government will soon be established in this State, and proper courts organized for the trial of offenses therein: Therefore,

Resolved, That the resolution above mentioned continue in force until the first day of July next, unless sooner repealed by this Convention or the future Legislature of this State." [2]

In March of 1778, the newly-established Albany Board of the Commissioners for Detecting and Defeating Conspiracies decided that the crime of treason was to be punished by "hanging by the neck until death," which was seen as a humane substitute for "the operation of English Law, so far as it related to the manner of putting offenders to death," which was characterized as "marked by Savage Cruelty, ["drawing and quartering"?] unnecessary for the purposes of public justice, and manifestly repugnant to that Spirit of Humanity, which should ever distinguish a free, a civilized, and Christian People." [3] Treason and espionage were thus likely to be seen to be synonymous.

Two years later, New York authorities took an even stronger stand against future British intelligence operations conducted behind American lines. On June 30, 1780, the Albany Board of the Commissioners for Detecting and Defeating Conspiracies passed an act whereby "...all persons who came from the British lines and were found lurking secretly in any part of the state, were to be tried by courts martial as spies." [4]

Kidnappings posed a special legal problem for the American authorities. Were they a kind of espionage, or merely a component of "irregular warfare" operations? In his book Broadsides and Bayonets: The Propaganda War of the American Revolution, Carl Berger mentions several

241

examples of kidnappings by Loyalists or British troops, including the December, 1776 seizure of Major General Charles Lee, aborted plans to carry off the Governor, Assembly, and Council of New Jersey, and the failed Loyalist-led plot to kidnap George Washington. With these experiences in mind, the American authorities took steps to make kidnapping a capital crime.

According to Berger, in February, 1778 the Continental Congress finally addressed the issue of kidnappings conducted in close proximity to Continental Army headquarters facilities: "…and, in a formal resolution, denounced the Loyalists who were banding together…for the purpose of seizing and secretly conveying to places in possession of the British forces such of the loyal citizens, officers, and soldiers of these states as may fall into their hands." Congress declared that all such persons (attempting these activities) were to be put to death "as a traitor, assassin or spy," if the offense was committed within seventy miles of the headquarters of any American Army."[5]

At the same time that they started to make the kidnapping of Americans a capital crime, however, Patriot authorities had begun to arrest Tories for the purpose of exchanging them for Rebel prisoners held by the British. Governor George Clinton began this program in July, 1778 when he ordered the Albany Board to send him the names of Loyalists who had refused to take the Loyalty Oath because he planned to use them in future exchanges of prisoners. In early September, the Board responded to a letter from Clinton by ordering that Henry Cuyler, James Dole, and Alexander White (all recalcitrant Tories who had signed paroles) "…be instantly removed down to Poughkeepsie and there deliver themselves up to the persons administering the government of the state." In November, Andries Ten Eyck, who had refused to take the oath, was "…informed that it is the determination of [the Governor] that he be sent with the next flag to New York which is to set off from Poughkeepsie on the 27th instant"[6]

This "forcible procurement" of Loyalists for use in prisoner exchanges remained in place for the rest of the conflict, and indeed the Board was eventually forced to re-imprison persons previously released on bail in order to use them in future exchanges. Unfortunately, the British authorities, and especially those in Canada, never had enough Rebel prisoners in their jails to match the number of Tories (especially the wives and children of those Loyalist men who had fled to Canada) and British prisoners being held by the Americans. As a result, from the outset kidnapping of Rebel leaders and other American citizens was one of the Tory Secret Service's most important missions.

To add to the confusion, the penalties imposed by Americans upon those convicted of spying during the War of Independence varied considerably. Simple treason—passing sensitive military information to the British—was, as in the case of Benedict Arnold, universally viewed as a capital offense. British military personnel or Loyalists caught with enemy dispatches, plans or orders, concealment devices, or lists of incriminating names in their possession were usually charged with espionage, but they did not always suffer execution if convicted. Sometimes their lives were spared if they provided information about the British military or other Loyalists who supported Secret Service operations. Tories were more likely to be tried and executed on espionage charges if they were captured while operating in their old neighborhoods.

However, the "weapons possession" issue in Tory espionage cases apparently remained undecided. On some occasions Loyalists apprehended carrying weapons behind

American lines were treated as POWs, rather than spies. A good example of the acceptance of this principle is provided by the case of two Tory scouts who were captured after having crossed the Connecticut River into New Hampshire in 1780. According to one source, the suspects, named Johns and Buel, were lucky: "Having arms with them, they could not, according to the rules of war, be treated as spies, and were therefore held under the more honorable distinction of prisoners of war."[7]

George Washington himself was clearly able to differentiate between an unarmed spy operating clandestinely and a "prisoner of war" wearing a uniform and carrying a weapon and operational orders or his commission papers. When warned by Governor William Livingston in January 1782 that Loyalist James Moody was threatening to kidnap a Member of Congress to avenge the execution of his brother John, Washington replied:

"It is a pity but that Villain Moody could be apprehended lurking in the Country, in a manner that would bring him under the description of a Spy. When he was taken before, he was in Arms—in his proper uniform—with a party—and had his Commission in his pocket. It was, therefore, a matter of great doubt whether he could be considered otherwise than a prisoner of war. It was said he had been inlisting [sic] men in the Country but no proof of the kind ever appeared." [8]

British threats of reprisal do not seem to have been very effective in stopping American espionage executions during the Revolution, largely because over time it became clear that such threats would not be carried out. This fact may explain the famous August, 1777 letter sent by US General Israel Putnam to former New York Governor Tryon concerning the fate of a Tory Provincial Corps officer named

Nathaniel Palmer. On the previous day Putnam had received a formal message from the British military leaders warning that they would "take reprisals" if Palmer was executed:

> Sir:
> Nathaniel Palmer, a lieutenant in your King's service, was taken in my camp as a Spy—he was tried as a Spy—he was condemned as a Spy—and you may rest assured, Sir, he shall be hanged as a Spy.
>
> I have the honour to be, & C.
>
> Israel Putnam
>
> P.S. Afternoon. He is hanged. [9]

The partisan struggle in northern New York produced a unique pattern of "high risk" participation by loyalists, ranging from volunteering for Provincial Corps and intelligence support duties, to helping pass British messages between Quebec and New York City, to managing TSS operations mounted from Canadian bases. In no other theater of the Revolutionary War did Loyalists become so deeply involved in the management, execution, and local support of complex Intelligence operations. The "intelligence warfare" conducted by both sides along the New York frontier with Canada was different from that carried out by the British and the Americans in the vicinity of New York City, and it had little in common with the British intelligence operations being pursued in lower New York, New Jersey, or North and South Carolina.

After Bennington and Saratoga, there were no large-scale battles in New York or Vermont in which Loyalist militia units played a major role. In Westchester County, New York throughout the War violence between roving

Rebel or Tory bands produced a pattern of ambushes, raids, and reprisals which eventually degenerated into banditry. General Henry Clinton occasionally obtained valuable intelligence from Loyalist bands known as the "Cowboys," but unlike the TSS, these bands were not part of a organized secret service run by Clinton's staff.

Like the Loyalists living along New York's northern frontier who supported the TSS, New Jersey Loyalists collected intelligence for the British, occasionally providing General Clinton's Headquarters in New York City with valuable information. But the militant Tories in New Jersey had their own operational priorities and agenda. Driven by the lack of British concern for the fate of Loyalist prisoners in Rebel hands, New Jersey's "Board of Associated Loyalists" tried to prevent executions of captured Tories by helping them escape from Rebel prisons and by kidnapping Rebel leaders for use as hostages. The New Jersey Board's dilemma was later described as follows:

"Was not the taking of Arms against the King, at least as high Treason, as the fighting against their new formd [sic] States? Yet our Generals suffered these Executions of the Loyalists to go on; without ever attempting to stop them by threatening to retaliate. Nay they would not permit the Associated Loyalists to save their Friends, by threatening to Execute any of those Rebels, whom these Loyalists had taken prisoners, and whom they held in their own custody."[10]

Perhaps the most notorious of the New Jersey Loyalists was Provincial Corps officer James Moody, who took part in a variety of intelligence operations. From April, 1777 to November, 1781 he recruited troops for Loyalist and British military units, freed Loyalist prisoners from Patriot jails, conducted "scouts" behind Rebel lines, attempted to kidnap New Jersey Governor William Livingston, and coordinated ambushes of several American military couriers. Moody was tasked with these operations by senior British officers in New York City, including General Clinton's Adjutant General, Colonel Oliver Delancey.

Moody's unsuccessful attempt to kidnap New Jersey Governor Livingston in May, 1780 had been ordered by Lieutenant-General Knyphausen. When Moody and a dozen of his men were captured by Rebel forces led by General Anthony Wayne in late July, a copy of the following operational orders were found on Moody's person and subsequently published in several Rebel newspapers. An article that appeared in the August 9th, 1780 issue of the New-Jersey Gazette noted that "The instructions found upon Moody, in order to give the better colour to his private directions of inlisting [sic] and assassinating, and to prevent his being treated as a spy from the military stile, which he was to produce, in case of his being taken prisoner, was as follows:"

"Headquarters, May 10th New York, 1780

SIR,
You are hereby directed and authorized to proceed without loss of time, with a small detachment, into the Jerseys, by the most convenient route, in order to carry off the person of Governor Livingston, or any other acting in public station, whom you may fall in with in the course of your march, or any person whom you may meet with, and whom it may be necessary to secure for your own security, and that of the party under your command.

"Should you succeed in taking Governor Livingston, you are to treat him according to his station, so far as lies in your power; nor are you, upon any account, to offer any violence to his person. You will use your endeavour to get possession of his papers, which you will take care of, and upon your return, deliver to head-quarters.

By order of his Excellency Lieutenant-General Knyphausen.

GEORGE BECKWITH, Aide de Camp,
To Ensign Moody, 1st Battalion, New-Jersey Volunteers"

The article's author went on to speculate about the fate of the recently-imprisoned James Moody: "And as to the most famous or infamous Ensign himself, the great taker of Governors and general gaol deliverer of Sussex, he is at present safely lodged at West Point, and if he has justice done him, it is generally supposed, as our correspondent observes, that he will be hanged for a spy, for inlisting [sic] our citizens in the British Army, and coming with a party as small as nine, and with weapons concealed, either of which are, according to the present construction of all the nations of Europe, characteristics of a spy." [11]

Amazingly, on the night of September 17th –only two days before his scheduled court martial--Moody managed to escape, and after a week of hiding and evasion supported by New Jersey Friends of Government, he returned to the safety of the New York border. A year later, James Moody published his famous advertisement in the August 25, 1781 issue of New York City's Royalist Gazette offering to pay "Two Hundred Quineas, true money" to "the person or persons who shall bring the said William Livingston alive into this city." He also mentioned that "In the mean time, if his whole person cannot be brought in, half the sum above specified will be paid for his EARS and NOSE, which are too well known, and too remarkable to be mistaken. . ."[12]

In late 1781 Moody helped his younger brother John mount an ill-conceived operation to steal documents from the Continental Congress' files in Philadelphia. The plot was betrayed by a Rebel "double agent," and John Moody and his colleague Laurence Marr were captured, tried, and sentenced to be hanged. Initially reported to have been executed, Marr was ultimately reprieved for providing useful information and given sanctuary behind British lines. Young Moody was hanged on November 13th, and a newspaper article two weeks later noted that "The enemy, who at this period seem equal to no exploits superior to robbing mails and stealing papers, may thank the monster Benedict Arnold, their beloved friend, for the untimely death of this young man, who was only in his 23rd year." [13]

In 1782 James Moody traveled to London, where he published a personal account of his Loyalist activities entitled <u>Lieut. James Moody's Narrative of His Exertions and Sufferings in the Cause of Government since the Year 1776,</u> in which he demanded £1719 pds. compensation for his personal losses. The book remained in print for several years, and Moody was eventually granted £1,608 pds. repayment by the Royal Commission. He and his family eventually settled in Weymouth, Nova Scotia. [14]

To their dismay, the British found the Loyalists in the Carolinas of little use when it came to intelligence collection or support. During 1780 Rebel partisan bands in North and South Carolina fought more than a dozen engagements (most of them successful) against combined British-Tory forces. Many of these battles and skirmishes were followed by summary executions and other atrocities directed against Tories. Perhaps because most Carolina Loyalists were Scots-Irish immigrants who lived in the western parts of the two states, British commanders used cavalry units and slaves and other local informants to gather tactical intelligence, but did not run networks of spies. Even after the British captured Savannah and Charleston, the chaos in the Carolinas did not lend itself to carefully-managed secret service operations.

Near the end of his book on the New York Loyalists, Philip Ranlet notes that: "One factor the British counted upon for victory was the presence of large numbers of Tories who would help them defeat the rebels. Time and time again, the British expected the loyalists to appear. But, in New York, the British were almost always disappointed. Even in the south, the expectation of a large turnout of Tories was a failure." Moreover, he concludes that "Toryism [in New York] declined steadily during the war and was of little help to the British…By the end of the war perhaps only 8 percent of New York's pre-war inhabitants still endorsed the king's cause."[15]

If this was the case, then what caused Loyalist families like that of Thomas Loveless family to remain loyal to the Crown until the very end of the war? Although they had escaped to Canada by the end of 1777, the Palmertown Lovelesses could have returned to Albany County, pledged their allegiance to the United States, and perhaps regained their property. The fact that they did not change sides after five years as refugees living a "hand to mouth" existence as wards of the British administration in the Province of Canada underscores the depth of their commitment. If the majority of Loyalists, both in New York and throughout the other colonies, had duplicated the sacrifices made by Thomas Loveless and his family, then the conduct, and even possibly the outcome, of the lengthy conflict might have been different.

If one considers the dangers associated with the higher levels of the "Pyramid of Risk" describing Loyalist support for the British during the war, the contributions of Thomas Loveless and his family were clearly exceptional. Beginning with a four-year Provincial Corps career, and continuing with two years as a guide and a member of the TSS, "Thomas the Spy" served for more than six years. He remained on duty with the King's Loyal Americans throughout and did not apply for invalid status, even when he reached the age of forty-two. As his two elder sons came of age, he encouraged them to volunteer for duty with British-sponsored military units. Whether such extraordinary commitment was the result of family tradition, patriotic zeal, or (later on) the realization that they had bet upon the losing horse and had to make the best of their new situation, the Loveless family supported the Crown's cause to the bitter end. Following the war, none of the Tory Spy's sons or daughters returned to New York or other parts of the United States.

As it did in throughout the colonies, the de facto British—Tory "alliance" in New York failed for a several reasons. The various "Tory management" policies mounted by British leaders in North America during the war were either condescending, hopelessly unrealistic, or applied too late to have any effect. Following the initial surge of Tory enlistments in late 1776, the Loyalists repeatedly failed to produce enough volunteers to fully man British-sponsored Provincial Corps or Militia units. Moreover, the "Intelligence advantage" which the British had expected to obtain from the Friends of Government (i.e. vital information about local terrain, the identities of Rebel leaders, and penetrations of Patriot military and political organizations) never fully materialized. This shortfall was particularly evident during such operations as Burgoyne's expedition into northern New York in 1777 and British operations in the Carolinas during 1779-1780.

British leaders' perception of their "betrayal" by Loyalists is humorously demonstrated by the text of a "tongue-in-cheek" dialogue between George III's son Prince William Henry and General Henry Clinton published in at least two Rebel newspapers in November, 1781. In this hypothetical exchange the Prince (who was visiting New York City at the time) learns of the defeat of Cornwallis' army at Yorktown and is then informed that "His Majesty's territory at present, in the thirteen revolted provinces, is confined only to the garrisons of New-York, Charlestown, and Savannah." Prince William than replies: "Why, Sir Harry, you have petrified me. Damn the Loyalists, all this comes from listening to their tales. They teased my father into this cursed war. I wish he may hang Galloway [Joseph Galloway a prominent Loyalist and the author of "Galloway's Plan of Union" in 1774] at the yardarm of a seventy-four...I will be revenged upon your vile Loyalists, who have divided the British empire, and brought this ruin upon my father's family." [16]

In his book <u>Loyalists and Redcoats</u>, Paul H. Smith summarizes the British leadership's creation of the "Loyalist Dilemma" as follows: "Perhaps the only accurate statement that can be made on the subject is that the Loyalists never occupied a fixed, well-understood place in British strategy. Plans to use them were in the main <u>ad hoc </u>responses to constantly changing conditions, and, like British strategy throughout the war, were developed to meet various peculiar situations. The immediate object of employing the Loyalists was not always solely to achieve a military end. At times they were organized for practically no other reason than to afford protection and to provide for their useful employment, at times to reduce military expenses, and at others to maintain Parliamentary support for continuing what many members of Parliament eventually came to believe was otherwise a hopeless war." [17] Some historians might argue that the British failed to comprehend the potential value of their Loyalist allies for the very same reasons that they underestimated the commitment and capabilities of those other "colonials" who were rebelling against British rule.

Why has the Topic of Revolutionary War Espionage Executions Been Ignored by American Historians?

Traditionally, nation-states have preferred to maintain a "veil of decency" concealing the more violent aspects of their founding, especially if they came into being as the result of protracted warfare and social conflict. Because the United States of America was the product of the first successful large-scale rebellion against British Imperialism, its citizens have nurtured an historical tradition that has consistently minimized the levels of social violence which accompanied their victory. Over the years, this myth has been strengthened by related mythologies concerning the inevitability of the American triumph and its relative lack of civilian and non-combatant casualties, especially when compared to those produced by the French, Russian, and Chinese revolutions.

Contrary to such mythology, America's revolutionary conflict was, in fact, classically bloody and divisive. Commenting upon the various missions routinely conducted by colonial militia during the war, military historian Michael Stephenson notes that "Apart from their checkered career in battle, the militias performed a critical task for the Patriot cause: to root out and ruthlessly suppress Loyalist opposition. To understand the nature of this activity, it is useful to look at the War of Independence through the lens of much more recent history. For example, the Communist political cadres of the Vietnam War, the IRA, and the "insurgents" of the second Iraq War were heavily invested in intimidating and killing those they perceived to be sympathetic to the occupying power. This is a constant element in an anti-colonial war. Some American historians are squeamish about making such long-range connections between, say, Vietnam (or Iraq) and the American War of Independence . . . but the connections are numerous and, indeed, inevitable. Colonial wars share a certain geometry."[18]

This reluctance is related to a larger problem—the refusal to admit the crucial role played by American secret diplomacy and overseas intelligence-gathering throughout the war, and especially that of Benjamin Franklin and Thomas Jefferson in Paris. Most serious students of the Revolutionary War will agree that the American victory was largely the outcome of three interrelated factors: 1). George Washington's success .in ensuring that the Continental Army remained a "force in being" throughout the war, 2). The British Army's defeat at Saratoga, which helped create the Franco-American Alliance, and 3). The victory of the French fleet at the Battle of the Virginia Capes, which made the surrender of Cornwallis's besieged force at Yorktown inevitable. Without Franklin's diplomatic and intelligence skills, there would have been no French Alliance. Without military supplies from France and the involvement of French land and naval forces, there would have been no "miracle" at Yorktown, and the war would have lasted much longer.

Yet the evidence contained in this book reveals that there was another Intelligence-related factor that contributed to the US victory: the effectiveness of the internal security, intelligence, and counter-intelligence operations mounted by the American civil and military authorities. Given the importance of these capabilities in determining the Revolution's outcome, it is ironic that so few American scholars have studied their impact upon the loyalist inhabitants of the thirteen newly-independent states as the war progressed. Likewise, within the more specialized field of Revolutionary War intelligence research, this is a story which has simply "fallen through the cracks"--too obscure, too deeply buried, and too embarrassing to be easily investigated and publicized.

Espionage and other forms of intelligence activity are integral components of revolutionary warfare, and these activities inevitably produce the need to improve security, thereby raising the possibility that enemy spies will be captured and possibly executed. The problem with discussing the role of "Tory spies" in the Revolution is that it highlights the reality of sustained, socially-diverse, high-risk resistance to America's War of Independence. The fact that large numbers of Loyalists were willing to risk their lives to prevent the rupture of the Colonies' ties to the British Empire remains difficult for Americans to accept. That their nation's founding was dependent upon the systematic intimidation and suppression (both official and unofficial) of Loyalist opposition is even harder for 21st Century Americans to recognize. Yet, the executions of British and Loyalist spies played an important part in this vital suppression campaign.

If Americans stop to consider the issue of Revolutionary War espionage executions at all, they tend to focus upon the experiences of two individuals: Nathan Hale and John André. The death sentences of both these men were clearly the result of having been caught, unarmed, conducting classic espionage activities in civilian clothes behind enemy lines. Moreover, the two hangings were carried out by military authorities after both men had admitted (either purposely or by accident) their guilt. This comforting perception of a highly complex phenomenon has been reinforced by many books and articles over the years. As a result, the true scope and magnitude of the espionage executions carried out by Rebel authorities during the Revolution have remained well-hidden. Ironically, Americans have been left with the impression that the British authorities were more likely to execute prisoners for espionage than the Patriots, when in fact the opposite was clearly the case.

The failure to understand the security and Intelligence-based roots of the American victory has caused US citizens to ignore the importance of fear and intimidation as vital means of maintaining public support for the war. Sponsored by both the State courts and the Continental Army, espionage trials and executions played an important role in the security and counterintelligence campaigns against the Loyalists. Ignoring the frequency and the capricious nature of the death sentences imposed upon British and Tory "spies" by Patriot authorities allows modern Americans to avoid one of the harsh realities of their Revolutionary heritage.

Why were Loyalists so Often the Targets of Patriot Espionage Executions?

A popular riddle among Patriots during Revolutionary War posed the question: "What is a Tory?" the answer to which was: "A Tory is a thing whose head is in England, and its body in America, and its neck ought to be stretched." Wallace Brown has quoted as an exaggeration the statement of a wealthy New York merchant, George Folliott, that the Rebels "…made a practice of hanging people up on a slight pretence." None-the-less, even a casual perusal of official documents, newspapers, and the personal correspondence associated with the American side of the war will reveal numerous references to the execution of Loyalists by both legally constituted and ad hoc authorities.

We will never know the exact number of espionage executions that took place during the American War of Independence, let alone how many of them were legally justified. Too many were carried out "in the field" at the discretion of commanders on the scene, or were conducted by angry mobs, rather than as the result of civil or military court proceedings. However, it is possible to make some educated guesses about the relative number of "spy" executions conducted by each side. Wallace Brown's research into the testimony of Loyalists before the post-war Claims Commission discovered only fifteen executions of Loyalists, but he noted that few of these cases involved the process of a legal trial. In his monumental 1959 summary of espionage activities in the American Revolution, John Bakeless cited about the same figure for the number of documented hangings of British spies by American authorities. Such figures have served as conventional wisdom for years, but are clearly too low to be credible.

The Rebels' obsession with espionage threats was a function of their relative military weakness. George Washington had a healthy respect for the kinds of damage that well-placed spies could do. As early as March, 1776 he was pushing for stronger Army counterintelligence efforts, insisting that "There is one evil [of the British] I dread, and that is, their spies. I could wish, therefore, the most attentive watch be kept...I wish a dozen or more of honest and diligent men, were employed...in order to question, cross question, etc.., all such persons as are unknown, and cannot give an account of themselves in a straight and satisfactory manner..."[19]

In fact, Washington was not over-estimating his opponents' use of spies. British intelligence efforts against their American colonists pre-dated the outbreak of hostilities and intensified as the conflict expanded. The role of

Loyalists in this information gathering effort was significant, and as a result British commanders in Boston, Philadelphia, and New York enjoyed some important intelligence successes. However, incomplete information obtained from a wide variety of American and British sources indicates that this aggressive campaign produced a much larger number of Patriot-sponsored espionage executions than Bakeless had estimated. Moreover, the following list of forty-five "spies" executed by American authorities between 1777 and 1782 includes the names of at least fifteen men who, like Thomas Loveless, were Loyalists:

Daniel Strang—Convicted at Peekskill, NY by "a fourteen-officer court" of espionage and recruiting volunteers for a Loyalist company commanded by "the infamous Robert Rogers" (January 27, 1777)

Moses Dunbar—A Connecticut Tory who was granted a Captain's commission in a Provincial Corps unit. He was convicted at Hartford of espionage and recruiting, and executed by hanging (March 19, 1777)

James Molesworth—Convicted as a spy and sentenced to death by a General Court Marshall held at Philadelphia (March 29, 1777)

Simon Mabee—Convicted by General Court Martial at Peekskill, NY of "being employed by the enemy as a spy and for enlisting men into their service," and sentenced to be hanged. (April 14, 1777)

Philip Wickwire and Robert Dunbar—Convicted and sentenced to death by a General Court Martial held in Stillwater, New York for "holding a correspondence with and giving intelligence to the enemy (their names were on two "passes" signed by Loyalist Philip Skene) and of "lurking about our encampments as spies" (August 5, 1777).

Nathaniel Palmer—A Provincial Corps Officer hanged by General Israel Putnam following a trial in August, 1777.

Daniel Taylor—A Lieutenant in the British Army caught carrying a concealed message from Sir Henry Clinton to be delivered to General Burgoyne. He was hanged at Hurley, New York (October, 1777).

Stephen Smith—Convicted "of being a spy" by a General Court Martial, Death sentence confirmed by Major General McDougall (January 6, 1778)

Matthias Colbhart—Convicted of "holding a Correspondence with the Enemy" and "living as a spy among the Continental Troops" (January 13, 1778)

Henry Mansen and Wendal Myer—"An officer in the British Army" and (Myer) "an inhabitant of this county" tried by General Court Martial at Lancaster, Pennsylvania and charged "with being spies, carrying on a traitorous correspondence and supplying the enemy with horses." Although they both made "discoveries" regarding several persons who aided them, they were executed (March 18, 1778).

Thomas Church—One of two spies caught by the Americans just prior to the British evacuation of Philadelphia. Before spying for General Howe, Church had been an Ensign in a Pennsylvania Regiment of the Continental Army (June, 1778)

Thomas Shanks—Convicted at Valley Forge by a Board of General Officers [which included Brigadier General

Benedict Arnold] of "being a spy in the service of the enemy" (June 3, 1778)

David Redding—A former Provincial Corps soldier convicted of espionage and "selling goods to the British" in Bennington, Vermont (June, 1778)

"M.A." and "D.C."—Two British spies executed by the General Orders of General John Sulllivan at Providence, Rhode Island (July 14, 1778)

George Spangler—Convicted of "serving the enemy last winter as a spy and guide through the country" and sentenced to death by a General Court Martial in Philadelphia, (August 15, 1778).

David Farnsworth and John Blair—Tried by Division Court Martial in Danbury, Connecticut and convicted of "being found about the encampment of the United States as Spies" (October 18, 1778)

Edward Jones—A Connecticut Loyalist captured in civilian clothes behind American lines, he was convicted of "guiding enemy troops and espionage" and hanged by order of General Israel Putnam (February, 1779)

Robert Land—Convicted and sentenced to death by a General Court Martial held in Minisink, New York for "spying" and "carrying intelligence to the enemy." (March 17-19, 1779)

Henry Hare—A Tory from Tryon County and "a Lieutenant under Butler," he was captured near Canajoharie, NY, tried by General Court Martial, convicted of spying, and hanged (June 21, 1779)

Sergeant William Newbury—Captured with Henry Hare. Tried as a spy, and executed. (June 21, 1779)

John Clawson, Ludwick Lasick, and John William Hutchinson—Convicted of "lurking as spies in the vicinity of the Army of the United States" (June 18, 1780)

Nathaniel Aberly and Reuben Weeks—Loyalist Provincial Corps soldiers sentenced to be hanged as spies by a General Court Martial held at West Point convened by order of Major General Benedict Arnold (August 20th and 21st, 1780).

Jonathan Loveberry—A Loyalist Provincial Corps soldier sentenced to be hanged as a spy by a General Court Marshall convened at the Township of Bedford at the request of Major General Benedict Arnold—(August 30th-31st, 1780) He later escaped.

John McMullen, Jacob Schell, and James Van Driesen—Charged under the act "subjecting all persons who shall come out from the enemy, and secretly lurk in any part of this State, to trials by Court Martial," they were convicted as British spies executed at Albany (October 27, 1780).

John Mason (a British Soldier) and James Ogden (a Loyalist)—Executed as spies for encouraging the mutiny against General Wayne's Continentals, near Trenton, N.J. (January 10, 1781)

Two unnamed British spies charged with fomenting the mutiny of the Pennsylvania Line At Morristown, New Jersey (Executed on January 11, 1781)

Stephen Edwards—of Eatontown, New Jersey, who had enlisted in a British-sponsored unit in 1778. Captured while clandestinely visiting his wife, he was convicted of spying and was hanged by Rebel militia Captain Joshua Huddy in 1781.

Abraham Ackerly, John Vermillion, and Henry Weeks—Hanged as "spies" at Poughkeepsie, New York. (April 21, 1781)

Solomon Baker—Charged as a "British spy" and hanged at Poughkeepsie, New York. (May 21, 1781).

John Moody—The brother of notorious Loyalist spy James Moody, he was captured, along with a colleague (Laurence Marr, who avoided death by providing information) and was executed in Philadelphia (November 13, 1781)

Joseph Bettis/Bettys--Convicted of "being a spy for General Burgoyne" and sentenced to death on April 6, 1778, but he escaped. Four years later he was captured at Ballstown, NY, and hastily executed at Albany (February, 1782)

John Parker—Captured with Joseph Bettys at Ballstown in March, 1782 and convicted of espionage. Executed at Albany (February, 1782)

Threats of hanging were frequently used to extract information from British and Tory prisoners, and phony hanging rituals and "near" hangings were used as extreme forms of interrogation. The previously mentioned case of Mathew Howard is a good example of this practice. In this regard, it is important to note the comment in Lieutenant Caleb Stark's letter to General Schuyler that the recently-executed spy Thomas Loveless had "made no essential discoveries" prior to his death. This suggests that General Stark and Colonel Van Vechten may have offered Loveless a lesser sentence in exchange for information of intelligence value to the Americans—an offer which Loveless evidently refused. His choice in this matter may have been driven by his own concept of personal honor, or by his sense of duty as a Loyalist officer. In either case, Thomas Loveless probably went to his grave surprised by his verdict but determined to prove to both his Rebel neighbors and his Tory colleagues in Canada, that he was willing to die for the cause he had chosen to defend.

While both sides in the Revolution's "Intelligence War" frequently threatened retaliatory hangings as a means of intimidating each other and protecting captured personnel, the actual number of such executions seems to have been very low. Indeed, the British never made good on such threats, and the Americans only rarely. One of the more famous such incidents involved George Washington's intervention in the case of Joshua Huddy, who had been murdered by New Jersey Loyalists for hanging Tory officer Stephen Edwards. In response, Washington threatened to execute an imprisoned British officer chosen by lot.

Young Alexander Hamilton was appalled by such a threat, and noted in a letter to General Henry Knox that "The death of André could not have been dispensed with; but it must still be viewed at a distance as an act of rigid justice; if we wreak our resentment on an innocent person, it will be suspected that we are too fond of executions. I am persuaded it will have an influence peculiarly unfavorable to the General's character."[20] Under political pressure from his French allies, Washington ultimately did not follow through on his retaliation threat.

Not all hangings of British or Tory spies were conducted on military parade grounds. Many took place on town squares, where the spectacle could be witnessed by the public at large, including those citizens who might already be secretly cooperating with the enemy, or considering changing sides in the future. Thomas Loveless' execution was held in an area close to General Stark's Old Saratoga garrison, on a bluff overlooking the Hudson River. The eyewitness' descriptions of the event make it clear that the hanging drew a considerable crowd, which probably included a number of Loveless' former friends and neighbors.

The ceremony of execution included participation by a clergyman (in Loveless' case a Baptist Minister), who prayed with the condemned man before his sentence was carried out. Loveless' hangman was apparently a Negro slave owned by Philip Schuyler who received items of the deceased man's clothing as partial payment for his services. All of this ritual undoubtedly added to the drama of the event, which in the 18th Century would have been seen by most people as a form of public entertainment.

However, even when conducted as the outcome of due legal processes, military executions of Tories convicted of espionage could be remarkably incompetent and amateurish. Take, for example, Bakeless' description of the February, 1779 hanging of Edward Jones, "…who may have been doing nothing worse than buying beef for the British Army," that was conducted under the command of General Israel Putnam:

"Jones's execution was an unusually ghastly business. He was brought to a twenty-foot gallows just in time to see the bleeding body of a deserter, whose uniform had taken fire from the muskets of the firing squad. Then, as poor Jones stood on the ladder with the noose around his neck, it was discovered that the executioner had lost his nerve and disappeared. From the ground, Israel Putnam shouted to the condemned man to jump—an order with which the spy excusably declined to comply; and eventually the ladder had to be turned over under him, throwing him into the air." [21]

In the same vein, Wallace Brown mentions the attempted execution of Benjamin Whitcuff, a free Negro from Long Island, whose father was serving in the American Army. He had spied for General Howe for two years before he was captured "at Cranbury in the Jerseys": Whitcuff "...maintained that having been caught as a spy he actually hung by his neck for three minutes before being cut down just in time by a detachment of British troops." [22]

How did the Patriot Cause benefit from Public Executions of Loyalist "Spies"?

Successful military operations have always benefited from effective security measures, especially when such measures are self-imposed by high levels of individual security awareness. Fear and indoctrination are equally powerful means of achieving such self-discipline, but in time of war, fear is the best means of ensuring heightened security. When a military force is under pressure and the outcome of its campaign is in doubt, security is more likely to be uppermost in the minds of soldiers of all ranks. But security concerns tend to diminish when wars are protracted, battles infrequent, and garrison duty more tedious.

In the 18th Century in particular, it was in times such as these that espionage executions proved most valuable in reinforcing the security commitments of both officers and enlisted men. Like other forms of publicly-enforced military discipline, the hanging of a spy could drive home to the most dull-witted soldier the penalties for disloyalty and the importance of routine security measures and awareness. As a result, during the War of Independence American commanders tended to see the hanging of spies as a useful means of indoctrinating and motivating their troops.

One does not have to be a sociologist to understand the potential power of rituals such as public hangings, especially when they take place in time of war. 21st Century Americans too often forget the uncertainty and enormous risks under which Patriot America fought its way to independence. Both the leaders and supporters of this unprecedented rebellion fully realized that they were engaged in a "life or death" struggle, the outcome of which was always in doubt. As the levels of sacrifice of blood and treasure rose, so did the fears that losing the war would bring both political and personal ruin for each and every Rebel, and that the hated Tories might emerge from the conflict stronger than ever.

Believing (as Doctor Samuel Johnson reputedly observed) that "Nothing so concentrates a man's powers as the realization that he is about to be hanged," the American authorities probably saw espionage executions as a means of bringing the brutal realities of the war home to both military personnel and to ordinary citizens, especially as some Patriots began to consider switching sides after 1778. A good example of the usefulness of publicly-staged espionage executions is provided by Bakeless' description of the hanging of Thomas Hickey, the Continental Army sergeant who was implicated in the abortive June, 1776 Loyalist conspiracy to kidnap George Washington:

"The military justice of the Revolutionary days moved swiftly. The man was guilty. Give him a day and a half for repentance. Then hang him. Four brigades were ordered to witness the execution and draw from the pinioned, twitching form of Sergeant Thomas Hickey such moral lessons as they might. Others, too, might profit. There were certainly more British agents in New York than anyone had yet discovered. Better give them something to worry about." In the wake of Hickey's execution, Washington informed Congress that he was "...hopeful this example will produce many salutary consequences and deter others from entering into like traitorous practices." [23]

Michael Stephenson has pointed out that pardons or reprieves often played a role in "instructive" military executions. He comments that "The deft use of the reprieve seems to have been a staple of eighteenth-century military and civil punishment," and notes that "In the War of Independence there were many instances of the gruesome ritual of execution, whether by firing squad or hanging, being interrupted with last minute pardons. Such mock executions were used by both armies, and the often drawn-out ritual was quite deliberately manipulated by commanders." [24]

As an example, Stephenson references an incident contained in the journal of Continental soldier Ebenezer Wild, in which ". . . the condemned were marched to the place of execution with their coffins preceding them. With the whole brigade in attendance the sentence was read out, the graves dug, and the coffins placed beside them. Each condemned man knelt 'beside his future resting place in mother earth while the executioners received their orders to load, take aim, and . . .' At this moment a messenger galloped up with a reprieve."[25] While it is unlikely that pardons were granted frequently in cases involving espionage, there are many unconfirmed stories about appeals being made to George Washington by the relatives of condemned Tory spies. Real or not, none of these petitions seems to have been successful.

The documentary record of yeoman farmer Thomas Loveless' Loyalist career reveals that he was a casualty of America's first civil war. In order to win the conventional conflict on the battlefield, at State and County levels Revolutionary America's civil and military leaders resorted to different forms of warfare that involved highly repressive tactics, including the frequent use of hangings as punishment for vaguely-proven charges of espionage. Confused and biased accounts by early historians, plus the ideological demands of American nationalism have created a pernicious mythology about the "bloodlessness" nature of America's Revolution. As a result, few US citizens today understand the extent of the personal bitterness and social upheaval caused by their country's secession from the British Empire.

This reluctance to admit that-- like virtually all of its international successors-- America's revolution required the adoption of highly coercive security measures in order to succeed, has contributed to what critics of US foreign policy call "American exceptionalism"—the naïve assumption that our revolution should serve as a model for the world. By downplaying the social violence which accompanied their own war of independence, the American people have been programmed to ignore the violent, coercive realities of other nations' revolutionary struggles. The assumption that foreign revolutionary movements can be "managed" by moderate political leaders (especially when provided with US support) and achieved without violent social change, has been a hallmark of America's foreign policy since its founding, and has repeatedly led to costly failures.

APPENDIX I:

THOMAS LOVELESS: A FAMILY AND PERSONAL CHRONOLOGY

The name Loveless [Lovelace] is uncommon in the Seventeenth and early Eighteenth century New England colonies. Except for two early New York Colonial Governors, Colonel Francis Lovelace (1668-1673) and his cousin Lord John Lovelace (1708-1709) and their immediate family members, the Lovelace/Loveless name is not seen again in New England until a group of Loveless names appears in the records of Westerly and Kingstown, Rhode Island between 1712 and 1747. This evidence suggests that the few Loveless/Lovelace families that do appear, especially within the same colony or community, are closely related.

About 1716, CT:	James Loveless (the father of the "Tory Spy") is born (based upon his age at the time of his militia enlistment in 1758)
Dec. 23, 1737, RI:	James Loveless of North Kingstown, R.I, "Cordwinder," sells 90 acres to Joseph Loveless of Westerly, (RI), "husbandman."
Before Jun. 27, 1738, RI:	James Loveless marries Lydia_____.
Jun. 27, 1738, RI:	Washington Co. Court of Common Pleas records:

	Christopher Curtis of South Kingstown, (SK) R.I. "vintner," Plaintiff vs. James Loveless & his wife Lydia Loveless of SK, "cordwainer," defendant.
Dec. 11, 1738, RI:	SK Town Council votes to cite James Loveless & others Who have "lately come into SK" to appear before them to give reasons why they should remain in town.
Jan. 8, 1738/9, RI:	SK Town Council votes that James Loveless has gained a settlement in South Kingstown, RI.
1739-1740	Thomas Loveless (the future "Tory Spy") is born. (He was 42 years old when executed in October, 1781)
1742, RI:	James Loveless junior is born (based upon his age at enlistment in 1760).
Feb. 1745/46	James Loveless senior and his family arrive in Dutchess County, NY. (He is on the tax lists from 1745/46-1758).
Jun. 24, 1746-Oct. 31, 1747:	James Loveless senior is an enlisted soldier in Capt. James

	Church's Co. in the Regt. of Foot of Col. Elisha Williams, Raised in the colony of CT, New London, for his Majesty's service in an expedition against Canada (in King George's War).
Oct. 13, 1756, NY:	James Lovelace? listed on muster roll of Capt. Nathan Hawley's Seventh Co. of Col. Nathan Whiting's 3rd Rgmt. James is Stationed "at Albany without leave." Roll signed on this date at "Camp at Fort William Henry."
Apr. 19, 1758, NY:	James Lovelace? Age 42 (b. 1716), Cordwainer, born in CT, enlisted in a company of provincials in the pay of the Province of NY, for Dutchess County, commanded by Joseph Crane, Esq.
1760	James Lovelace died (name appears on a 1760 list of "Deceased soldiers, 1756-62, whose heirs received the pay due them at the time of their death."
1760, NY:	Thomas "Lovelace" appears for the first time in Dutchess Co., NY. He is on the Southern Precinct (modern day Putnam

	Co.) tax lists from 1760-1771, and then on the lists of Fredericksburg (partitioned from Southern Precinct) through 1773. If James was the father of Thomas, it is plausible that Thomas took over the farm after his father died in this same year.
Apr. 4, 1760, NY:	Joshua Loveless age 17, [b.1743, son of Joseph, and probable cousin of Thomas, the "Tory Spy"], laborer, born in RI, enlists in the Dutchess County Militia, (Capt. Livingston's Co.)
Apr. 15, 1760, NY:	James Loveless [brother of the "Tory Spy"], age 18, farmer, born in RI, enlists in Dutchess County Militia (Capt. Bogardus' Co.)
Abt. 1761	Thomas Loveless, ("Tory Spy") marries Lois_____.
Abt. 1762:	James Loveless (eldest son of the "Tory Spy") is born, (based on his age of 19 at the time of his father's death in 1781, as stated in his 1786 claim for compensation from The Crown.
1765, NY:	Both Thomas Loveless & Joseph

	Loveless were named as creditors in a suit brought by Ithiel Towner in Dutchess Co.
May 1, 1768, NY:	Thomas Loveless and Josiah Benjamin were in possession of a farm in lot 8, [present town of Southeast] in Phillips Patent.
July 9, 1768, NY:	Thomas Loveless was a customer at the Sleight Store in Beekman, Dutchess Co., where he bought rum, two hats and coffee for 14s 71/2p.
April 25, 1769, NY:	Thomas paid his account at the Sleight Store with 3 bushels and 6 quarts of wheat and cash, total L1/9/1.
1774, NY:	Thomas "Lovelace" disappears from the tax lists in Dutchess County.
1775, NY:	Thomas Loveless (the "Tory Spy") purchases "100 acres of land near Saratoga" from Cornelus Tabout and 100 acres of "wild land" in Jessup's Patent.
Bet. 1762 and 1776:	"Thomas the Spy" and his wife produce seven surviving

	children (five boys and two girls).
November, 1776:	Thomas Loveless joins "The King's Loyal Americans," a Provincial Corps unit raised by the Jessup brothers.
October, 1777:	Loveless provides vital logistics support to Burgoyne's Army, is forced to surrender, and is paroled to Canada, where his family had already sought refuge.
1778-1779:	Along with the rest of the King's Loyal Americans, Loveless is employed in "works" duties, building roads, fortifications, and housing for refugee Loyalist families.
Late 1779:	Loveless volunteers for "secret service" missions, guiding British troops on operations behind American lines.
1780--1781:	Thomas Loveless begins to carry out solo "secret service" missions. In 1781 he joins the TSS," conducting "scouts" until the capture of his party at Old Saratoga, New York on September 25th,. Convicted of espionage, he is executed by hanging on October 8th.

APPENDIX II:

PHOTOCOPIES OF AMERICAN DOCUMENTS CAPTURED BY THE TORY SECRET SERVICE, AND SIGNED BY:

--John Hancock

--George Washington

--Patrick Henry

--Thomas Jefferson

--Benjamin Franklin

--Silas Dean

--General Jean Baptise Rochambeau

--Governor George Clinton

John Hancock

The DELEGATES of the UNITED STATES of New-Hampshire, Massachusetts, Rhode-Island, Connecticut, New-York, New-Jersey, Pennsylvania, Delaware, Maryland, Virginia, North-Carolina, South-Carolina, and Georgia, TO *Monsieur Mottin de la Balme* —

WE, reposing especial Trust and Confidence in your Patriotism, Valour, Conduct and Fidelity, DO, by these Presents, constitute and appoint you to be *Inspector General of the Cavalry of the Armies with the Rank and Pay of Colonel* — in the Army of the United States, raised for the Defence of American Liberty, and for repelling hostile Invasion thereof. You are therefore carefully and diligently to discharge the Duty of *Cavalry* by doing and performing all manner of Things thereunto belonging. And we do strictly charge and require all Officers and Soldiers under your Command, to be obedient to your Orders of *Cavalry* — And you are to observe and follow such Orders and Directions from Time to Time, as you shall receive from this or a future Congress of the United States, or Committee of Congress for that Purpose appointed, or Commander in Chief for the Time being of the Army of the United States, or any other your superior Officer, according to the Rules and Discipline of War, in Pursuance of the Trust reposed in you. This Commission to continue in Force until revoked by this or a future Congress.

DATED at *Philadelphia* ye *July 8, 1777*.

By Order of the CONGRESS,

John Hancock PRESIDENT

Cha Thomson secy

George Washington

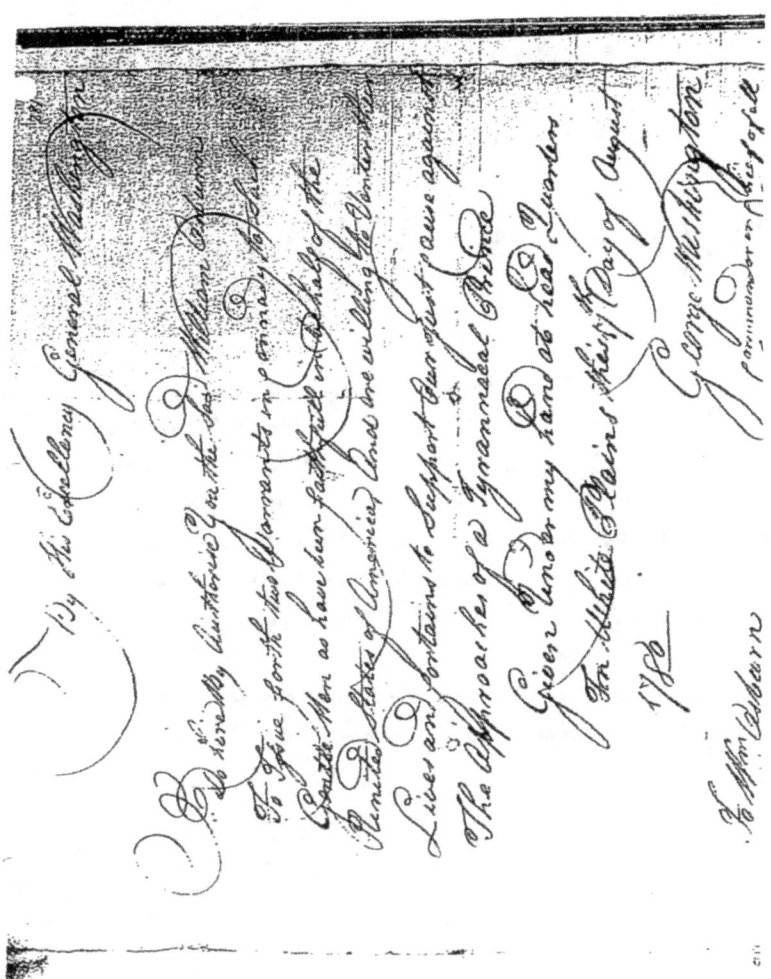

By His Excellency General Washington

You are hereby authorized on the last William Cabeman
To Issue forth two Warrants in Country to such
Continental Men as have been faithful in behalf of the
United States of America and are willing to Volunteer
Lives and Fortunes to Support our present ensueing against
The Approaches of a Tyrannical Force

Given Under my hand at Head Quarters
at White Plains this 11th Day of August
1782

George Washington
Commander in Chief of all

To Wm Cabeman

Patrick Henry

ealth of Virginia

Greeting:

which is repofed in your Patriotifm, Fidelity, Courage, and good inted *Major* — of Militia in the County of *Monongalia* Duty of *a Major* — of the Militia, by doing and pay a ready Obedience to all Orders and Inftructions which from er of this State for the Time being, or any of your fuperiour General Affembly. All Officers and Soldiers under your Command and to aid you in the Execution of this Commiffion, according to

mmonwealth, at *Williamsburg*, under the Seal of the Commonwealth, Year of the Commonwealth, Annoq. Dom. 1779

Thomas Jefferson

silver or paper dollars were intended, and in what rate of depreciation they were estimated. The price of commodities in hard money or paltry will serve as a standard for you to fix the rate of depreciation. I must put you on your guard not to confide too much in Shannon as he has proved here that it would be misplaced.

Many reasons have occurred lately, for declining the expedition against Detroit. want of men, want of money, scarcity of provisions, are of themselves sufficient, but there are others more cogent which cannot be trusted to a letter. we therefore wish you to decline that object, and consider the taking post on the Mississippi and chastising the hostile Indians as the business of this summer.

There is reason to apprehend insurrection among some discontented inhabitants (Tories) on our South Western frontier. I would have you give assistance on the shortest warning to that quarter should you be applied to by the militia officers, to whom I wrote on the subject. nothing can so soon produce so dangerous a diversion of our force as a circumstance of that kind if not crushed in the infancy.

The withdrawing the whole of your men from the Illinois country seems very expedient & necessary unless there be powerful reasons against it unknown to us. Colo Todd I hope will get their militia into such training and subordination as that they will be in no danger from the Indians.

I am Sir with great respect
Your most humble servt

To
G R Clark

Benjamin Franklin

known for that service. As he has otherwise an excellent Character, I take the liberty of recommending him to my friends as a Stranger of merit worthy of their Notice and to the Congress as an Officer who if employed may greatly serve a cause which he has sincerely at heart. With great respect I have the honor to be, Sir, Your most obedient Humble Servant

B Franklin

Cha Thomson

Silas Dean

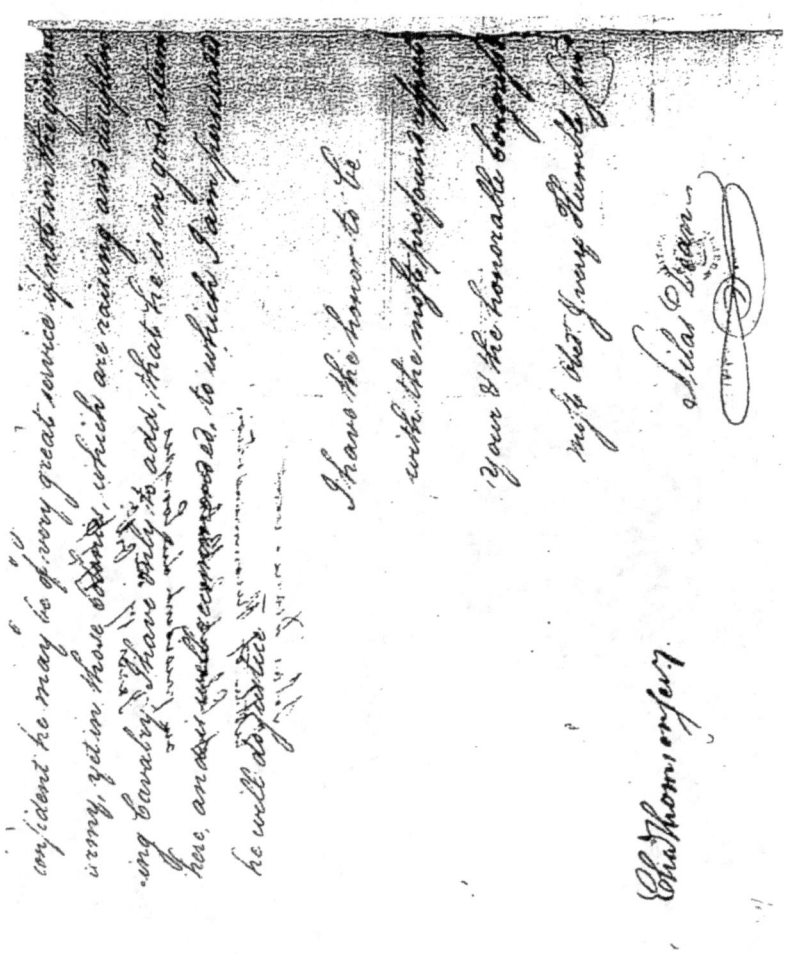

confident he may be of very great service if put on that footing
is very get in those others, which are more or less
ing Cavalry. I have only to add, that he is in good health
here, and anxiously wishes to be employed, to which family views
he will do justice.

I have the honor to be
with the most profound respect

Your & the honorable Congress
most obedient very humble serv.

Silas Deane

Cha. Thomson esq.

General Jean Baptise Rochambeau

Governor George Clinton

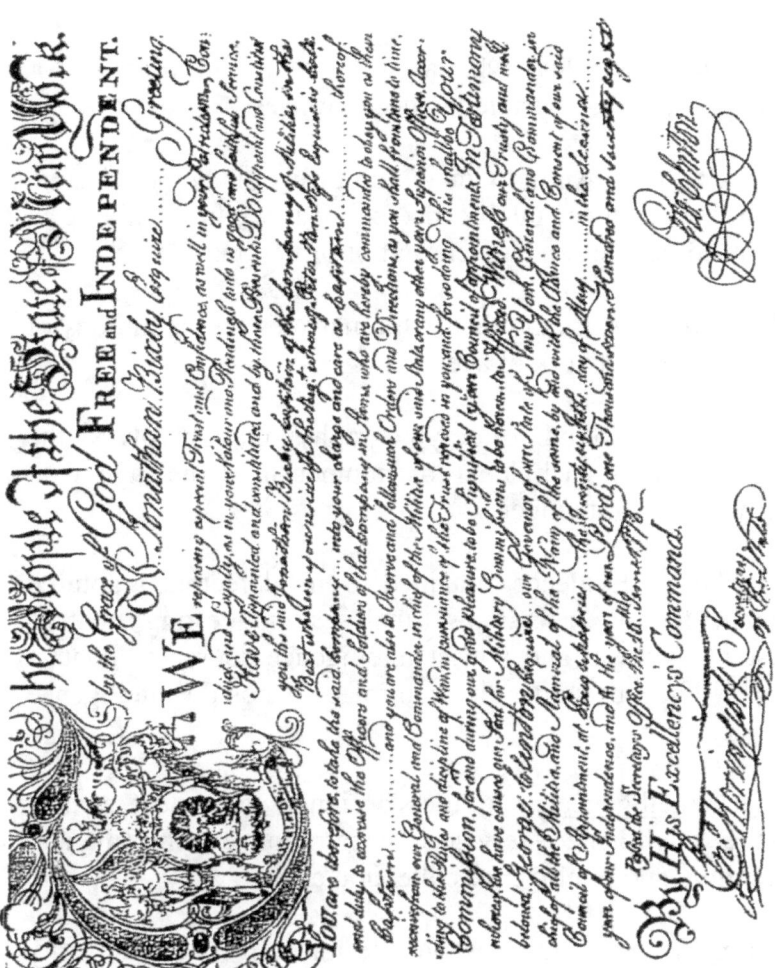

APPENDIX III:

A GLOSSARY OF RELEVANT INTELLIGENCE TERMINOLOGY:

Agent: An individual who acts to obtain information for intelligence or counterintelligence purposes.

Agent-in-Place: An individual who offers his/her services to another country (or intelligence service) while remaining in his job so that he can pass current information.

Case Officer: An individual who manages the operations of an agent or a network of agents.

Cipher: A method of cryptography that involves the replacement of each letter or number in a message with another letter or number.

CI "Flags." Evidence obtained from defectors, captured documents, or operations analyses suggesting that a presumably loyal and honest intelligence source or contact may, in fact, be under the control of a hostile intelligence service.

Counterintelligence: Activities designed to protect against hostile intelligence services' penetration, disinformation, deception, and intelligence collection efforts.

Courier: A messenger responsible for delivery and security of classified documents or other classified material.

Cover: Protective measures used by Intelligence personnel or organizations too prevent their identification with clandestine activities.

Covert Action: Activities carried out in a concealed or clandestine manner in order to make it difficult to trace the activities back to the sponsoring intelligence service.

Dead Drop: A prearranged location for depositing and picking up messages or money in a clandestine manner.

Deception: Measures designed to mislead an enemy Intelligence service by manipulating, distorting, or falsifying information to induce a mistaken perception.

Defector: A person who claims to repudiate his country and may be in possession of information of value to the country to which he defects.

Denied Area: An area containing targets of intelligence value, but inaccessible to most human source collection operations due to enemy security countermeasures..

Disinformation: The creation and dissemination of misleading or false information to discredit or confuse an opposing Intelligence service.

False Flag: A hostile intelligence officer who misrepresents himself as a citizen of a friendly country or a member of its Intelligence service.

Hard Target: A foreign country or intelligence service which is extremely difficult to penetrate.

Human source, or "HUMINT" Operations: Intelligence collection which primarily makes use of human beings to gain access to denied information.

Indications and Warning (I&W): Intelligence activities intended to detect and provide warning about short-term military threats to a country or its allies.

Penetration: The recruitment or placement of agents within an Intelligence organization in order to gain access to its secrets.

Safe House: A building or other structure used by an intelligence service to support its clandestine or covert activities.

Secret Writing: The use "invisible" organic inks such as lemon juice or vinegar to conceal written messages.

Special Operations: A wide variety of paramilitary activities, which can include punitive raids, sabotage, and military reconnaissance.

Strategic Intelligence: Intelligence Information employed in the formulation of long-term national-level policy and military plans.

Tactical Intelligence: Intelligence used to plan or support short-term military operations at the theater or unit level. It is concerned with the enemy's short-term capabilities and immediate intentions.

Tradecraft: Proven techniques—such as the use of concealment devices, encrypted communications, and dead drops--used in espionage operations.

NOTES

Chapter 1:

1. The Asa Fitch MSS, Vol. 1, p. 78, the Account of Jacob Bitely.

2. Michael Kammen, "The American Revolution as a Crise de Conscience: The Case of New York," in Richard M. Jellison (Ed.) <u>Society, Freedom and Conscience: The American Revolution in Society, Freedom Virginia, Massachusetts, and New York</u>. pp. 188-189.

3. Roger Kaplan. "The Hidden War: British Intelligence Operations During the American Revolution," <u>The William & Mary Quarterly</u>, Vol. 47, no. 1, pg. 117.

4. Esmond Wright. "The New York Loyalists: A Cross-section of Colonial Society," in East and Judd (Eds.) <u>The Loyalist Americans: A Focus on Greater New York</u>. pg. 79.

5. Wallace Brown. <u>The King's Friends: The Composition and Motives of the American Loyalist Claimants.</u> pg. 81.

6. Wright. "The New York Loyalists." pg. 80.

7. Piers Macksey. <u>The War for America, 1775-1783.</u> pg. 526

8. See: Philip Katcher and Michael Youens. <u>The American Provincial Corps, 1775-1784</u>. pg. 7.

9. The Haldimand Papers, Reel 81, July 26, 1779.

10. Janice Potter-Mackinnon. While the Women Only Wept. pg. 22.

Chapter Two:

1. Stephan Stratch. Some Sources for the Study of the Loyalist and Canadian Participation in the Military Campaign of Lieutenant-General John Burgoyne, 1777. pg. 4.

2. Kaplan. "The Hidden War," pg. 122.

3. See: Stefan Bielinski, "Albany County," and Paul R. Huey, "Charlotte County," in Tiedemann & Fingerhut, (Eds.) The Other New York: The American Revolution Beyond New York City, 1763-1787. pp. 155-178 and 119-222.

4. Brown. The King's Friends. pg. 106.

5. Henry Steele Commager and Richard B. Morris (Eds.) The Spirit of Seventy-six: The Story of the American Revolution as Told by Participants. pg 333.

6. Ibid., pg. 347.

7. Don R. Gerlach. Proud Patriot. Pg. 207.

8. Whisker. The American Colonial Militia, Vol. IV., pg. 30.

9. The Haldimand Papers, Reel 92, pg. 226.

10. Hazel Mathews. <u>Frontier Spies: The British Secret Service, Northern Department, During the Revolutionary War</u>. pg. 86.

11. Paul R. Huey. "Charlotte County," in Tiedemann & Fingerhut, <u>The Other New York</u>. pg. 204.

12. Sung Bok Kim "The Impact of Class Relations and Warfare in the American Revolution: the New York Experience," <u>The Journal of American History</u>, Vol. 69, no. 2 (September, 1982), pg. 345.

13. See: Wallace Brown. "The American Farmer During the Revolution: Rebel or Loyalist?" <u>Agricultural History.</u> Vol. 42, no. 4 (October, 1968), pp. 334-338.

14. <u>The Haldimand Papers</u>. Reel 85.

15. Potter-Mackinnon. <u>While The Women Only Wept.</u> pg. 39.

16. Mary Beacock Fryer. <u>King's Men: The Soldier Founders of Ontario.</u> pp. 184-185.

17. As quoted in Fryer. <u>King's Men</u>. pg. 187.

18. <u>The Haldimand Papers. Memorials from the Provincial Corps and Loyalists</u>, Vol. I, B-214).

19. <u>Ibid.,</u> Vol. I, B-162..

20. (For a well-illustrated summary of the evolution of KLA uniforms, see: Chartrand, René, American Loyalist Troops, 1775-1784, pg. 45 and Plate E)

21. Brown. The King's Friends. pp. 78-80.

22. Potter-MacKinnon. While the Women Only Wept. pg. xv.

Chapter Three:

1. As quoted in Caleb Stark. Memoir and Official Correspondence of Gen. John Stark. pp. 51 and 53.

2. Ibid., pg. 69.

3. As quoted in Catherine S. Crary., The Price of Loyalty: Tory Writings from the Revolutionary Era. pp. 303-304.

4. Katcher. The American Provincial Corps. pg. 11.

5. Letter of August 20, 1777 to Germaine. Whitehall., November 1, 1777 [Letters]

6. As quoted in Crary. The Price of Loyalty. pg. 306.

7. Mark M. Boatner III. Encyclopedia of the American Revolution, 3rd Edition, pg. 689.

8. As quoted in Fryer. King's Men. Pg. 194.

9. As quoted in Mathews. <u>Frontier Spies.</u> pg. 31.

10. See: <u>The Haldimand Papers</u>, Reel 85.

11. <u>Ibid.</u>, Reel 81.

Chapter Four:

1. John Grenier. <u>The First Way of War</u>: pg. 162.

2. <u>Ibid.</u>, pg. 164.

3. Flick. <u>Loyalism in New York During the American Revolution</u>, pg. 65.

4. Stephan Beilinski. "Albany County" in Tiedemann & Fingerhut (Eds.) The Other New New York. pg. 165.

5. Palstits. <u>Minutes</u> Vol. II, pp. 41-42.

6. <u>Ibid.</u>, pg. 42.

7. Crary. <u>The Price of Loyalty.</u> pp. 225-226.

8. See table in Philip Ranlet. <u>The New York Loyalists</u>, pg. 149.

9. Palstits. <u>Minutes,</u> Vol. I, pg. 46.

10. Spaulding. <u>New York in the Critical Period, 1783-1789.</u> pg. 123.

11. Palstits. <u>Minutes,</u> Vol. I, pg. 97.

12. Ibid., pg. 109

13. Ibid., pg. 128

14. Ibid., pp. 147-148.

15. Ibid., pg. 238

16. Palstits. Minutes. Vol. II, pg.405

17. Ibid., pp. 417-418

18. Ibid., pg. 539

19. Ibid., pg. 554

20. Ibid., pp. 600-601

21. The Massachusetts Spy. June 14, 1775.

22. The Haldimand Papers. Memorials from the Provincial Corps and Loyalists, Vol. I, B-214)

23. Palstits. Minutes. Vol.I, pp.. 142-143.

24. Ibid., Vol. II, pg. 304

25. Ibid., pp. 454-455

26. Ibid., pg. 702.

27. As quoted in Potter-Mackinnon. The Women Only Wept. pg. 40.

28. Palstits. Minutes. Vol. II, pp. 762-763

29. The Haldimand Papers. Reel 81.

30. Fryer. King's Men. pg. 180.

31. As quoted in Ibid., pg. 225.

32. The Haldimand Papers. Reel 81.

33. Fryer. King's Men. pg. 15.

34. Potter-Mackinnon. "Loyalists and Community," pg. 182.

35. Potter-Mackinnon. While the Women Only Wept. pg. 118.

36. Fryer. King's Men. pg. 16.

37. Censuses of Canada, 1665-1871. Statistics of Canada, Vol. Fourth [sic], pp. 14-16.

Chapter Five:

1. Mackesy. The War for America. pg. 525.

2. Haldimand Papers, Reel 232. Letter dated August 1, 1767

3. Haldimand Papers. (Reel 83) December 10, 1780, Robert Mathews to Edward Jessup.

4. Ibid., (Reel 83), January 1, 1781, Mathews to Edward Jessup.

5. Ibid., (Reel 91), January 22, 1781. Mathews to Justus Sherwood.

6. Mathews. <u>Frontier Spies</u>. Pg. 109.

7. Haldimand Papers. (Reel 100) June 5, 1782.

8. <u>Idem.,</u>

9. See: William L. Stone. <u>Life of Joseph Brant</u>. pg. 153.

10. The University of Michigan, William L. Clements Library, <u>Sir Henry Clinton Papers</u>, Vol. 160, item 6.

11. Pemberton. "The British Secret Service," pg. 135.

12. <u>Haldimand Papers</u>. (Reel 100)

13. <u>Ibid.,</u> (Reel 91C), Mathews to Smyth, May 18, 1782.

14. Ibid., (Reel 92)

15. <u>Ibid.,</u> (Reel 81), Loveless to Mathews, September 2, 1780.

16. <u>Haldimand Papers</u>, (Reel 92) Sherwood to Mathews, May 25, 1781.

17. <u>Ibid.,</u> (Reel 92) Sherwood to Mathews, June 2, 1781.

18. The Archives of Ontario. <u>The Edward Jessup Papers,</u> MS 521., Reel F-485.

19. <u>Haldimand Papers</u>. (Reel 81), Letter of Benjamin Patterson, January 7, 1782.

20. (The original copy of this letter was obtained from the French and reprinted in the November 11, 1779 issue of <u>The Massachusetts Spy</u>).

21. See: Mathews. <u>Frontier Spies</u>. pg. 78.

22. <u>Haldimand Papers.</u> (Reel 89) Sherwood to Smyth, April 5, 1782.

23. Winston Adler (Ed.). <u>Their Own Voices.</u> pp. 104-105.

24. <u>Haldimand Papers</u>. (Reel 83), Mathews to Smyth, April 30, 1781.

25. Samuel Eliot Morison. <u>John Paul Jones, A Sailor's Biography.</u> pp. 324-325.

26. <u>Haldimand Papers</u>. (Reel B-176) pg. 293.

27. <u>Ibid.,</u> (Reel B-179-III) pg. 185.

28. John Bakeless. <u>Turncoats, Traitors and Heroes</u>. Pg. 28.

29. <u>Haldimand Papers</u>. (Reel 81) Letter to General Haldimand, October 22, 1780.

30. <u>Ibid.,</u> (Reel 92) pg. 245

31. As cited in Ian Pemberton, "The British Secret Service in the Champlain Valley During the

Haldimand Negotiations, 1780-1783," <u>Vermont History,</u> Vol. 44 (1976), pg. 134.

32. As quoted in James Flexner. <u>The Traitor and the Spy</u>. pg. 384.

33. Katcher. <u>The American Provincial Corps.</u> pg. 26.

34. As quoted in Morton and Penn Borden (Eds.) <u>The American Tory</u>. pg. 61.

Chapter Six:

1. Caleb Stark. <u>Memoir.</u> pg. 276, footnote.

2. Based upon information contained in <u>The Regimental Order Book of the Loyal Rangers,</u> formerly in the possession of Lt. Col. H.D. Jessup of Prescott, Ontario, CN.

3. As quoted in Stone. <u>The Life of Joseph Brant</u>. pp. 152-153.

4. <u>Haldimand Papers</u>. B-180, pg. 348.

5. Palstits. <u>Minutes.</u> Vol. II, pp. 686-687.

6. <u>Ibid.,</u> pp. 55-56.

7. <u>Ibid.,</u> pp. 25-26.

8. <u>Ibid.,</u> pg. 26

9. <u>Ibid.,</u> Vol. II, pg. 696.

10. <u>Ibid.,</u> pg. 735.

11. James Moody. <u>Lieutenant James Moody's Narrative of His Exertions and Sufferings in the Cause of Government, Since the Year 1776.</u> London, 1783. pg. 55.

12. <u>Haldimand Papers</u>. (Reel 92) Sherwood to Mathews, May 25, 1781.

Chapter Seven:

1. Gerlach. "Philip Schuyler and the New York Frontier in 1781," pg. 333.

2. Hastings. <u>The Clinton Papers,</u> Vol. VI, pp. 771-772.

3. Additional Manuscripts, <u>Haldimand Papers</u>. 21794/85-86, as quoted in Gerlach, "Philip Schuyler and the New York Frontier," pg. 348.

4. Pemberton, "The British Secret Service," pp. 134-135.

5. Fryer. <u>John Walden Meyers, Loyalist Spy.</u> pg. 145.

6. <u>Haldimand Papers.</u> (Reel 81) Smyth to Mathews, September 2, 1781.

7. As quoted in Gerlach. "Philip Schuyler and the New York Frontier," pg. 354.

8. Stone. <u>The Life of Joseph Brant</u>. pg. 178.

9. John Benson Lossing The Field Book of the Revolution. Vol. I, pg. 32.

10. Haldimand Papers. (Reel 81) David Jones to Smyth, August 20, 1781.

11. Idem.,

12. Idem.,

13. Haldimand Papers. (Reel 178) pp. 451-456.

14. Caleb Stark. Memoir. pg. 325.

15. Haldimand Papers. (Reel 91) Mathew to Sherwood, September 20, 1781.

16. Caleb Stark, Memoir. pg. 63-64.

17. As quoted in Ibid, pg. 69.

18. As quoted in Ibid., pg. 173.

19. As quoted in Ibid., pp. 184-185.

20. Haldimand Papers. (Reel B-178). p. 102.

21. Caleb Stark. Memoir. pp. 250-251.

22. Isabel Tarant. New Hampshire: Years of Revolution. pg. 12.

23. Boatner. (Ed.) The Encyclopedia of the American Revolution, 3rd Edition, pg. 1053.

Chapter Eight:

1. Haldimand Papers. (Reel 91) pg. 113.

2. Fishkill (Dutchess County, NY) newspaper article of October 4, 1781.

3. Palstits. Minutes. Vol. I, pp. 406 [Note], and Vol. II, pp. 704-705, and 766-767.

4. Lossing. Pictorial Handbook of the Revolution. Vol. I, pg 93.

5. S. De Witt Bloodgood. (Ed.) The Sexagenary: or, Reminiscences of the American Revolution. pp. 195-198.

6. Caleb Stark. Memoir. pg. 259.

7. Ibid., pp. 259-260.

8. The Fishkill article was subsequently reported in the Massachusetts Continental Journal (October 11, 1781) and the Pennsylvania Evening Post (October 15, 1781)

9. As contained in Bloodgood. The Sexagenary. pg. 109.

10. Lossing, Pictorial Fieldbook of the Revolution, Vol I, pg. 93.

11. Caleb Stark. Memoir. pg. 85.

12. Bloodgood. The Sexagenary. pp. 199-200.

13. <u>Haldimand Papers</u>. (Reel 91) Sherwood to Haldimand, October 18, 1781.

14. <u>Ibid.</u>, (Reel 91) Mathews to Smyth, November 1, 1781.

15. New York Public Library. <u>The Philip Schuyler Papers.</u> Box 35, Reel 17.

16. Hastings. <u>The George Clinton Papers</u>. Vol. VII, pp. 391-392.

17. William Abbatt (Ed.) <u>Memoirs of Major-General William Heath, by Himself.</u> pg. 15.

Chapter Nine:

1. Caleb Stark. <u>Memoir.</u> pg. 265.

2. Hastings. <u>The George Clinton Papers</u>. Vol. VII, pg. 391.

3. Caleb Stark. <u>Memoir.</u> pg. 271.

4. Ibid., pg. 294.

5. Ibid., pg. 281.

6. Ibid., pg. 286.

7. Ibid., pg. 303.

8. <u>Haldimand Papers</u>. (Reel 88) pg. 123.

9. Ibid., (Reel 91B) pg. 176.

10. Ibid., (B-177-I, Reel 89) pg. 179.

11. Ibid., (Reel 91D) Mathews to Smyth, August 19, 1782.

12. Ibid., (Reel 88) pp. 123-124.

13. Ibid., (Reel 91D) Mathews to Smyth, September, 1782.

14. G. J. A. O'Toole. Honorable Treachery. pp. 64-65.

15. Haldimand Papers. (Reel 91C) Sherwood to Mathews, May 24, 1782 and Mathews to Sherwood, May 28, 1782.

16. Ibid., (Reel 91B) Haldimand to Smyth, pg. 149.

17. Ibid., (Reel 92B) Smyth to Mathews, pg. 165.

18. Ibid., (Reel 91C) pg. 218.

19. Idem., Mathews to Smyth, May 18, 1782.

20. Idem., Mathews to Sherwood, May 21, 1782.

21. Haldimand Papers. (Reel 89) B-177-I, pg. 170.

22. Palstits. Minutes. Vol III, pp. 548, 699-700, 736, and 764.

23. Stone. The Life of Joseph Brant. pg. 12.

24. Ibid., Vol. II, pp. 212-213.

25. Ibid., Vol. II, pg. 213.

26. From Jean H Higby's poem 'The Rime of the Ancient Traveler." (Brookside Museum of the Saratoga Historical Society)

27. <u>Haldimand Papers</u>. (Reel 84) Letter from Mathews, February 3, 1782.

28. Ibid., (Reel 83) Haldimand to Sherwood and Smyth, January 31, 1782.

29. Ibid., Letter from Mathews to Major Edward Jessup, October 14, 1782.

30. Ibid., (Reel 85) document dated March 1, 1782.

31. Ibid., Series B, Vol. 178, pp. 187-190.

32. See: <u>The Public Archives of Canada, War Office Records,</u> M.G. 13, W.O. 28 Vol.10, part 4).

33. See: Ibid., (B-167), pg. 398 and Reel 85, Early 1783.

Chapter Ten:

1. As quoted in Jeanne Winston Adler. <u>In the Path of War</u>. pg. 115.

2. All six of these examples were obtained from photocopies of original documents held by the US National Archives (NARA), <u>Revolutionary War Pension and Bounty Land Warrants,</u> M804.

3. Heath. <u>Memoirs</u>. pp. 287 and 289.

4. Sylvester. <u>History of Saratoga County.</u> pg. 28.

5. William Stone. <u>Visits to the Saratoga Battle-Grounds, 1780-1880.</u> pg. 77.

6. Brandow, <u>The Story of Old Saratoga.</u> pg. 101.

7. Letter from Francis Ronalds, Superintendent of the Morristown National Historical Park to Superintendent, Saratoga National Historical Park, dated June 25, 1947.

8. US National Park Service Case Incident Record #870120, concerning "reburial of human remains," dated June 18, 1987.

9. H. C. Burleigh. <u>The Bones of David Redding</u>. pg. 5.

10. See: John Spargo. <u>David Redding: Queen's Ranger, Who was Hanged in Bennington, Vermont June 11, 1778.</u>

11. Lossing. <u>The Pictorial Field-Book of the Revolution.</u> Vol. I, pp. 92-93.

12. Lorenzo Sabine. <u>Biographical Sketches of Loyalists of the American Revolution</u>. pg. 91.

13. A.W. Holden. <u>A History of the Town of Queensbury.</u> pg. 431.

14. Caleb Stark. <u>Memoir.</u> pp. 84-85.

15. Ibid., pg. 86.

16. Stone. <u>Visits to the Saratoga Battle-Grounds</u>. pg. 285.

17. Mahoney and Mahoney. <u>Gallantry in Action</u>. pg. 228.

Chapter Eleven:

1. As contained in Coldham, (Ed.) <u>American Loyalist Claims.</u> pg. 388.

2. <u>Haldimand Papers</u>. (Reel 81) Sherwood to Mathews, December 5, 1781.

3. Ibid., (Reel 83) Mathews to Unknown, December 10, 1781.

4. Ibid., (Reel 81) Major John Nairne to Haldimand, January 27, 1782.

5. Ibid., (Reel 82) Letter of Edward Jessup, April 12, 1783.

6. Idem., pg. 387.

7. Mathews. <u>Frontier Spies.</u> pg. 198.

8. Fryer. <u>Rolls of the Provincial Corps</u>. pp. 82-83.

9. Fryer. <u>The King's Men</u>. pg. 300.

10. W. Stewart Wallace. <u>The United Empire Loyalists</u>. pg. 46.

11. The Dictionary of Canadian Biography. "Sir Frederick Haldimand," pg 16.

12. Wallace. The United Empire Loyalists. pp. 45-46.

13. Maya Jasanoff. "The Other side of the Revolution: Loyalists in the British Empire," The William and Mary Quarterly, Vol. LXV, no. 2 (April, 2008), pp211 and 222.

14. Brown. The King's Friends. pp. 78 and 86.

15. Flick. Loyalism in New York. Pp. 212-213

16. Alexander Fraser. (Archivist) 2nd Report of the Bureau of Archives for the Province of Ontario, 1904. No. 49, pp. 152-153.

17. Fryer. King's Men. pg. 301.

18. Spaulding. New York in the Critical Period 1783-1789. pp. 123-124.

19. Caleb Stark. Memoir. pg. 309.

20. Ibid., pg. 137.

21. Roger Brown. The Republic in Peril: 1812., pg. 102

22. Bloodgood (Ed.). The Sexagenary. pp. 139-140

23. Fryer. John Walden Meyers. pg. 254.

24. Tom Pocock. Nelson's Women. pg. 195.

25. Haldimand Papers. (Reel 178) pp. 330-331

26. Mathews. Frontier Spies. pg. 113.

27. Flick. Loyalism in New York. pg. 213.

28. Certificate of the Board, dated Council-Chamber, Quebec, February 17, 1789.

Chapter Twelve:

1. Fryer. King's Men. pg. 204.

2. Caleb Stark. Memoir. pg. 254.

3. Idem.

4. Caleb Stark. Memoir. pp. 256-257.

5. Ibid., pg. 257.

6. Gerlach. "Philip Schuyler and the New York Frontier in 1781," pp. 360-361.

7. Philip Schuyler Papers, Box 35, Reel 17, "Letters Received, 1781-1785," October 8, 1781.

8. Gerlach. Proud Patriot. pg. 463.

9. Caleb Stark. Memoir. pp. 228-229.

10. Ibid., pg. 233.

11. Ibid., pp. 236-237

12. Ibid., p. 262.

13. Fernow. New York in the Revolution. passim.

14. Moody. Narrative. pp. 32-33.

Chapter Thirteen:

1. Bakeless. Turncoats, Traitors and Heroes. pp. 19-20.

2. State of New York. Journal of the Provincial Convention, Vol. I, Pt. 2, pp. 856-857.

3. Palstits. Minutes. Vol. I, pg. 59.

4. Idem., pg. 46.

5. Berger. Broadsides and Bayonets. pg. 166.

6. Palstits. Minutes. Vol III, pp. 223, 239, 286.

7. As quoted in D. Hamilton. A History of Sullivan County, New Hampshire. Philadelphia, 1886.

8. The David Library of the American Revolution. no. 2206, Washington to Livingston, January 12, 1782.

9. Bakeless, Turncoats, Traitors & Heroes, pg. 146.

10. James Moody. Narrative, pg. 8.

11. The New Jersey Gazette, August 9, 1780.

12. The Royal Gazette, August 25, 1781

13. The New England Chronicle, November 29, 1781

14. Susan Burgess Shenstone. So Obstinately Loyal, passim.

15. Ranlet, The New York Loyalists. pp. 188 & 186

16. The Continental Journal, November 8, 1781.

17. Paul Smith, Loyalists and Redcoats, pg. ix.

18. Stephenson. Patriot Battles. pg. 19.

19. Refalko. A Counterintelligence Reader, Vol. I. pg. 2.

20. (From a letter of June 7, 1782 to General Henry Knox).

21. Bakeless. Turncoats, Traitors and Heroes. pp. 271-272.

22. Brown. The King's Friends. pg. 79.

23. Bakeless. Turncoats, Traitors and Heroes. pg. 107.

24. Michael Stephenson. Patriot Battles: How the War of Independence was Fought. pg. 97.

25. Ibid., pp. 97-98.

309

BIBLIOGRAPHY:

Sources

This book is intended for a popular, rather than an academic audience, and does not pretend to have exhausted all the primary and secondary sources relevant to its topic. Wherever possible, however, I have used excerpts from original documents to tell my story. While much has been published on the general topic of Tories and Loyalism, few books or articles experience of "high risk" Tories in individual colonies such as New York. Perhaps the best of these is Canadian Susan Burgess Shenstone's 2002 biography of notorious New Jersey Loyalist officer James Moody entitled <u>So Obstinately Loyal</u>. Only a handful of books have been written about Loyalist military participation during the war (Mary Beacock Fryer's 1980 book entitled <u>King's Men: The Soldier Founders of Ontario</u> is the best wrap-up of New York Loyalists' participation in British Provincial Corps units). Even less information has been published--especially by American authors--that deals specifically with Tory participation in British Intelligence operations.

As for the exploits of the "Tory Secret Service" in northern New York during 1780-1783, the best previous works are Hazel Mathews' privately-published 1971 paperback volume entitled <u>Frontier Spies</u>, Ian Pemberton's brief article on "The British Secret Service in the Champlain Valley" contained in Volume 44 (1976) of the journal <u>Vermont History,</u> and two biographical volumes (dealing with commissioned officers Justus Sherwood and John Walden Meyers) written by Canadian author Mary Beacock Fryer and published in the early 1980s. With the exception of some superficial newspaper articles, nothing has been published that focuses upon the life and career of Thomas

Loveless or any of the other "rank and file" veterans of the "Tory Secret Service."

Like Mathews, Pemberton, and Fryer, I have made extensive use of the "papers" documenting General Frederick Haldimand's tenure as Governor-General of Canada during 1778-1784. This book is the first to include (both as illustrations and in the Appendices) readable photo copies of original "Tory Secret Service" documents contained in the Haldimand Papers. Additional documentation has been obtained from The Public Papers of Governor George Clinton, Caleb Stark's Memoir and Official Correspondence of Gen. John Stark, The Edward Jessup Papers, and the Memoirs of Major-General William Heath. As a means of cross-referencing the events Thomas Loveless' espionage career with New York security and counterintelligence activities, I have made good use of the transcripts of the Albany County Sessions (1778-1781) contained in the Minutes of the Commissioners for Detecting and Defeating Conspiracies in the State of New York, and the Journals of the Provincial Congress, Provincial Convention of Safety of the State of New York (1775-1776-1777).

Primary Sources:

The Haldimand Papers, 115 microfilm reels. (Passim).

The Carleton Papers, 110 microfilm reels. (Passim).

Abbatt, William (Ed.) Memoirs of Major-General William Heath, by Himself. Originally published in Boston in 1798. Republished in New York: William Abbatt. 1901.

The David Library of the American Revolution. Letter no. 2206, (Washington to Livingston, January 12, 1782).

Government of Canada. "Censuses of Canada, 1665-1871," Statistics of Canada, Vol. Fourth [sic].

Hastings, Hugh (Ed.) Public Papers of George Clinton, first Governor of New York, 1777-1795, 1801-1804. Albany, (10 Volumes). Published by the State of New York, 1899-1914.

Loyalist Claims. Public Record Office, AO/12 and 13. Microfilm, National Archives of Canada.

Miscellaneous newspapers of the period, including articles from: The New Jersey Gazette, The Royal Gazette, The New England Chronicle, and The Continental Journal.

Moody, James. Lieut. James Moody's Narrative of His Exertions and Sufferings in the Cause of Government, Since the Year 1776; authenticated by proper certificates. London: 1782; Harvard University Houghton Library, Document Number CW3304176504). Repr. New York: The New York Times and Arno Press, 1968.

New York Historical Society. Minutes of the Committee and of the First Commission for Detecting and Defeating Conspiracies in the State of New York, December 11, 1776—September 23, 1778. (2 Vols.) New York: 1924.

New York State Legislature. Journals of the Provincial Congress, Provincial Convention, Committee of Safety and Council of Safety of the State of New York, 1775—1776—1777., Albany: Printed by Thurlow Weed, Printer to the State, 1842.

New York Public Library. The Philip Schuyler Papers, Box 35, Reel 17, "Letters Received, 1781-1785".

Palmer, Gregory (Ed.). A Bibliography of Loyalist Source Material in the United States, Canada, and Great Britain. Meckler Publishing, 1981.

Palstits, Victor Hugo (Ed.) Minutes of the Commissioners for Detecting and Defeating Conspiracies in the State of New York, Albany County Sessions, 1778-1781. Originally published by the State of New York: Albany, 1909.

_____. (Ed.) Minutes of the Committee and of the first Commission for detecting and defeating conspiracies in the State of New York, December 11, 1776-September 23, 1778: with collateral documents, to which is added Minutes of the Council of Appointment, state of New York, April 2, 1778-May 3, 1779. New York Historical Society. (2 Vols.) 1924-1925.

Stark, Caleb. (Ed.) Memoir and Official Correspondence of Gen. John Stark. Concord: New Hampshire, Edson C. Eastman, 1877. (Reprinted by Heritage Books, 1999).

State of New York. Journal of the Provincial Convention, Vol. I, pt. 2.

Simcoe, John Graves. A Journal of the Queen's Rangers.

The Appendices of United Empire Loyalists lists compiled by the Crown Lands Department, Toronto, Canada.

Archives of Ontario. The Edward Jessup Papers, 1773-1915. (on microfilm) MS 521, Reel F485.

_____. 2nd Report of the Bureau of Archives for the Province of Ontario. United Empire Loyalists: Enquiry into the Losses and Services in Consequence of their Loyalty—Evidence in the Canadian Claims. Toronto. 1905.

University of Michigan, The William A. Clements Library, The Sir Henry Clinton Papers. Vol. 160.

US National Archives (NARA). Revolutionary War Pension and Bounty Land Warrants. M804.

US National Archives, War Department, Judge Advocate General's Office, Records of Court Martial. US no. O-13, US no X-161, and Military Monitor, Vol. I, no. 23, Feb. 1, 1813

Secondary Sources:

Adler, Winston (Ed.). Their Own Voices: Oral Accounts of Early Settlers in Washington County, New York. Interlaken, New York: Heart of the Lakes Publishing, 1983.

Allen, Robert S. Loyalist Literature: An Annotated Bibliographic Guide to the Writings on the Loyalists of the American Revolution. Dundurn Press Limited, 1982.

Anderson, Fred. Crucible of War: The Seven Years War and the Fate of Empire in British North America, 1754-1766. Alfred A. Knopf, 2000.

Bakeless, John. Turncoats, Traitors & Heroes: Espionage in the American Revolution. Da Capo Press, 1998.

Beilinski, Stephan. "Albany County," in Tiedemann and Fingerhut (Eds.) The Other New York: The American Revolution Beyond New York City. pp. 155-178.

Blakely, Phyllis R. and John N. Grant, (Eds.) Eleven Exiles: Accounts of Loyalists of the American Revolution. Dundurn Press Limited, 1982.

Bloodgood, S. De Witt. (Ed.). The Sexagenary: or, Reminiscences of the American Revolution. (Author unknown, originally published in 1833). Albany, N.Y., J. Munsell, 1866.

Boatner, Mark M. (Ed.) The Encyclopedia of the American Revolution. (3rd Ed.).

Borden, Morton, and Borden, Penn (Eds.). The American Tory. Prentice-Hall, 1972.

Brandow, John Henry. The Story of Old Saratoga and History of Schuylerville., Saratoga Springs, 1901.

Brown, Roger. The Republic in Peril: 1812. W.W. Morton & Co., 1988.

Brown, Wallace. The King's Friends: The Composition and Motives of the American Loyalist Claimants. Brown University Press, 1965.

_____ and Senior, Hereward. Victorious in Defeat: The American Loyalists in Exile.Facts on File. 1984.

_____. The Good Americans. New York: Morrow, 1969.

_____. "The American Farmer During the Revolution: Rebel or Loyalist? Agricultural History. Vol. 42, no. 4 (October 1968), pp. 327-338.

Burleigh, H.C. The Bones of David Redding. Adolphustown Museum. 1975.

Calhoun, Robert. The Loyalists in Revolutionary America, 1760-1781. New York: Harcourt, Brace & Jovanovich, 1973.

_____ and Barnes Timothy and Rawlyk, George A. (Eds.). Loyalists and Community in North America. Greenwood Press, 1994.

Callahan, North. Flight from the Republic: The Tories of the American Revolution. Bobbs-Merrill, 1967.

Chartrand, René American Loyalist Troops, 1775-1784. Osprey Publishing Ltd. 2008

Coldham, Peter Wilson. (Ed.) American Loyalist Claims. Washington, D.C., National Genealogical Society, 1980.

Commager, Henry Steele, and Morris, Richard B. (Eds.) The Spirit of Seventy-six: The Story of the American Revolution as told by Participants. Harper & Row, 1975.

Cometti, Elizabeth (Ed.). The American Journals of Lt. John Enys. Syracuse University Press, 1976.

Coolidge, Guy Omeron. The French Occupation of the Champlain Valley from 1609 to 1759. Harbor Hill Books, 1979.

Cooper, James Fenimore. The Spy: A Tale of the Neutral Ground. Penguin Books, 1997.

Crary, Catherine S. The Price of Loyalty: Tory Writings from the Revolutionary Era. New York: Mcgraw-Hill, 1973.

Cruikshahk, Ernest A. and Watt, Gavin K. The History and Master Roll of the King's Royal Regiment of New York, Global Heritage Press, 2006.

Cuneo, John R. Robert Rogers of the Rangers. Oxford University Press, 1959.

Curtis, Edward E. The Organization of the British Army in the American Revolution. Corner House Historical Publications, 1998.

Dictionary of Canadian Biography. ___Edition., Vol___.

Draper, Theodore. A Struggle for Power: The American Revolution. Times Books, Random House, 1996.

East, Robert A. and Judd, Jacob. (Eds.), The Loyalist Americans: A Focus on Greater New York.. Sleepy Hollow Restorations, 1982.

Eckert, Allan W. The Wilderness War. Bantam Books, 1982.

Edgar, Walter. Partisans and Redcoats: The Southern Conflict that Turned the Tide of the American Revolution. William Morrow. 2001.

Fernow, Berthold. New York in the Revolution (Vol. 15 of Documents Relative to the Colonial History of the State of New York, Albany 1887.)

Fish, Hamilton. New York State: The Battleground of the Revolutionary War. Vantage Press, 1976.

Fitch, Asa. Their Own Voices: Oral Accounts of Early Settlers in Washington County, New York.. (Originally published in the mid-19th Century. A version edited by Winston Adler was republished in 1983 by Heart of the Lakes Publishing, Interlaken, NY.)

Flexner, James. The Traitor and the Spy: Benedict Arnold and John André. Syracuse University Press, 1991.

Flick, Alexander C. Loyalism in New York During the American Revolution. Originally published in 1901 by Columbia University as volume XIV, No.1 of "Studies in History, Economics, and Public Law. Republished in 1970 by AMS Press of New York).

Ford, Corey. A Peculiar Service. Little, Brown, 1965.

Fryer, Mary Beacock. John Walden Meyers: Loyalist Spy. Toronto: Dundurn Press, 1983.

_____. Buckskin Pimpernel: The Exploits of Justus Sherwood, Loyalist Spy. Toronto: Dundurn Press, 1981.

_____. King's Men: The Soldier Founders of Ontario. Dundurn Press, 1980.

_____. Rolls of the Provincial (Loyalist) Corps.

_____. and Christopher Dracott. John Graves Simcoe, 1752-1806, a Biography. Toronto and Oxford, 1998.

Gerlach, Don R. "Philip Schuyler and the New York Frontier in 1781," pp. 331-365 of The New York Historical Society, Narratives of the Revolution in New York, 1975.

_____. Proud Patriot: Philip Schuyler and the War of Independence, 1775-1783. Syracuse University Press, 1989.

Greene, Jack P., Bushman, Richard L., and Kammen, Michael. Society, Freedom, and Conscience: The American Revolution in Virginia, Massachusetts, and New York. New York: W.W. Norton & Co., 1976.

Grenier, John. The First Way of War: American War Making on the Frontier, 1607-1814. New York: Cambridge University Press, 2005.

Halsey, Francis Whiting. The Old New York Frontier: Its Wars with Indians and Tories, Its Missionary Schools, Pioneers, and Land Titles. Charles Scribner's Sons, 1902.

Hamilton, D. (Ed.) A History of Sullivan County, New Hampshire. Philadelphia, 1886.

Hibbert, Christopher. Redcoats and Rebels: The American Revolution Through British Eyes. New York: Avon Books, 1990.

Higby, Jean H. "The Rime of the Ancient Traveler," Poem in the collection of the Brookside Museum at the Saratoga Historical Society.

Holden, A.W. A History of the Town of Queensbury. Albany, Joel Munsell, 1874.

Huey, Paul R., "Charlotte County," in Tiedemann & Fingerhut (Eds.) The Other New York: The American Revolution beyond New York City, 1763-1787., pp. 1119-222).

Hickey, Donald R. Don't Give Up the Ship: Myths of the War of 1812. University of Illinois Press, 2006.

Jasanoff, Maya. "The Other Side of the Revolution: Loyalists in the British Empire," The William and Mary Quarterly, Vol. LXV, no.2 (April 2008), pp. 205-232.

Jellison, Richard M. (Ed.) Society, Freedom, and Conscience: The American Revolution in Virginia, Massachusetts, and New York. New York: W.W. Norton & Co., 1976.

Kammen, Michael. Colonial New York: A History. Oxford University Press, 1975.

Kaplan, Roger. "The Hidden War; British Intelligence Operations during the American Revolution," The William & Mary Quarterly, Vol. XLVII, no. 1 (January, 1990), pp. 115-137.

Katcher, Philip and Youens, Michael. The American Provincial Corps, 1775-1784. Osprey Publishing, 1973.

Ketchum, Richard M. Divided Loyalties: How the American Revolution Came to New York. Henry Holt & Co., 2002.

Kim, Sung Bok. "Impact of Class Relations and Warfare in the American Revolution: The New York Experience. The Journal of American History. Vol. 69, no.2 (Sept. 1982), pp. 326-346.

Launitz-Schurer, Leopold S. Loyal Whigs and Revolutionaries: The Making of the Revolution in New York, 1765-1776. New York University Press, 1980.

Leach, Douglas Edward. Roots of Conflict: British Armed Forces and Colonial Americans, 1677-1763. University of North Carolina Press, 1986.

Loescher, Burt Garfield. The History of Roger's Rangers, Volume I, "The Beginnings." Heritage Books, Inc. 2001.

_____. Genesis: Roger's Rangers: The First Green Berets. Heritage Books, 2000.

_____. The History of Roger's Rangers, Volume III, "Officers and Non-Commissioned Officers." Heritage Books, 2001.

Lossing, Benson J. The Pictorial Field-Book of the Revolution. Two Vols., New York, Harper & Brothers, 1852.

MacKinnon, Neil. This Unfriendly Soil, the Loyalist Experience in Nova Scotia, 1783-1791. McGill-Queen's University Press, 1986.

Macksey, Piers. The War for America, 1775-1783. University of Nebraska Press, 1993.

Marston, Daniel. The French-Indian War, 1754-1760. Osprey Publishing, 2002.

Mathews, Hazel C. Frontier Spies: The British Secret Service, Northern Department, During the Revolutionary War. The Ace Press, 1971.

_____. The Mark of Honour. University of Toronto Press, 1965.

Moore, Christopher. The Loyalists, Revolution, Exile, Settlement. Toronto: McClelland & Stewart, 1994.

Morison, Samuel Eliot. John Paul Jones: A Sailor's Biography. Little, Brown, 1959.

Morton and Penn Borden (Eds.) The American Tory.

Niles, Hezekiah (Ed.). Principles and Acts of the Revolution in America. 1876.

O'Toole, G. J. A. Honorable Treachery: A History of US Intelligence, Espionage, and Covert Action from the American Revolution to the CIA. The Atlantic Monthly Press, 1992.

Palmer, Gregory. Biographical Sketches of Loyalists of the American Revolution. London: Meckler Publishing. 1984.

Pemberton, Ian. "The British Secret Service in the Champlain Valley During the Haldimand Negotiations, 1780-1783," Vermont History. Vol. 44 (1976), pp. 134-____?

Phelps, M. William. Nathan Hale: The Life and Death of America's First Spy. Thomas Dunne Books, 2008.

Phillips, Kevin. The Cousins' Wars: Religion, Politics, & The Triumph of Anglo-America. Basic Books, 1999.

Pocock, Tom. Nelson's Women. London: Andre Deutsch, 1999.

Potter-Mackinnon, Janice. While the Women Only Wept: Loyalist Refugee Women. Mc-Gill-Queen's University Press, 1993.

_____. "Loyalists and Community," in Robert M. Calhoon, et.al. (Eds.) Loyalists and Community in North America. Greenwood Press, 1994.

Rafalko, Frank J. (Ed.) A Counterintelligence Reader: Vol. I., American Revolution to World War II. National Counterintelligence Center (NACIC), 1996.

Ranlet, Philip. The New York Loyalists. New York & Oxford: University of Tennessee Press, 1986. (2nd Edition published by University Press of America, Inc., 2002

Rogers, Robert. Journals of Major Robert Rogers. Various publishers and editions, 1765- 1769.

Rubicam, Milton. The Old United Empire Loyalists List. Originally published in Toronto in 1885 as "Centennial of the Settlement of Upper Canada by the United Empire Loyalists." (Reprinted under new copyright in 1984 by Genealogical Publishing in Baltimore).

Sabine, Lorenzo. Biographical Sketches of Loyalists of the American Revolution. Boston: Little, Brown & Co., 2 Vols., 1864. (Reprinted by Kennikat Press, 1966).

Schama, Simon. Rough Crossings: Britain, the Slaves, and the American Revolution. Harper-Collins Publishers, 2006.

Shenstone, Susan Burgess. So Obstinately Loyal: James Moody, 1744-1809. McGill-Queen's University Press, 2002.

Smith, Paul H. Loyalists and Redcoats: A Study in British Revolutionary Policy. University of North Carolina Press, 1964.

———. "The American Loyalists: Notes on Their Organization and Numerical Strength," William and Mary Quarterly, 3d ser., 25 (1968): 259-277).

Spargo, John. David Redding: Queen's Ranger, Who was Hanged in Bennington, Vermont, June 11, 1778. Vermont: Bennington Museum, 1945.

Spaulding, E. Wilder. New York in the Critical Period, 1783-1789. Columbia University Press, 1933.

Starbuck, David R. The Great Warpath: British Military Sites from Albany to Crown Point. University Press of New England, 1999.

Stark, Caleb. Memoir and Official Correspondence of Gen. John Stark. Originally published in 1877, reprint published by Heritage Books, Inc.,1999.

Stephenson, Michael. Patriot Battles: How the War of Independence was Fought. Harper-Collins, 2007.

Stone, William L. Life of Joseph Brant—Thayendanegea, Including the Border Wars of the Revolution. Buffalo: Phinney & Co., 1851

Stratch, Stephen G. Some Sources for the Study of the Loyalist and Canadian Participation in the Military Campaign of Lieutenant-General John Burgoyne, 1777. Eastern National Park and Monument Association, 1983.

Sylvester, Nathaniel Bartlett. A History of Saratoga County. Chicago. 1893.

Taylor, Alan. The Divided Ground: Indians, Settlers, and the Northern Borderland in the American Revolution. Knopf. 2006

Tebbenhoff, Edward H. "The Associated Loyalists: an Aspect of Militant Loyalism,"The New York Historical Quarterly. Vol. 63, no.2. (April, 1979).

Tiedemann, Joseph S. and Fingerhut, Eugene R. (Eds.) The Other New York: The American Revolution Beyond New York City, 1763-1787. State University of New York Press, 1980.

Tiedemann, Joseph S. Reluctant Revolutionaries: New York City and the Road to Independence, 1763-1776. Cornell University Press, 2008.

Tiedemann, Joseph S. (Ed.) The Other Loyalists: Ordinary People, Royalism, and the Revolution in the Middle Colonies. State University of New York Press, 2009.

United Empire Loyalists Centennial Committee. The Old United Empire Loyalists List. (Originally published in 1885). Re-published by the Genealogical Publishing Company, 1969.

Van Buskirk, Judith. Generous Enemies: Patriots and Loyalists in Revolutionary New York. University of Pennsylvania Press, 2002.

VanDerwerker, Mrs. J.B. Early Days in Eastern Saratoga County. Empire State Books, 1994.

Van Tyne, Claude Halstead. <u>Loyalists in the American Revolution</u>. Corner House Historical Publications, 1999.

Wallace, W. Stewart. <u>The United Empire Loyalists</u>. Toronto, 1914. (Reprinted by Kessinger Publishing, 2000.

Ward, Harry. M. <u>Between the Lines: Banditti of the American Revolution</u>. Praeger Publishers, 2002.

Whisker, James Biser. <u>The American Colonial Militia</u>. Vol IV. The Edwin Mellen Press, 1975.

Wright, Esmond. "The New York Loyalists: A Cross-section of Colonial Society," in East and Judd (Eds.) <u>The Loyalist Americans: A Focus on Greater New York</u>. Sleepy Hollow Restorations, 1982.

INDEX

Albany Board, 56-58, 60-64, 117-120, 172, 241-243; definition of a spy, 241

Albany County, 11, 23-24, 26-27; African-Americans, 61-64; hard target for TSS operations, 130; map of key towns in 1781, 21; Native Americans, 64-65; population, 24; post-war reprisals against Loyalists, 211-212

Albany militia, 72

Allen, Ethan, 77-78, 93-94

American espionage executions: a partial list, 258-262

American execution of spies, 238-239

American intelligence: effectiveness, 254-255

American obsession with espionage threats, 257-258

American Revolution, casualty numbers, 3; success factors, 8, 253-254

André, John (Major), 108-112; impact of execution, 112-113; trial, 110

Arnold, Benedict, 109, 110, 112

Bain, Mary Gillespie, 99, 181

Bennington, Battle of, 43-46, 136, 141; Treatment of Loyalist prisoners, 45-46

Bettis, Joseph, 85, 103, 172-173, 196, 262; capture; Stone's account, 174; capture in Ballston, 169; elopement, 131; reaction, 131-132; newspaper account, 171; poem, 174-175; Sabine's account, 172

Bettys, Joseph. *See* Bettis, Joseph

Bitely, Jacob: story about Lovett the spy, 181

Black Tories, 61-64

Bloodgood, Simon, 57

Board of Commisioners for Detecting and Defeating Conspiracies in the State of New York. *See* Albany Board

British Army's Northern Department, 14

327

British execution of spies, 238, 255-256
British Military Commands: communication, 97
Burgoyne, John (General), 43, 46, 48, 50
Canadian population growth, 71
Carleton, Guy Sir, 97
Charlotte County, 24, 33
Clinton, George (Governor), 108, 122, 220; post-war career, 214
Clinton, Henry (General), 10, 79, 99
Clinton, James (General), 83
Committees of Safety, 31
Counterintelligence, 104-105, 129-130
Courier intercept capabilities, 126-127
Courier intercept operations, 101
Courier missions, 97-98
Couriers, 99-100
Crocker, Ephraim, 107, 217
Crocker, Levi, 134, 217
Crowfoot, William, 99, 170-171
Crown Point, 24, 27, 38, 43, 72, 124, 168, 227

Double agents, 106-107, 129, 171
Dunham, Hezikiah, 134, 143, 194; biographical summary, 147; post-war career and legend, 215
Dunham, Holton, 134, 143, 182; arrest for treason, 147-148
Espionage: definition; weapons possession, 243; penalties, 239-242
Espionage execution: ceremonies and rituals, 264-265
Espionage executions: ceremonies; benefits of reprieves, 267; effectiveness, 265-267
Espionage Executions: interrogation tool, 262
Fishkill (near Old Saratoga, 50
Friends of Government, 7, 105, *See* Loyalists
Gage, Thomas (General), 97
Gates, Horatio (General), 47, 217
General Stark, The, 137
Haldimand, Frederick, 79; apology to Philip Schuyler, 133; as spymaster, 75, 81, 90; attack of Fort Edward, 96; background, 73-74;

Bettis elopement, 132; Bettis execution; retaliation threat, 169-170; counterintelligence concerns, 129; fear of French intervention, 126; oposition to kidnapping, 130-131; orders dissolution of the TSS, 177; places Tories in charge of the TSS, 75; *portrait*, 76; post-war career, 215; provisions, 71; refugee families, 69; replaces Carleton, 73; Vermont negotiations, 77-78, 167

Hale, Nathan: betrayal by Robert Rogers, 230-231

Hazen, Moses, 36, 164

Heath, William (General), 162, 184, 194, 220; views on deception in war, 160

Howard, Matthew: capture, 131

Howe, William (General), 97

Huddy, Joshua, 261, 263

Intelligence warfare, 2, 5, 245

Iroquois, 53

Jessup, Ebenezer, 19-20, 37-39, 52, 65, 68, 116, 217-218

Jessup, Edward, 19-20, 37-38, 49, 52, 217-218 attack of Fort Edward, 96

Jessup's Corps, 37-40; discharge of its men, 178

Jessup's Landing, 19

Jessup's Rangers--See Loyal Rangers, 116

Jessup's Corps, 14

Johnson, John, 66

Jones, David, 47; failure to kidnap Major John McKeinster, 133-135

Jones, John Paul, 102

Kidnappings, 241-243

Kidnappings by the TSS: driven by prisoner exchange requirements, 121-122

Kidnappings by TSS: failure of, 131

King's Loyal Americans, 37-39, 48, 50, 51, 67; uniforms, 40

King's Loyal Americans, 38-40, 66

KLA. *See* King's Loyal Americans

Lands in Canada granted to Loyalists: compensation guidelines, 202-203

Loveless, James (father), 15

329

Loveless, James (son): compensation, 211; compensation claim, 209-210

Loveless, Lois, 18, 41, 177, 198, 204; pension, 198; remarriage, 199

Loveless, Thomas, 48; atttempt to become an Ensign, 67; burial, 2, 185-186; capture; Bloodgood account, 148-151; Heath's account, 184; Lossing account, 148; newspaper account, 151-152; casualty of America's first civil war., 267; children, 200, 210; Ebenezer, 201; Elizabeth, 201; James, 200; resettlement, 203-204; Thomas jr., 200; William, 201; chosen as a scout, 75; enlists in the KLA, 37; execution, 1; accounts by Patriot Militiamen, 181-184; British reaction, 158-159; General Heath's view, 160; Lossing account, 154; officially reported, 154-155; retaliation, 168; Sexagenary account, 155; Sherwood report, 156; father, 15-16; intelligence reports, 92-94; official Death Warrant, 154-155; orders, 144-145, 194; Pyramid of Risk, 250; trial, 152-154; Becker account, 153; Lossing account, 154

Loveless, Thomas--the nature and value of his property in New York State, as described in the claim for compensation submitted by his son James in July, 1786, 210-211

Loveless/Lovelace Family: participation in Revolution, 233-234

Loyal Block House, 74, 77, 86, 88, 123, 170; base for scouts, 175; construction of, 85; security screen for, 85

Loyal Rangers, 67, creation of, 116; manpower 1781, 116; Muster Roll 1783, 178-179, resettlement, 202

Loyalist Dilemma, 252-253

Loyalist Provincial Corps: resettlement, 201-202

Loyalist Provincial Corps: units in Canada; pensions, 176-177
Loyalist refugees, 68-69; provisions, 70-71; quality of life, 69
Loyalist-manned Provincial Corps units, 13-14
Loyalists: military recruitment, 22-23; social class, 8-9, 18, 20, 36-37; and threats of invasion, 55
Loyalty oaths, 31-32, 242
Mathews, Robert (Capt.), 77, 81, 85, 90, 101, 132, 137, 143, 164, 165; post-war career, 215-216; reaction to Loveless execution, 158; response to Bettis & Parker executions, 170; retaliation proposed, 159
McRae, Jane, 47
Meyers, John Walden, 103, 196; Schuyler kidnappping attempt, 132
Moody, James, 120, 237, 244, 246, 247, 248; postwar activities, 249
Moody, John, 249
Munro, Hugh (Capt), 48
Native Americans, 64-65

Naughton, Andrew: biographical data, 198
New Hampshire, 213
New Jersey Loyalists, 120-121, 246
New York, 214; Response to Loyalist espionage threats, 240-241
New York Loyalists, 10-14; compensation claims, 209; Lower Hudson, 12; Military Support, 12; New York City, 11, 22; reprisals, 211-212; Upper Hudson, 12; value to British, 249-250, 251-253; Westchester County, 245
New York State: counter-espionage laws and statutes, 219, 240-241
Palmertown, 18, 19, 20
Patriot internal security programs, 255
Persecution of Loyalists, 40-41, 212
Peter's Corps, 38
Peters, John, 38, 44, 46; post-war career, 218
Powell, Watson (General), 72
Prisoner exchanges, 121-122, 130, 165-166
Provincial Corps: officers; second-class status, 68;

331

recruiting requirements, 67-68
Provincial Marine, 49
Pyramid of Risk (The), 9
Queen's Loyal Rangers, 38, 40, 50, 51, 67, 82
Rebel executions of Tories for spying--often amateurish, 264-265
Removal of Tories, 118-119
Reprisals for executions, 158-159, 168, 171, 244-245
Republic of Vermont, 78, 82, 115
Revolutionary War espionage executions,255-262
Rogers, Robert, 231, 233
Rogers' Rangers, 17, 227-228
Saratoga, Battle of, KLA participation, 48-51
Schuyler, Philip, 25, 26, 29, 36, 50, 60, 61, 64, 79, 94, 108, 115, 123; agent network in Canada, 124; courier intercept activities, 126; intelligence sources in Canada, 223; kidnapping plot, 127; *portrait*, 125; post-war career, 215; spymaster, 124, 236; stolen silver plate, 133; use of deception ploys, 126-127
Sherwood, Justus, 62, 77, 84, 88, 90, 91, 94, 103, 107, 108, 123, 129, 135, 136, 143, 164, 168, 169, 171, 196; background, 81-82; postwar career, 216; role in prisoner exchanges, 78
Skene, Philip, 12, 43, 46, 58; postwar career, 218
Smyth, George, 25, 116; agent in Albany, 83; background, 82-84; his pseudonym Hudibras, 82; uncovers Rebel agents in Canada, 129; on Bettis elopement, 131-132; post-war situation, 216-217
South Carolina Loyalists, 249-250
Stark, Caleb (grandson), 193
Stark, Caleb (son), 155, 159
Stark, John, 49, 115, 123, 136-137, 151; account of Loveless capture, 151; at André trial, 110; attitude towards Tories, 138-142, biographical summary, 136-137; decision to execute

Loveless, 145; decision to hang Thomas Loveless, 235; Loveless execution, 154-155; *portraits*, 139, 221; postwar attitude towards British, 213; post-war career, 212; his Tory relatives, 229; and prisoner exchanges, 225-226; reputation for insubordination, 141-142
Taylor, David, 99
Thomas the Spy. *See* Loveless, Thomas
Tories. *See* Loyalists
Tory Secret Service, 2; logistics supply of, 88; courier operations, 98-101; CI countermeasures, 104-107; comparision to Rebel Intelligence organization, 236; consumption of rum and spruce beer, 88; counterintelligence problems, 104-106; courier intercept operations, 101; dissolution, 177; effectiveness, 105-106, 108, 196; efforts to counter Rebel agents in Canada, 129; guide duties, 96; Headquarters, 85; kidnapping missions, 130-131; missions, 77, 89-90; morale, 175; more dangerous operational environment, 127; operations security, 169; origins, 75; pay scales, 89; personnel, numbers, motivation, 86; Philip Schuyler kidnapping attempt, 132; Rebel disinformation, 166; recruiting efforts, 94; role in Vermont negotiations, 78; sabotage operations, 102; Crown Point raid, 168; scouting parties; dangers of, 96-97; security issues, 175-176; security problems, 102-103; security techniques, 103-104; sources of intelligence data, 91; subordination of, 75; tasking by Haldimand, 90; theater of operations, 78-79; use of term, 75; Vermont negotiations, 93; weaknesses, 129-130

Tory Spy rib, 188
Tory Spy skull, 185-188;
Treason, early Rebel definitions of, 239-241
United Empire Loyalists, 6, 208
Van Vechten, Cornelius (Colonel), 61, 145; 146; assassination attempt, 219; biographical summary, 146; legend, 214; post-war career, 214; target of Thomas Loveless' mission, 143
VanVetchen, Colonel Cornelius, 135
Vermont negotiations, 105

War Scare of 1781, 161-162, 223-224; factor in John Stark's decision, 219; messages exchanged between Patriot leaders, 220, 222-224
War Scare of 1782, 166
Washington, George, 53, 54, 110, 112, 113, 115; as spymaster, 10, 114-115, 124, 126, 166; definition of a spy, 244; on espionage threats, 257; plot to kidnap, 242, 266
Yorktown: impact, 162-165

www.ingramcontent.com/pod-product-compliance
Lightning Source LLC
Chambersburg PA
CBHW070229230426
43664CB00014B/2249